Bridges to L

Books from Heinemann
on
Reading Recovery
by Marie M. Clay

• • •

Bridges to Literacy

Learning from Reading Recovery

Edited by

DIANE E. DeFORD
The Ohio State University

CAROL A. LYONS
The Ohio State University

GAY SU PINNELL
The Ohio State University

Heinemann
Portsmouth, NH

Heinemann
A Division of Reed Elsevier Inc.
361 Hanover Street, Portsmouth, NH 03801-3912
Offices and agents throughout the world

We would like to thank the teachers, children, and parents who have given their permission to include material in this book. Every effort has been made to contact copyright holders for permission to reprint borrowed material where necessary, but if any oversights have occurred, we would be happy to rectify them in future printings of this work.

The editors and publisher wish to thank the following for permission to include reprinted material in this work:

Chapter 1, "Reading Recovery: Learning How to Make a Difference," was previously published in the January 1990 issue of The Reading Teacher and is reprinted with permission.

Pages 93, 94: Figures 4–10a and 4–10b, Opportunities and Purposes for Writing (Early Stages), previously appeared in an article entitled "Shared Writing," by Moira McKenzie, which was published in Language Matters Nos. 1 and 2 (1985), copyright the London Education Authority's Center for Language in Primary Education. The diagrams are used here with the permission of the author.

Reading Recovery ™ is a registered trademark of The Ohio State University

Library of Congress Cataloging-in-Publication Data

Bridges to literacy : learning from reading recovery / edited by Diane
   E. DeFord, Carol A. Lyons, Gay Su Pinnell.
      p. cm.
   Includes bibliographical references.
   ISBN 0-435-08575-1
   1. Reading—Remedial teaching. 2. Reading disability. 3. Reading
teachers—Training of. 4. Teacher-student relationships.
   I. DeFord, Diane E. II. Lyons, Carol A. III. Pinnell, Gay Su.
   LB1050.5.B75 1991
   372.4'3—dc20   91-6551
                                           CIP

Design by Maria Szmauz
Printed in the United States of America
98 97 96   EB 10 9 8 7 6

CONTENTS

....

3

INTRODUCTION

··

*I*n 1982, Charlotte Huck read a newspaper report of the failure rate of first-grade children in the Columbus, Ohio, schools. At that time, more than 30 percent of first graders in this large school district were being retained. Charlotte had always believed in the power of books to change children's lives. She had invited Dorothy Butler to speak at the annual Children's Literature Conference that is sponsored by Ohio State University's Language, Literature, and Reading Program. Dorothy had written in 1979 about a young physically disabled child, Cushla, whose life had been enriched far beyond initial predictions because of the books that were presented to her by her parents. Charlotte had also followed the work of another New Zealand educator, Marie Clay. Her book *The Early Detection of Reading Difficulties* was first published in the United States in 1979, and the results of the early intervention program, Reading Recovery™, described in that volume looked promising. Charlotte felt that something must be done to change what was happening in her own city.

In the same way that the plot of a novel may unfold in surprising ways, Charlotte Huck, Martha King, and Gay Su Pinnell began a journey that led to an unexpected, but significant, conclusion. These three Ohio State University faculty members went to New Zealand to see Marie Clay's Reading Recovery program in operation. They wanted to implement this program in the Columbus school system. They had talked with administrators, the State

Department of Education, and teachers who were excited to begin such an endeavor.

After they saw the intensity of the teacher-training program and its success in New Zealand schools, however, Charlotte, Martha, and Gay decided their proposal was unrealistic. They could not implement the program without significant help and training from Marie. So they returned and began their plans with renewed effort. Two grants and a Distinguished Visiting Professorship brought Clay and Barbara Watson, the national director of the Reading Recovery program in New Zealand, to Columbus. During the 1984–85 school year, a pilot program was established and tested in a collaborative effort among Ohio State University, the Ohio Department of Education, and the Columbus public schools. Many people watched this first effort, including an Ohio representative in the Ohio General Assembly. After seeing the program in operation, he ushered through legislation to fund a statewide effort to implement the Reading Recovery program in Ohio schools. Instead of just initiating a program in the Columbus schools, Charlotte, Gay, and Martha were responsible for the development of a statewide program. The success of the Ohio Reading Recovery program with children throughout the state led us to suggest this text, *Bridges to Literacy*. The story of the Reading Recovery implementation is, in itself, a case study of institutional and interpersonal collaboration—the kind of collaboration that is necessary to create positive change in education.

ABOUT THE PROGRAM

The Reading Recovery program is described by Marie Clay as a "prevention strategy designed to reduce dramatically the number of children with reading and writing difficulties in an education system" (1987, p. 36). To accomplish this goal, the program operates on several levels within a given education system, encouraging:

1. Change on the part of teachers.
2. Change on the part of children.
3. Organizational changes in schools achieved by teachers, parents, and administrators.
4. Social-political changes in funding by controlling authorities.

First-grade children who are identified as having the lowest ability in reading and writing are selected for individual lessons within the Reading Recovery program. After they are able to work comfortably around the average level of their class, the children leave the program. The average length of time children receive tutoring is twelve to fifteen weeks, but the program may last as long as twenty weeks for some children. Currently, more than 80 percent of these lowest achieving students reach average levels of their class at program sites in Ohio, Illinois, Texas, Virginia, Arizona, South Carolina, and Toronto, Canada.

New Reading Recovery sites were established in Wisconsin, Oregon, Idaho, New York, Kentucky, West Virginia, and Halifax, Nova Scotia, during the 1989–90 school year. In that same year, six new states (Utah, Massachusetts, Georgia, Michigan, Tennessee, and New Hampshire) sent district or university representatives to Ohio State University, and five states (Texas, Oregon, New York, Illinois, South Carolina) initiated their own teacher-leader training program. New teacher-leader training sites will be established in Michigan and West Virginia in the 1990–91 school year, and Illinois will add a second site in the northern portion of the state.

ABOUT THE TRAINING

Teacher leaders are involved in a one-year educational program that includes a clinical practicum experience, a theoretical seminar, a supervision practicum, and a district apprenticeship. These teachers work daily with four children and apprentice with an experienced teacher leader in addition to taking university coursework (at Ohio State, twenty-one hours at the graduate level). Teacher leaders must have at least a master's degree and primary teaching experience. Once the year of coursework, apprenticeship, and work with children is completed, these leaders return to their districts to implement the Reading Recovery program.

Within each district, the teacher leader works with classroom and special reading teachers who are in training to be Reading Recovery teachers. This leader carries out continuing contact sessions and site visits to supervise previously trained teachers in their work with children. The leader conducts districtwide inservice as necessary to support the program, and continues to work with four children. The leader also conducts "awareness sessions" as part of the National Diffusion Network dissemination plan, to inform administrators and teachers within the program area of the goals and operation of this intervention. (An early intervention program for children who are "at risk" of failure but who have yet to fail is harder to sell than a long-term remedial education program.)

The second level of teacher training is directed at regular class-room teachers or special reading teachers within each site (the boundaries of the site may cross district lines). Reading Recovery teachers should have at least three years of primary teaching experience before they are selected for training. The teachers-in-training participate in a year of inservice after school, or during school hours in some sites, to become Reading Recovery teachers. They receive nine hours of graduate course credit for this year. Throughout the year, they work with four children (one-on-one) in daily tutoring sessions and attend class once a week. The other half day they conduct their regular jobs within the district (half time first grade or kindergarten, or half time special reading teacher). Once trained in the Reading Recovery procedures, they continue to work with four children and carry out district responsibilities the other half of their day. They attend six yearly continuing contact sessions and are visited by their teacher leader as necessary to support their teaching. Because of the intensity of this one-on-one teaching, teachers seldom teach as Reading Recovery teachers full time.

The unique aspect of the teaching-training model is the demonstration lessons accompanied by peer critique; these take place on a weekly basis throughout the year of training. Teachers and teacher leaders use this model during their training year and afterwards in continuing contact sessions (see diagram below).

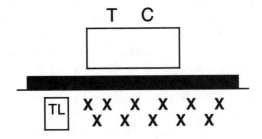

The teacher and child (T and C) conduct a normal lesson that is observed by the teacher's peers (X's) behind a one-way mirror. The observers are being guided by a teacher leader (TL). Usually, two such lessons occur consecutively, then all of the group come together after the lesson to discuss issues that were raised in the talk behind the glass. The total session lasts for two and a half hours. The child's progress and the group's learning are central to the discussions held. An individual teacher may not get specific feedback about particular points in teaching, but the teacher leader will meet with those teachers who taught the lessons after the session to address any questions.

The goal of this teacher education program is to learn how to improve the teaching of at-risk learners. Often, however, all of us must "unlearn" previously held views and assumptions that do not work in one-on-one teaching or that get in the way of helping children achieve accelerated progress. In many replications of this program in New Zealand, Australia, and the United States, the necessity of the yearlong intensive teacher education program and the continuing contact has been justified. New learning is taking place, and many local and political factors can interfere with the success of the program. Teachers and school authorities must learn how to provide for and support the learning of these children. This commitment involves learning to work with children who have not succeeded in the regular program, learning to teach with the intensity necessary to reach the goal of accelerated learning, and learning to use children's individual strengths to foster their progress. The support of colleagues within this learning community continues as long as a teacher works with a child utilizing Reading Recovery procedures.

ABOUT THE LESSONS

Lessons begin after the children recommended by teachers are given the Diagnostic Survey and after those selected have had an extended evaluation period referred to as "roaming around the known." During this time, the teacher is cautioned not to "teach," but to explore further what the child can do through the child's reading, the teacher reading to and with the child, and through the child's writing, the teacher writing for and with the child.

The Reading Recovery lesson frame was developed by Marie Clay and teachers working together (Clay 1985). After observing good readers and noting instructional practices from good holistic classroom settings, the teachers and research team put together and tested lesson frames that combined knowledge from clinical (one-on-one) settings and classroom settings to devise the most accelerative framework possible. Many instructional experiences, such as reading to children, were tried, and those that did not facilitate the development of a self-improving, independent reading process in a short period of time were dropped. The following set of experiences was settled upon to allow the teacher flexibility in decision making and teaching opportunities and to give the child as many opportunities as possible within a thirty-minute time period to develop reading and writing strategies able readers use:

1. Reading familiar materials.
2. Reading yesterday's new book.
3. Writing.
4. New book introduction and first reading.

In the familiar-reading portion of the lesson, the child reads books aloud that were enjoyed in previous lessons. This experience closely approximates bedtime story readings for the very young child, only in this instance, these favorite books are read by the child. The teacher and child enjoy books together, with laughter. They comment about the story and its meaning, and the teacher remarks on strategies the child is using. The child or the teacher may choose these books. They should be easy, fluently read texts that will help the reader orchestrate a well-balanced set of strategies. They are read as often as the child is still learning from them and enjoying the love of reading.

While the child reads the new book from yesterday's lesson, the teacher is taking a running record (Clay 1985). Using a blank sheet of paper, the teacher monitors the text during the child's reading, marking what the reader says. In the following sample, the actual text is written underneath what the child has said, to illustrate the technique (the Reading Recovery teacher would not have the text written on the running record sheet, however):

Marking: ✔ <u>dog</u> ✔ <u>•</u> ✔
     boy very

Text: The boy ran very fast.

Reader: The dog ran fast.

After the running record, one or two important teaching points are selected. The comments made during the reading of familiar materials and the running record and the teaching points emphasized are decisions teachers learn to make. Nothing children can do for themselves should be done by the teacher. Weaknesses should not be emphasized. Consequently, the teacher must choose the most powerful examples from the child's reading to further the child's literacy development. The teacher must know what the child does well and must work from this basis of strength to teach the child how to do whatever is needed to improve the reading process. The abilities to ask the most appropriate question, to direct the child's use of important cues and strategies during reading, and to conduct the teaching points are the hallmarks of an experienced Reading Recovery teacher.

The writing portion of the lesson is a joint process. Very early in lessons, the child writes what he or she can, with the teacher writing everything else. The writing vocabulary and dictation sub-tasks from the Diagnostic Survey and information gathered from the ten sessions of "roaming around the known" are used to guide the teacher in initial lessons. As the child learns, the teacher must do less and less. The examples below show how this takes place for one child across three early lessons. Working on the practice page (upper portion), the teacher and child explore written language through the use of boxes (hearing sound in words), taking high frequency words to fluency and generating like words from known forms. The child thereby constructs and writes a message. In this section, the teacher makes notes on lesson plans about the child's contributions, including written inventions attempted and strategies

for writing (rereading, self-corrections, etc.). At the bottom of the page the message is written conventionally, so the child can reread it in future lessons.

The new book is carefully selected by the teacher to be just a bit more difficult than the text read that day and also to bring new learning into focus. If the child needs to use syntactic or structural cues more effectively during readings, a highly patterned text like *Cat on the Mat* (Wildsmith 1982) or *The Chick and the Duckling* (Ginsburg 1972) might be introduced. The best way to characterize the new book introduction and first reading is the notion of "scaffolding" (Bruner 1973). The teacher sets the main theme and action of the book and guides the child as they both examine the pictures and predict story outcomes. Simultaneously, the language of the book is woven into their talk, and the child is asked to examine aspects of the text. During the first reading, the teacher questions for strategies and facilitates complex learning. The teacher and child may then read the book again together to gain fluency. This book will then be read independently during the next lesson.

ABOUT THIS BOOK

Reading Recovery is based on the notions that children and teachers are lifelong learners and that any innovation in education must become part of the system in order to create change. The chapters in *Bridges to Literacy* explore what can be learned by teachers, administrators, and parents from our work with students who are at risk in our educational settings. The discussions provide insight into how we can work together to create an environment in which children and teaching are the focus of literacy learning.

REFERENCES

Bruner, J. S. 1973. "Organization of Early Skilled Action." *Child Development* 44: 1–11.

Clay, Marie M. 1985. *The Early Detection of Reading Difficulties*. 3d ed. Portsmouth, N.H.: Heinemann.

———. 1987. "Implementing Reading Recovery: Systemic Adaptations to an Educational Innovation." *New Zealand Journal of Educational Studies* 22 (1): 35–58.

Ginsburg, M. 1972. *The Chick and the Duckling*. New York: Macmillan.

Wildsmith, B. 1982. *Cat on the Mat*. New York: Oxford University Press.

1

On Reading Recovery

●●●●●●●●●●●●●●

This section describes how Reading Recovery operates, how it is implemented, and what surprises have come out of the use of this program in four countries (New Zealand, Australia, the United States, and Canada). The chapters discuss the following hallmarks of Reading Recovery as they have been set out by Marie Clay in The Early Detection of Reading Difficulties:

First, a shift to one-to-one instruction allows the teacher to design a program that begins where the child is, not where the curriculum is. Any grouping of children for teaching forces a compromise on this position.

Then, daily instruction increases the power of the intervention.

The teacher strives to make the child independent (to overcome one of the major problems of remedial tuition), never doing for the child anything that he or she could be taught to do for him- or herself.

Acceleration is achieved by all the above means and also because the teacher never wastes valuable learning time teaching something the child does not need to learn. The teacher moves the child to a harder text as soon as this is feasible, but backs such progressions with quantities of easy reading.

From sound theory of the reading process the child is taught how to carry out operations to solve problems in text, how to monitor his or her reading, how to check options, how to be an independent processor of print.

ONE

••••••••••

Reading Recovery:
Learning How to Make
a Difference

GAY SU PINNELL   MARY D. FRIED
ROSE MARY ESTICE

Let me tell you about my eleven-year-old son. Billy started kinder-garten, age five and a half, had done average work, went on to first grade. They waited till spring to tell me he was just immature; by now he was seven. I let them hold him back. I then started to watch more closely; halfway through the second year of first grade, he still couldn't read! They tested him (at my request); they said he had atten-tion disorder. They assigned him to special education; he went through second grade with a class of seven students in his room that were disabled. Billy didn't read but I felt he didn't belong there. Our doctor said they had made a mistake and would not order Ritalin. I put him in one year of vision therapy, and three years of expensive tutors, and two more years in a reading study group at the university which is also expensive and wears us all out running back and forth. Now we wouldn't mind any of the above if some improvement had been made. At age eleven he's a normal all-boy child in every way; he shows a lot of common horse sense at home and play. Halfway through the fourth grade Billy does other subjects well, but he still isn't reading.

••••••••••••••••••••••••••••••   ••••••••••••••••••••••••••••••

*B*illy's story is a familiar one to us and to many reading teachers who try to reduce reading failure and the frustration that goes along with it. Several years ago we began to think hard about those children who were having difficulty learning to read in the early years of school. As teachers of reading, we had tried many methods and used a variety of materials. We had learned about how children learn to talk, read, and write and tried to incorporate approaches such as process writing and whole language in our own work. With most children we succeeded, but some always seemed to be in trouble even though we were doing very good teaching.

As Clay (1985) suggests, our own experience told us that we could see the reading process going wrong in the first year of school. Clay's research (1979, 1984, 1985) helped us expand our knowledge about how young children learn to read. We began to understand that young readers must learn to "orchestrate" their knowledge of language, of the world, and of print and how it works. Our poor readers did not seem to achieve this orchestration.

We investigated Reading Recovery, the program developed in New Zealand to give extra help to children having trouble learning to read. In 1984, with the help of Marie Clay and Barbara Watson, we began implementing Reading Recovery in our Ohio schools. This chapter represents our experiences as teachers of children and teachers of teachers in Reading Recovery. First we will describe the program, the teaching procedures, and the research base. Then we will outline some important understandings we have gained. In additional material, we will take a look at Reading Recovery through the eyes of one of us, Rose Mary, who served as a Reading Recovery teacher.

WHAT IS READING RECOVERY?

Reading Recovery is an early intervention program for young readers who are experiencing difficulty in their first year of reading instruction. The program is designed to serve the lowest achieving readers in a first-grade class. In Reading Recovery, children receive individual daily lessons from a specially trained teacher. These lessons do not take the place of good classroom instruction. As they say in New Zealand, Reading Recovery is "something extra" (New Zealand Department of Education 1987).

Reading Recovery is not intended to be a long-term or permanent program. Teachers provide daily, thirty-minute lessons during which they involve children in reading many little books and in writing and reading their own stories and messages. During each lesson, teachers work hard to be sure that children are actively involved in reading and writing. The materials, the written messages, and the way teachers respond to children on a minute-to-minute basis vary according to the individual child's strengths, needs, and interests. The teacher carefully observes the child reading and writing text and finds opportunities to draw attention to the details of print and to work on letter-sound associations and spelling patterns within those activities. The goal is to teach children to use their knowledge and to see the purpose for it. Reading Recovery is designed to help these initially low-achieving children make accelerated progress and catch up with their peers. Then, they are released from the program as successful readers. When that happens for an individual child, the program is discontinued, and another qualified child begins to receive individual tutoring.

A READING RECOVERY LESSON

The Reading Recovery lesson is an intimate situation. It has some characteristics of the lap story in which a parent and child are involved in a collaborative literacy activity focusing on meaning and learning detail in the process (Snow & Ninio 1986). In Reading Recovery lessons, the teacher and child sit side by side, reading and writing collaboratively. This setting provides opportunities to use oral interaction to support literacy learning. Reading Recovery teachers try to follow the child, observing precisely and recording systematically so that they know and can take advantage of the discoveries children are making for themselves while they are engaged in reading and writing. The teacher has a theory of the reading process and experience in observing for behavioral evidence of reading strategies. The teacher watches for those moments when the child demonstrates awareness and then responds, sometimes just giving attention to the good things children are doing and sometimes actively teaching new ways of operating. This deliberate analysis and teaching is different from the lap story setting but similar to it in that the focus is on meaning. By selecting appropriate texts and adjusting their own interactions, teachers make it easy for children to use what they know and to behave as readers and writers.

To illustrate the framework of a lesson, we will use examples from one student, Dante. At the end of this chapter, his teacher, Rose Mary, has provided a longitudinal case history of Dante. In this section, we describe some of the teacher-child interactions during one day of Dante's program. At this time, Rose Mary had worked with him for twenty-five days; he had already made considerable progress, and his increasing competence shows throughout the various components of this thirty-minute session.

A Reading Recovery lesson includes the following five components:

READING OF FAMILIAR STORIES • As books are introduced, they are placed in the child's own box, ready to be read again. Each day the child begins by rereading several of these familiar books. Some of the books may be preselected by the teacher because they offer certain teaching and learning opportunities; others may be chosen by the child. Rereading provides the opportunity to engage in fast, fluent reading because the child does not have to work so hard that the reading process breaks down. Selected texts provide some remaining challenges (e.g., difficult words or unfamiliar book language), thus providing opportunities for problem solving that must be done "on the run" while reading a text.

Dante first chose to read *Lazy Mary* (Melser 1980), a predictable book based on the song. Rose Mary encouraged him to read fluently so that he made it sound like a story. Next, he read *Three Little Ducks* (Melser & Cowley 1980). Although the text was easy for him, a few language structures provided some challenges, such as "Come and hide, said Mother Duck. And very, very quietly, they did" (p. 12–13). At first, Dante read, "Came and hid, said Mother Duck." He stopped and repeated the sentence. Then, he returned to the beginning of the line, this time reading accurately. He was using visual information on the first attempt but was able to monitor and self-correct in a subsequent attempt based on language structure and meaning. The teacher was encouraged to see that Dante was using several sources of information on the run while reading. She said, "That's right. What you read first didn't make sense. I like the way you fixed that up yourself. Going back really helped you." Dante read one more familiar book that also offered opportunities to do some reading work, that is, problem solving while reading text.

TAKING A RUNNING RECORD OF TEXT READING • Every day the teacher assumes the role of a neutral observer for the purpose of taking a record of the child's independent reading behavior. The child is expected to read a book that was read once the previous day for the very first time; the teacher records the reading using a kind of shorthand miscue recording technique. While the teacher may help by telling a word when the child is completely stopped, this reading generally proceeds on an independent basis. The material is new, so the text will be just a bit difficult. The child is not expected to read this book with complete accuracy, but it should not be so difficult that the child has to struggle. An accuracy check confirms the teacher's selection of the right level of difficulty. If the child is reading at about 90 percent to 95 percent accuracy, the text is probably in the appropriate range.

While the child is reading, the teacher watches for and records behaviors such as substitutions, self-corrections, omissions, and insertions. After the lesson, the teacher analyzes the record, making inferences as to the child's use of cues—for example, meaning, language syntax, or visual information in print—and hypothesizing about the child's use of strategies. This analysis helps the teacher make decisions about the next day's selection of texts and about how to direct teacher and child attention during the lesson.

Dante independently read *Cats and Kittens* (Scott Foresman 1971) while Rose Mary took a running record (see Figure 1–1). His substitutions indicated that Dante was attending to visual information and letter-sound correspondence, but his reading did not always make sense. He was not consistently using meaning to monitor his reading of the passage. For example, Dante read "Cats hoot" for "Cats hunt."

After the reading, Rose Mary had to decide the most productive teaching points to make. First, she commented on Dante's independence in reading (he tried to work on the hard parts himself) and pointed out his self-correction on page 10. Then she

• •

FIGURE 1–1   RUNNING RECORD OF DANTE'S READING

Text	Record of Reading	Analysis Errors	Self-corrections
p. 6 - Cats keep clean. They lick their fur.	✓ ✓ ✓ ~~there~~/there ~~look~~/look ~~they~~/they ~~lick~~/lick ✓ ✓	m s ⓥ m s ⓥ	
p. 7 - Cats keep their kittens clean too.	✓ ✓ ✓ ✓ ✓ ✓		
p. 8 - Cats hunt.	✓ hoot/hunt	m s ⓥ	
p. 9 - Kittens hunt, too.	✓ hut/hunt ✓		
p. 10 - Cats get mad. Their fur stands on end. Their tails puff up.	✓ ✓ ✓ ✓ fura/fur sits/sc stands ✓ ✓ ✓ ✓ ✓	ⓜ s ⓥ m s ⓥ	ⓜ s v

turned to page 8, saying, "You were working hard on this page. You said, 'Cats hoot.' That word does start like 'hoot.' Does 'Cats hoot' make sense? Try it again and think what the cats and kittens are doing in the story." This time, Dante read the pages accurately. Many other teaching opportunities were present in the lesson. Rose Mary selected her responses based on previous observations of Dante's behavior. She was searching for the most powerful examples to help Dante learn to solve his own problems.

WORKING WITH LETTERS • If a child is just beginning to learn about letters and the features of print, the teacher may work with the child using plastic letters and a magnetic board. This activity may occur at various points in the lesson as children write words in their writing books and on the chalkboard. Later, as opportunities occur during reading, children use these magnetic letters to construct words or engage in word analysis. Dante's strengths indicated that he did not need specific work on letter identification, so in his case, lesson time was not devoted to this component. Instead, more time was spent on writing activities. For children who have very low letter knowledge, the teacher would spend a brief period working with the magnetic letters, perhaps beginning by having the child make his or her name.

WRITING A MESSAGE OR STORY • Every day the child composes a brief message, usually one or two sentences long, and, assisted by the teacher, writes it in a special book. Sometimes these messages are extended over several days and become stories. The child uses a blank writing book opened and turned sideways. The child's message or story is written on the bottom page; the top page, called the practice page, is used for working out the words (see Figure 1–2).

The message is written word by word; the child writes known words and attempts unknown words with the help of the teacher. When appropriate, the teacher invites the child to say the word slowly and to predict the letters that represent the sounds in the words. In this supported situation, children learn to analyze words and to make links between sound and letters. Sometimes the teacher might decide to write the word for the child.

After the message is written, the teacher quickly writes it on a sentence strip and then cuts it apart for the child to reassemble. The written message is always read as a whole text, both from the writing book and from the cut-up sentence. Writing gives children the chance to examine the details of written language in a situation

FIGURE 1–2   DANTE'S WRITING IN READING RECOVERY

where they already know what the message means and where the language is their own. The writing component is a collaborative effort, and, as in the reading, the literacy activity is constantly supported through oral language interaction.

After seeing an assembly provided by Artists in the Schools, Dante composed this sentence for his writing in Reading Recovery: "The man put make up on his face." (His writing book is shown in Figure 1–2.) He already knew the words *the* and *man* and wrote them independently. He did not know the word *put*, so the teacher quickly drew three connected boxes on the practice page. She asked Dante to "say the word slowly," then said, "What can you hear?" First, Dante put in the *t*; then, saying the word again, he wrote the *p*. The teacher supplied the *u*. A similar process was followed with *make* (and later *face*), using three boxes, one for each sound. When Rose Mary said, "Does that look right?", Dante was able to add the silent *e* to *make*. It was not important at this time to insist that *makeup* be written as one word.

Up and *on* were familiar words, and he immediately wrote them. These were words that he could read and write independently as a result of prior instruction. It is helpful to children to have complete control of some high-utility words that they can write quickly and independently. Accordingly, when an appropriate word comes up in the child's story, the teacher might ask the child to write it several times on the practice page and on the chalkboard. In Dante's lesson, no appropriate new high-utility words were in his story, so Rose Mary did not engage him in these activities.

By this time in his program, however, Dante had learned quite a few words. He had acquired some useful information that would allow him to use what he knew to figure out what he did not yet know, a process that is evident in his work on the next word, *his*. Rose Mary knew that Dante could write the word *is*. She quickly drew out magnetic letters and asked him to make *is*. Then she placed an *h* at the beginning and asked, "Could that be *his?*" Dante made the word with the magnetic letters several times, wrote it once on the practice page, and put it in his story.

When the writing was completed, Dante read his sentence several times, and Rose Mary copied it on a sentence strip. She cut the sentence into words, and Dante quickly reconstructed and read the sentence again to check it. This writing activity provided the opportunity for Dante to examine the details of written language, sort out letter-sound relationships, search for information, analyze words, use known information, and check his own work. The language in the message was his; the content emerged from his own experience. He was making written language his own, not by learning any *particular* word or sound but by learning how to *use* his knowledge of letters, sounds, and words.

The writing component described here is only one example; the experience is different for every child. The variability depends on the teacher's split-second decisions related to (a) what the child already knows; (b) the child's responses during the lesson; and (c) the opportunities in the text composed by the child.

READING A NEW BOOK • Every day the child is introduced to a new book and then reads it for the first time. In the introduction, the teacher does not read the book to the child; instead, the teacher and child look at and talk about the pictures in the whole book. Through oral language, the child has a chance to become familiar with the plot, the important ideas, and some of the language of the story. The introduction will vary according to the strengths and needs of a particular child at a particular point in time. For example, if the child is just about ready to be released from Reading Recovery, the child may simply look at the book alone and ask questions as needed. Then, the child reads the book with assistance as necessary from the teacher.

ROSE MARY'S REFLECTIONS ON BEING A
READING RECOVERY TEACHER
••••••••••••••••••••••••••••••••

I was respected as a good primary teacher. I was successful with most of my students, but every year there were always a few whom I just couldn't reach. Usually those few were good language users and intelligent, but I couldn't seem to help them learn to read. They were confused. I worked hard on their weak areas. I didn't know what to do, except more of the same program. My first year of training as a Reading Recovery teacher changed my teaching.

Soon after I started the Reading Recovery training course, I began to notice new things about children's reading and writing. For example, I noticed that if I waited instead of jumping in and correcting or telling the word, children would actively search for an appropriate response. They looked at the pictures to help them with the meaning, and I realized then how important the pictures were. I had never seen that kind of behavior as a strength before. In our basal readers, the pictures were not always helpful, and that worked against the strengths children were bringing into school.

I always had lots of books in the classroom, but I used to feel a little uneasy when I noticed a child just exploring a book instead of reading. I read to children, but didn't do much with it, and I never counted that as reading instruction.

Now I began to realize the importance of rereading texts, both those I read aloud to children and those they read independently. What happened when students were encouraged to reread? They were more willing to take risks and to learn from their own mistakes. And, they could practice what worked for them.

I did journal writing in my classroom before I started in Reading Recovery, so I had a sense that first graders could write, and I had studied writing as a process. Reading Recovery training helped me understand the connections between reading and writing. I observed that children make up stories using their own oral language, and then they try to write the words by using their knowledge of sound-to-letter relationships and visual memory. In my classroom, many children were inventing spellings. Writing and reading their own stories gave students more chances to examine print and letter-sound relationships closely within a context that was familiar and meaningful to them. The Reading Recovery students needed more intensive instruction to learn to use letters to represent the sound for words they wanted to write. Using a Reading Recovery procedure, the students were able to learn to hear the sounds in words and use letters to record those sounds.

Even that first year I began to alter my classroom reading program to provide all of my students with more opportunities to read and write. My view of reading changed, and my instruction began to look quite different. The children learned to solve problems for themselves. I spent less time on systematic drill and practice and more time teaching children to use knowledge of words, letter-sound relationships, and

> spelling patterns while they were actually reading and writing. My teaching became more efficient.
>
> I finally feel like a reading teacher. I know how to observe children systematically. I can hypothesize about their knowledge and possible confusions. I can now plan more effective and appropriate instruction. I no longer have to rely on someone else's preconceived notions of what my students need to learn.

Rose Mary selected *The Carrot Seed* (Krauss 1945) as Dante's new book because it has a strong story line and would provide opportunities to make predictions, although the language is not overly patterned. The teacher and child talked about the story and looked at the pictures. Dante knew that seeds grow into plants, but he was not familiar with all of the concepts of caring for plants. The teacher explained some of the concepts and used some of the specific language structures in the book, such as "sprinkled the ground with water" and "just as the little boy had known it would." In this latter phrase, Dante was able to locate the word *just* after Rose Mary asked him to predict what letter he would expect to see at the beginning. Immediately after the introduction, Dante read the story with some support. He would read it independently the next day for the running record.

The lesson framework as described has been found to provide the flexibility within which teachers can respond to individual children, but the decision maker is the teacher: "Individual variations in lesson plans are always possible, providing there is a sound rationale based on a particular child's response to lessons" (Clay 1985, p. 56).

READING RECOVERY TEACHER-TRAINING MODEL

Before they even begin the Reading Recovery inservice course, teachers know that their training is going to be different. The first difference they notice is the time commitment. Reading Recovery inservice training is not the typical one- or two-day session; instead, teachers volunteer for a full year of inservice training for which they earn nine quarter-hours of university credit.

Teachers begin their training by attending a thirty-hour workshop that is held before the opening of the school year. Classes are held at a school-based training center. During the summer training sessions, they learn to administer and analyze the six-part Diagnostic

Survey Test (Clay 1985). The skills and understandings gained in early training allow the teachers to begin assessment testing with first-grade children, thus illustrating the direct application of newly learned skills, another unique characteristic of Reading Recovery training.

Throughout the school year, teachers attend weekly two-and-a-half-hour classes held after school in which they learn the components of the lesson and the basic procedures. Simultaneously the teachers apply and expand their new knowledge as they work with children in their classrooms. This learning process is integral to Reading Recovery. Teachers learn, apply, receive feedback, and refine their teaching skills. These processes are consistent with elements suggested to be characteristic of effective training models, but in Reading Recovery there are some additional components.

Before they begin their regular training classes, many of the teachers have already heard about the special feature of the Reading Recovery training called "teaching behind the glass." Three times during their training year, each teacher brings a child to the training site and teaches a lesson behind a one-way glass in a sound-equipped room. Other teachers in the class observe and discuss the child's behavior and the effects of the teacher's instructional decisions. This lively discussion is guided by a teacher leader who challenges the observers with questions that require analysis.

Early in her training year, one teacher, Mary Jo, threw up her arms, covered her ears, and said: "Stop asking so many questions! I just want to sit and see what's happening!" However, Mary Jo and the other teachers soon began to understand and develop their skills as active participants in the talk behind the glass, simultaneously observing, offering comments, and listening to others.

The lessons behind the glass are not a demonstration of "how to do" the procedures. They are authentic experiences for teacher learning. Teachers use these lessons to help the group understand the procedures, observe the immediate effects of a teacher's decisions when teaching a child, analyze what might be happening, provide specific evidence to back up their assumptions, and relate what they are observing and learning to their own teaching. In the course of the year, teachers gradually shift their levels of thinking about the lessons, and they build a theoretical base for their own teaching.

After two behind-the-glass lessons, the demonstrating teachers join the teacher leader and classmates in a lesson discussion. Often, the group can increase the teacher's understanding by describing the child's or teacher's behaviors. The demonstrating teacher is often amazed at what the group has observed. Observers on the other side of the glass also reflect on their own teaching and often recognize some less effective techniques they may be using in their own Reading Recovery lessons.

The role of the leader is to get the teachers to think and to analyze their own teaching decisions for each of the children they teach. The inservice training course is not designed to train the teachers to use a fixed set of procedures for *the* Reading Recovery program. Reading Recovery has a lesson framework and a menu of possibilities. Each option has the potential to succeed or fail, depending on its appropriate use for a particular child, at a particular time, and in a particular context. Teachers have to learn to be expert decision makers in order to choose appropriate books and to select the most effective and powerful procedures for each child. This individualizing aspect is initially difficult for some teachers to understand and accept.

In the long run, perhaps the most important benefit of Reading Recovery for teachers is the insight they acquire in the process of analyzing and articulating their own teaching decisions. They look more closely at the students they are teaching and find it easier to see strengths; further, they begin to change their views of the reading process and to develop a more refined theory of how children learn to read. In one study, Pinnell and Woolsey (1985) analyzed informal discussions held after class sessions throughout the year (sponsored by the Research Foundation of the National Council of Teachers of English). The focus of teachers' comments gradually shifted from a concern for practicalities (how to do it) to reporting detailed observations of children and finally to articulating generalizations and theories. We learned from this study that long-term staff development, with opportunities to talk with and be challenged by a supportive group of peers, is essential if teachers are to link theory and practice.

Interviews with teachers indicate that the inservice course challenged their views and helped them grow professionally (see Rose Mary's "Reflections on being a Reading Recovery teacher"). Rentel and Pinnell (1987) analyzed transcripts of group discussions following the behind-the-glass sessions. They noted that the number of statements teachers made that were supported by evidence—that is, either examples of behavior or reference to informational sources and research—increased over time. These findings indicate that teachers may be learning a kind of pedagogical reasoning process through which they can argue about educational issues and make instructional decisions.

These results are promising, but more research is needed. We hope to take more detailed looks at the work of children and teachers. We still do not know much about how teachers tailor and adjust their minute-to-minute responses to each child, and we are just beginning to examine how talk assists teachers in their own learning.

THE RESEARCH BASE FOR READING RECOVERY

Reading Recovery was constructed from a research base and has been tested and evaluated in three countries and in hundreds of different locations.

NEW ZEALAND STUDIES • In the 1970s, Clay (1985) undertook a research program to determine whether it was possible to use early intervention to reduce reading failure. Clay's team of practitioners met regularly to observe each other teach, to discuss pupil and teacher responses, to assess and refine procedures, and to analyze and justify teaching decisions. The idea of articulating the basis for instructional decisions emerged from the research program as Clay and her team piloted teaching techniques. Clay (1985, p. 84) says, "A large number of techniques were piloted, observed, discussed, argued over, related to theory, analyzed, written up, modified and tried out in various ways, and, most important, many were discarded."

The procedures were refined over a period of three years and then the team prepared for the field trials in 1978 and replications in 1979 (described in Clay 1985). The procedures were tested with remarkable results. The majority of children served made accelerated progress and achieved average reading levels. At the end of the year, discontinued Reading Recovery children compared favorably to a group of higher achieving children who were not selected for the program because they were higher achievers from the beginning and did not need extra help. Reading Recovery children had caught up with their higher achieving peers. Follow-up studies indicated that children continued to make progress comparable to that of average groups of students. These results appeared to be consistent across ethnic, economic, and language groups.

The New Zealand studies provided evidence that, given appropriate instruction in an individual setting, the lowest achievers can learn effective reading strategies that enable them to read at average levels for their class or school. Since that time, these findings have been replicated in New Zealand, Australia, and many school districts in the United States.

PILOT STUDY IN OHIO • Three years of investigation and fund seeking preceded Ohio's first pilot test of Reading Recovery (Huck & Pinnell 1985). In autumn, 1984, Ohio State University awarded a distinguished professorship to Marie M. Clay, and separate grants from the Martha Holden Jennings Foundation and the Columbus Foundation provided the services of Barbara Watson, national director of Reading Recovery in New Zealand. Clay and Watson spent most of the school year in Ohio, and during that time conducted a preparation program that included one class each of teacher leaders and Reading Recovery teachers. They also taught one professor to train teacher leaders.

The program began in October with teachers learning the diagnostic procedures and then beginning to work with children as they learned to use Reading Recovery procedures. We were cautious about early intervention. New Zealand children begin school on their fifth birthday; if, after one year of reading instruction, they are having difficulty, they enter Reading Recovery. Our children had spent a year in a half-day kindergarten program, the curriculum of which emphasized the learning of letters and sounds but not reading and writing. Would our students need more time in school before the need for Reading Recovery could be determined?

Children did not enter the program until January when the first failing notices were sent to parents. Then teachers selected children and tested them, noting that the lowest performing children had made very little progress since September even with good classroom instruction. The children who participated in Reading Recovery that year were compared with another group of low performing children from randomly selected classrooms. Results showed that Reading Recovery children performed better than the comparison group and that they also performed comparably to the first graders in those schools.

THE FIRST YEAR IN OHIO • The next school year (1985–1986), Reading Recovery teachers in training, taught by the teacher leaders who were trained by Clay and Watson, selected children in late September. First-grade children from six schools who scored the lowest on a pretest were randomly assigned either to Reading Recovery or to another compensatory program (see Pinnell, DeFord, & Lyons 1988). The alternative program provided extra service in the classroom that was closely linked to basal reader lessons. Reading Recovery students with the lowest scores were selected for the program first and received daily tutoring. As these children were discontinued from the program, having reached average levels and demonstrated an independent reading level, the next children on the list were admitted. Reading Recovery children received an average of sixty-seven lessons during the year, and 73 percent of those children who received at least sixty lessons were successfully discontinued. Comparison children received daily instruction all year.

At the end of the year, all children were tested. Results showed that Reading Recovery children performed better than the comparison group on the following measures (see Pinnell et al. 1988): (a) *text reading:* the level of text in a series of lengthy graded passages that the child can read at 90 percent accuracy; (b) *writing samples:* a writing sample, produced in response to a standard prompt, holistically scored by blind raters; (c) *letter identification:* identification of the accurate name or sound for fifty-four characters; (d) *word test:* recognition of isolated words in a list drawn from a standard list; (e) *concepts about print:* appropriate responses to series of questions about print conventions in the context of a book; (f) *writing vocabulary:* the number of words the child can write within a ten-minute time period with the tester using a standard set of prompts and also encouraging the child to write personal words such as names; (g) *dictation:* accurate representation of phonemes in a dictated sentence. Further, when compared to an average band of performance for first graders (constructed by taking .5 standard deviations above and below the mean of a random sample), the group of discontinued Reading Recovery children performed well within the average range.

LONGITUDINAL STUDY • We followed this group of children for two years after the initial intervention to find out whether they could retain their gains and continue to make progress in reading (Pinnell et al. 1988). One and two years later, we asked all children in the study, as well as random samples of children at appropriate grade levels, to read progressively more difficult levels of texts. These texts consisted of a series of graded passages from one to thirty. The texts were lengthy, whole stories for the easier levels and up to 500 words for harder levels. Passages were drawn from grade-level materials and tested with children. Levels ranged from materials at kindergarten through eighth-grade difficulty.

Testing was performed by individuals who did not know the group designation of the children. Both early intervention groups had continued to make progress, but the Reading Recovery children could read significantly higher levels of text than could the comparison children. In May 1987, the text level score for Reading

Recovery children was 14.39 and the score for comparison children was 11.23. In May 1988, Reading Recovery children scored 19.70 and comparison children scored 16.71 (data from Pinnell et al. 1988).

THE STATE PROJECTS • In Ohio there are now twenty-two sites offering Reading Recovery training for teachers. The program has been tested at each site, and each time the majority of children have been shown to make accelerated progress and to reach average reading levels for their particular school or district. More important, running records of children's reading indicate that they can orchestrate a range of strategies to construct meaning while reading. Qualitative data obtained from questionnaires and interviews indicate that teachers, administrators, and parents have responded enthusiastically to the program. Last year in Ohio, 86 percent of program participants were successfully discontinued. (For more information see Pinnell et al. 1988; and Slavin 1987.)

In the 1986–1987 school year, Reading Recovery was implemented in Fairfax County, Virginia. The next year, the program was implemented at several other locations including Arizona, South Carolina, Texas, and Ontario, Canada. In the 1989–1990 school year, Reading Recovery projects were implemented in Illinois, Idaho, Kentucky, New York, West Virginia, and Wisconsin, as well as Nova Scotia, and Scarborough, Canada.

In addition to this formal research evidence that documents the success of Reading Recovery, we present Rose Mary's "Story of Dante" vignette as a case study of one specific student's success with the program.

SUMMARY AND CONCLUSIONS

Reading Recovery is not a quick fix or easy answer. The program requires hard work, a long-term commitment, and a willingness to solve problems. As with any innovation, Reading Recovery may challenge existing programs and generate resistance among educators who have invested a great deal in them. Those promoting new programs like Reading Recovery sometimes become impatient and forget to acknowledge what has been learned through existing programs and how it contributes to new ones. The decision to implement Reading Recovery should be made with sensitivity to existing programs and the past contributions of individuals.

Reading Recovery is promising, but it is not *the* answer. There is no one answer to problems in education. Many of the children served by Reading Recovery remain in the potentially-at-risk category because of economic circumstances. Children may learn to *read* through Reading Recovery, but they do not turn into different children even though many adopt a much more positive attitude toward school. Poor children are still poor. Highly mobile families still move. Many have family problems. Some children's work habits are still not very good even though their reading ability has improved. Some continue to be discipline problems.

Classroom experience is another variable. If children have few books at home *and* they have little opportunity to read in the classroom, then it is difficult for them to continue their growth in reading ability. Children develop into mature readers by reading challenging and interesting material. Without personal attention and a rich school curriculum, some of the more vulnerable children may not continue to make good progress. Reading Recovery must not be the only good teaching children experience in their school careers. As in the case of Dante (see Rose Mary's "The Story of Dante"), children need continuous classroom literacy experiences and knowledgeable, observant teachers (called "noticing teachers" in New Zealand) who can help children further develop their competence.

Finally, ethical questions may arise. Since we know we *can* provide this powerful instruction, are we *obligated* to provide it to those who need it despite the cost? We hope that longitudinal studies will show that the initial costs are offset by fewer retentions and referrals for special services as well as more effective teaching in classrooms and other settings by teachers who have been trained in Reading Recovery. Gathering this evidence will require controlled studies of large numbers of children over a long period of time.

In this collaborative project, we are required to perform several roles simultaneously, usually within the same day. We are all teachers of children, teacher educators, and researchers. We work together closely, and we constantly evaluate and analyze our work; the problems of innovation demand that process. As we reflect on our last five years of effort, we realize that we have generated some understandings that now guide our practice as reading educators. These understandings are not unique to Reading Recovery but are likely to arise when educators from different perspectives work together on teaching and research, observe children closely, and reflect on their work. We present some of these understandings as a conclusion to this chapter. As teachers of children we understand that:

- Even children appearing to know very little can learn to be good readers. If we look closely, every child has competence and knowledge that can be used effectively. Just because a child is in the lowest portion of the class does not mean he or she will have to remain there.
- Instruction in beginning reading must include massive amounts of reading and writing. Teachers must use all their ingenuity to increase reading and writing time.
- The most effective texts to support young readers do not have controlled vocabulary but present real stories with language close to the child's own. As the child increases in knowledge and understandings, texts should not only present new challenges but should always be meaningful and enjoyable.
- The most powerful teaching builds on competence instead of deficits. Programs must be designed around each child's strengths; prescriptive, inflexible programs are not adequate; skilled teaching is required.
- Instruction must be focused at the strategy level and take into account the complexities of the reading and writing processes. Children must be assisted to learn the "how to" of the reading process rather than specific, sequenced bits of information presented in isolated ways.

As teachers of teachers we understand that:

- Teachers can change their views and expand their theories, but they need long-term staff development and a supportive group in which to articulate understandings and get feedback on teaching decisions.
- Teaching is a decision-making process that involves systematic observation, in-depth analysis, hypothesis testing, and self-evaluation. Teacher education must take into account the complexities of this process and recognize that decision making must be done on the run while teaching.
- Teaching is learning. We have found that we as teacher educators and researchers must continue to learn from our own teaching of children. We need to experience *responsibility* for children's learning as we use techniques consistent with our new theories. We cannot make brief, occasional visits to classrooms and then expect full understanding of the world of teachers and children.

- Every child is different. Our experiences with each child remain part of our teaching forever. Through these experiences we build theory on a case-by-case basis, changing as we learn more.

As educational change agents, we understand that innovations such as Reading Recovery must have school-system support to be successful (Clay 1987). Examining the essential characteristics of this successful program can provide insights for establishing even more comprehensive efforts to help young children learn to read and write. We are taking advantage of this opportunity to learn because we want to prevent the problems evident in Billy's story and because, even though we know continuing effort is needed, we want to make possible more stories like Dante's.

THE STORY OF DANTE
••••••••••••••••••••••••••••••••••

At the beginning of the year, Dante was typical of many of the low achieving students I had had in first grade over the years. Everything seemed difficult for him. He knew just a few of the sounds and words that were the core of the readiness program in kindergarten. The worksheets that accompanied the basal were hard for him. His journal entries consisted of a picture and a few random letters, as shown in example (a). His participation in group activities was limited; he seemed to be inexperienced and to lack the confidence that would enable him to join in.

(a) EARLY CLASSROOM WRITING BY DANTE (FIRST GRADE)

Dante was chosen to participate in the Reading Recovery program because he was one of the lowest achieving students in my first-grade class. When he was asked to complete the Diagnostic Survey (Clay 1985) in October to determine eligibility for the program, he could write his first name, *a* and *cat*, and he could hear and record the sounds for *b, s, t,* and *l*. He did not understand that the words on a page had to match his spoken language; for example, he read "No" for "No, no, no" in *Where's Spot* (Hill 1980) after the first seven pages had been read *to* him.

After twelve weeks of classroom instruction using a basal series and additional help from an instructional aide, Dante was again asked to complete the individual tests. The results showed that he had indeed made some progress but was still clearly at the bottom of my class. By December he could write fifteen words, many of which were words introduced in the basal program, and he could hear and record twenty-one sounds; however, he was not able to apply these skills in the real task of reading. His instructional reading level was the first preprimer. My experience told me that Dante was very much at risk of failing first grade. How could he possibly make the gains necessary for promotion when nearly half of the school year was behind him?

Dante began receiving Reading Recovery lessons in January. Our early lessons consisted of reading together many short books with repetitive patterns and clear illustrations. We also wrote some messages cooperatively, and these stories were used for rereading. An example is shown in (b).

$$\underline{I} \, l \underline{i} \, \text{ke} \, \underline{Z} e \, \text{bra} \, s.$$

(b) DANTE'S WRITING IN MIDYEAR (FIRST GRADE) AFTER BEGINNING READING RECOVERY LESSONS (UNDERLINING SHOWS WHAT HE CONTRIBUTED)

As we moved through the lessons, Dante learned to check on his own reading, self-correct many of his errors, and search for cues in an effort to attempt unknown words (see Figure 1–1). In writing, he learned to write more high-frequency words, to hear and record sounds in words in order to analyze unknown words, and to write useful letter chunks, such as *s* and *ing*.

Then Dante really began to make accelerated progress. By the end of April, he was reading higher-level books quite easily and could write a couple of sentences daily for his story, both with very little help from me, as shown in example (c).

After fifteen weeks in Reading Recovery, Dante was reading with the middle group in my classroom, and he was able to write fifty-four words in ten minutes and hear and record thirty-six out of a possible thirty-seven sounds in a dictated sentence. His newfound abilities and confidence were evident throughout the school day. He stacked books on his desk in preparation for independent reading time and often chose to read in

We went on our
trip. We had fun.
We went to the
flower shop
We made flowers and
saw a movie.

(c) DANTE'S WRITING LESSON #46 (HE CONTRIBUTED ALL BUT THE U IN OUR, THE A IN SAW AND THE I IN MOVIE)

his free time. He wrote stories, messages, and journal entries regularly, like that in example (d). He checked out books from both the classroom and school libraries, and he even talked about playing school at home.

Friday in Saturday
in Sunday I'm
going to spin a
night over Judy's
house I'm going
to play with
my cosen
May 23, 1985.

(d) DANTE'S CLASSROOM WRITING AFTER READING RECOVERY (END OF FIRST GRADE)

We wanted to be certain that Dante maintained his reading abilities even after being discontinued, so he was tested again at the end of May. At that time he was able to read in a second-grade book with an accuracy level above 90 percent. He finished his first-grade year as a strong, average student who could profit from classroom instruction without extra help.

I knew Dante had become a reader the day the neighborhood librarian came to my classroom to explain the summer library program. She spoke to Dante, and he to her, on a first-name basis. Afterward, I asked how she knew Dante. She said he was a regular at the library, who stopped in for story hour and to check out books. I don't mind saying that I had a personal and emotional response to this information. Dante was taking the initiative on his own to find reading materials.

At the end of second grade, Dante was able to read at the fourth-grade level with 97 percent accuracy; at the end of third grade, he was able to read at sixth-grade level with an accuracy rate of 95 percent. Most of his errors could be attributed to lack of prior experience with the particular word or concept. For example he read *appetis* for *apparatus*, *refence* for *reference*, and *tenically* for *technically*. His classroom instruction for both second and third grade was at grade level.

I caught up with Dante again in April of his fifth-grade year. His teacher described him as a strong B/C student and was pleased with his progress. She was instructing Dante in the fifth-grade book of a basal series. When tested, Dante was able to read at the eighth-grade level (Text Level = 30) with 96 percent accuracy. He tried to pronounce the unknown words and often came close, such as *nature-a-list* for *naturalist* and *forfeet* for *forfeit*, but lack of prior experience with those words and concepts made it difficult for him to self-correct. In spite of these kinds of errors, Dante was able to explain what happened in the stories he read. Dante also read a selection from *The Indian in the Cupboard* by Lynne Reid Banks (1981), and my discussion with him following the reading indicated that Dante had indeed comprehended what he had read. Dante asked to borrow the book and more books like it.

Dante had also grown in writing ability. His fifth-grade teacher described his abilities in writing as strong average. Example (e) shows his work at this time.

Because Dante had caught up by the end of first grade, he was able to take advantage of the learning opportunities that were to follow. Without Reading Recovery, he probably would have remained in the low achieving group, year after year, as many of my students like him had done in the past.

Dante has made excellent progress in his elementary years, but he may still be at risk educationally because of factors that have nothing to do with his abilities or potential. Dante has attended six schools in as many years. If this pattern of mobility continues, it is possible that such instability will affect Dante's progress or attitude toward school, especially as he is approaching middle school. Family problems, including economic difficulties, may also interfere with his educational progress. Because of mobility and his economic status, teachers may not hold high enough expectations for him.

Dante M.   ALL About Me!   3-30-89

Essay-You (3 essays)

I like a lot of things like football, basketball, hiking, fishing, camping, and helping people. When I grow up I am going to be a doctor, a professional one maybe. I hope I be rich when I grow up. Some of the things I like the most is hiking, camping, and helping people. I like helping people because its nice helping people do things, and some day the might help you. My special interests is doing things with my family. My best friend is a boy called Tyrone Valentine. When I lived on 20th we used to do a lot of things like: go for a long, long walk, go make money, go to the store. I do stuff with my cousin Timmy like go to Northern lights, and Schottenstein's. Now I do things with my cousin like go for a walk, scavenger hunt, throw rock in the creek, collect cans, go to the store. I also do things with my Uncle Micheal I walk with him to places. Well this is the end of All About Me.

(e) A FIRST DRAFT BY DANTE IN FIFTH GRADE

The fact that in classroom instruction Dante is reading at a level well below his measured capability (i.e., he could read a Level 30 text—eighth-grade level—quite well) indicates that he is not being challenged or expected to excel. If this can happen in elementary school where teachers know students well, what may occur in middle and high school?

Dante likes learning, and he likes school. He still reads on his own time. He is a young man with high motivation and aspirations, well on his way to success. I hope that the school will provide the support he needs. He does not need remediation. What could we do to help Dante during the difficult middle school years? We might:

- Provide personal attention—perhaps a mentor or role model—so he can receive the extra encouragement and help he must have.
- Prepare teachers to be better observers so that his strengths will be recognized.
- Provide a challenging instructional program that gives him real and frequent opportunities to read and write.
- Provide rich experiences to help him expand his background knowledge in content areas.

In a time when highly educated minority leaders are needed, it is important to help children like Dante achieve their true potential. As a reading teacher, I contributed by giving him a start. Now he needs the opportunity to keep going.

REFERENCES

Banks, L. R. 1981. *The Indian in the Cupboard*. Illus. by Brock Cole. New York: Doubleday.

Clay, M. M. 1979. *Reading: The Patterning of Complex Behavior*. 2d ed. Portsmouth, N.H.: Heinemann.

———. 1984. *Observing Young Readers*. Portsmouth, N.H.: Heinemann.

———. 1985. *The Early Detection of Reading Difficulties*. 3d ed. Portsmouth, N.H.: Heinemann.

———. 1987. "Implementing Reading Recovery: Systemic Adaptations to an Educational Innovation." *New Zealand Journal of Educational Studies* 22 (1): 35–58.

Hill, E. 1980. *Where's Spot?* New York: Putnam.

Huck, C. S., & G. S. Pinnell. 1985. *The Reading Recovery Project in Columbus, Ohio: Pilot Year 1984–1985*. Technical Report. Columbus: Ohio State University.

Krauss, R. 1945. *The Carrot Seed*. New York: Harper & Row.

Melser, J. 1980. *Lazy Mary*. Auckland, New Zealand: Shortland.

Melser, J., & J. Cowley. 1980. *Three Little Ducks*. Auckland, New Zealand: Shortland.

New Zealand Department of Education. 1987. *Something Extra*. Reading Recovery Program (Videotape). Auckland, New Zealand: University of Auckland.

Pinnell, G. S., D. E. DeFord, & C. A. Lyons. 1988. *Reading Recovery: Early Intervention for At-Risk First Graders*. Arlington, Va.: Educational Research Service.

Pinnell, G. S., & D. Woolsey. 1985. *A Study of Teacher Change During a Research-oriented Project*. Urbana, Ill.: NCTE Research Foundation.

Rentel, V. M., & G. S. Pinnell. 1987. "Reasoning in Reading Recovery Instruction." Paper presented at the National Reading Conference, December, St. Petersburg, Fla.

Scott Foresman Co. 1971. *Cats and Kittens*. Reading Unlimited. Glenview, Ill.: Scott Foresman Co.

Slavin, R. E. 1987. "Making Chapter 1 Make a Difference." *Phi Delta Kappan* 69: 110–119.

Snow, C. E., & A. Ninio. 1986. "The Contracts of Literacy: What Children Learn from Learning to Read Books." In Teale & Sulzby, eds., *Emergent Literacy: Writing and Reading*, 90–115. Norwood, N.J.: Ablex.

TWO

....

Maintaining the Integrity of a Promising Program: The Case of Reading Recovery

COLIN DUNKELD

.... *I* ....

n the United States, we have an unprecedented opportunity to enable thousands of failing first graders to learn how to read. The Reading Recovery program was first introduced in the United States in Columbus, Ohio, in 1984–85. As of autumn 1990, this program is operating in 268 school districts in the state of Ohio, in more than 50 school districts across the United States, and in 12 sites in Australia, Canada, and England. It is firmly established in New Zealand, the country of its origin, where it is a national early intervention program. Reading Recovery is the outcome of more than thirty years of observations of the reading and writing behavior of high- and low-progress readers. It was designed and implemented by educational psychologist Marie Clay and her associates at the University of Auckland, New Zealand.

Reading Recovery teachers, Reading Recovery teacher leaders, and trainers of teacher leaders participate in a yearlong professional education sequence, and the program is steadily spreading nationwide. Since 1989, more than forty new states have sent district personnel to an established training program. Reading Recovery is well designed; it has enabled 86 percent of the 13,000 at-risk first-grade readers receiving a full program in the United States to reach average reading levels in their first-grade classrooms. When Reading Recovery is carefully implemented, it has the potential, not to eliminate, but to reduce reading failure dramatically by attacking the problem very intensively when children are first learning to read.

However, promising programs have come and gone. If this one is to fulfill its promise, it must be properly implemented and properly maintained.

The first part of this chapter briefly sketches the structure of the entire program and the preparation of teachers at all levels. It draws attention to the less apparent, but essential, features of its administrative design. The second part raises and responds to questions of implementation and maintenance, including issues that threaten the program and need to be dealt with if the program is to flourish and its integrity be preserved.

THE STRUCTURE OF THE READING RECOVERY PROGRAM

Reading Recovery is an intensive, individualized intervention program for children in the first grade. Children at risk of reading failure are identified in the first few weeks of the first-grade year. These children then receive individually taught, thirty-minute lessons every day until they are able to read and write as well as the average children in their class.

From 70 percent to 95 percent of the children selected for this program—all of whom at the time of selection are in the bottom 20 percent of their class—reach the average level of their class and are discontinued from the program within an average of twelve to fifteen weeks. A longitudinal follow-up study of one group of children in Columbus, Ohio, shows that the reading performance of these children, as a group, was within the average band ($\pm.5$ standard deviation) of randomly selected children at the end of grades two, three, and four. In the words of one member of an independent evaluation team, "we are talking about seeing effects, substantial effects, three years later, four years later" (Allington 1989).

Diagnostic tests, instructional procedures, and the results of early studies in New Zealand are described in *The Early Detection of Reading Difficulties* (Clay 1985) and in a recent publication in the *New Zealand Journal of Educational Studies* (Clay 1990). The longitudinal study in the Columbus public schools, annual reports from sites around Ohio, and technical reports from Ohio State University document the success of the program in the United States. Comprehensive descriptions of all aspects of Reading Recovery, with good summaries of its research studies and suggestions for implementation are also available (Pinnell 1990; Pinnell, Fried, Estice 1990 [reprinted as Chapter 1 in this book]; Pinnell, DeFord, & Lyons 1988; Lyons 1989; Lyons & White 1990; DeFord, Tancock, & White 1990).

PROFESSIONAL DEVELOPMENT • An important feature of Reading Recovery is its comprehensive and innovative design for teacher education. The educational program lasts an academic year. At the district level, the course of study is offered by teacher leaders who have successfully completed one year of supervised training. Only successful, experienced teachers should be selected for the program, and they begin by learning how to give and interpret diagnostic tests in order to select children for the program. Once the children have been selected, teaching begins. Implementation is therefore simultaneous with training.

Teachers learn the framework of the lessons and more complex decision-making skills in a variety of ways. For half of their time, they learn "on the job" as they teach four children every day in individual tutorials. In weekly seminars, they study and use the text, *The Early Detection of Reading Difficulties* (Clay 1985), and teachers take turns teaching a child "behind the glass." While a teacher teaches behind a one-way observation window, other teachers in training observe, describe, and discuss the behavior of the child and the instructional decisions the teacher makes. And finally, they participate in lecture discussions on both theoretical and procedural matters. It is a collaborative learning model as all teachers involved study teaching and learning while teaching and learning occur.

In addition to the activities described above, teachers are visited at their schools during their training year. Site visits continue as long as teachers remain in the program. Each site also schedules continuing contact sessions for its experienced teachers in which teacher leaders guide class activities based on the needs they have observed during their site visits. A trained teacher periodically volunteers to bring a child and teach a lesson behind the glass, in the same way as was done in the initial training year.

Reading Recovery teachers, therefore, receive regular consultation and inservice education. Their learning is never complete and they are never alone.

TEACHER-LEADER TRAINING • A course of study for Reading Recovery teacher leaders, including a theoretical class and a practicum, was developed at the University of Auckland in New Zealand and has been taught there since 1979. In the 1984–85 school year, Marie Clay and Barbara Watson, national director of Reading Recovery in New Zealand, were in residence at Ohio State University. Since that time, Ohio State University has trained sixty-one teacher leaders for the state of Ohio and thirty-six teacher leaders for school districts across the United States and Canada. Six new sites have since been added at which the teacher-leader class and practicum are offered: Portland State University, Texas Woman's University, University of Illinois, New York University, Clemson University, Western Michigan University. In the near future, North Carolina, West Virginia, Georgia, Massachusetts, Missouri, and Arizona will implement this level of training for Reading Recovery.

Teacher-leader training takes a full year. It includes all of the requirements for training as a Reading Recovery teacher and a number of other activities—an additional theory course, an internship, site visits, and written reports. Teacher leaders learn to work with administrators, classroom teachers, parents, and the public; to supervise teachers; to make presentations about Reading Recovery to a wide range of audiences; and to collect data and summarize research for their site report. They also continue to work with children.

Candidates for teacher-leader training must hold a master's degree and must be nominated either by a school district, a university, or a school district consortium. The school district must also make commitments regarding implementation after the training year. Those commitments include the construction of an adequate training facility with an observation room for behind-the-glass demonstrations, provision for site visits beyond the training year, continuing contact sessions, and participation at two annual national meetings. Two site visits from the training institution are required during the implementation year. Site visits are provided on request after that time. Teacher leaders keep up to date by attending a national Reading Recovery conference every February and they participate in policy decisions and program development by attending a Reading Recovery institute every June.

PREPARING TEACHER-LEADER TRAINERS • The first trainers of teacher leaders in the United States were prepared at Ohio State University by Marie Clay and Barbara Watson in 1984–85. Two additional faculty members at Ohio State were subsequently trained to launch a statewide program in 1985–86. In 1989–90, teacher-leader trainers from New York University, Portland State University, and the University of Illinois spent the year at Ohio State University. In the same year, one experienced Reading Recovery teacher leader completed additional coursework to prepare as a trainer of teacher leaders and accepted a faculty position at Texas

Woman's University in Denton, Texas. Beginning in 1989, therefore, teacher-leader training became available at New York University, Portland State University, Texas Woman's University, and the University of Illinois. Western Michigan University and Clemson University sent faculty members that year, and they will have teacher-leader programs in place either in 1990 or 1991.

Trainers of teacher leaders must hold a doctorate and have successful experience in college or university teaching. They complete all of the requirements to become teacher leaders, work very closely with the staff at Ohio State University, study the development of the teacher-leader curriculum, and accompany trainers of teacher leaders on site visits. The numbers are small; the training therefore resembles an apprenticeship.

ADMINISTRATION AND THE SUPPORT SYSTEM • Reading Recovery is a system intervention. Once a district adopts Reading Recovery, it becomes part of a growing network that is continually supporting and contributing to the program. At each site, teacher leaders, in addition to teaching children and training teachers, play a vital role in supervising, providing support, and collecting data. At many sites an administrator serves as site coordinator, allowing the teacher leader to concentrate on teaching and supervision.

For each region, the trainers of teacher leaders provide similar supervision and support for their teacher leaders. This three-tiered design is not always apparent to either teachers or administrators. Yet, the long-term integrity of the program depends upon the recognition and willing acceptance of this thorough and disciplined support system.

The essential features of Reading Recovery and its support system are these:

1. Only successful, experienced teachers are selected to receive training as Reading Recovery teachers.
2. Teacher training lasts one full year. Implementation is immediate.
3. A Reading Recovery teacher begins by learning how to give diagnostic tests and identify children who are having difficulties.
4. A Reading Recovery teacher works individually with four of the lowest-achieving first-grade children every day.
5. The instructional emphasis is on helping children learn strategies for the reading and writing of whole texts. Teachers make

moment-to-moment instructional decisions to meet the needs of each child.

6. Record keeping, the diagnostic appraisal of children's reading and writing behaviors, and data collection are part of each teacher's daily responsibilities.

7. Teacher training follows a collaborative, participatory model and is carried out only by trained teacher leaders.

8. Teacher leaders and trainers of teacher leaders remain current—and credible—by continuing to teach children in addition to their other responsibilities. Most teacher leaders teach four children every day. Trainers of teacher leaders work with at least one child every day.

9. The teacher leaders provide continuous support to all Reading Recovery teachers both in their training year and beyond.

10. Teacher leaders arrange for continuing contact (i.e., inservice sessions) for all trained Reading Recovery teachers every year they continue to teach Reading Recovery children.

11. Teacher leaders collect data about every child admitted to and released from the program, send those data to Ohio State University for analysis, summarize those data, and write site reports.

12. The teacher leaders send out questionnaires to parents, teachers in training, classroom teachers, and administrators and summarize the responses in the site report.

13. Each new site is supported during its implementation year. Site visits are available on request in subsequent years.

14. Each Reading Recovery site has a site coordinator (sometimes this is the teacher leader) to take care of room assignments, class schedules, ordering supplies and materials, arranging college credit, and so on.

15. Ohio State University collects data from each site every year, summarizes those data, and issues reports. Reading Recovery staff also voluntarily compile and distribute a quarterly newsletter.

16. Until 1988–89 teacher-leader training in the United States was offered only at Ohio State University in Columbus, Ohio. Commencing in 1989–90, a small number of teacher leaders will also be trained at Clemson University, South Carolina; New York University, New York; Portland State University, Portland, Oregon; Texas Woman's University, Denton, Texas; and the University of Illinois, Champaign-Urbana, Illinois. In 1990–91,

programs will begin at Western Michigan University, Kalamazoo, Michigan. In 1991–92, programs will begin at the Graduate School in West Virginia; Leslie College, Boston, Massachusetts; University of North Carolina, Wilmington; Southeast Missouri State, Cape Girardeau, Missouri; and University of Arizona, Tucson, Arizona.

17. Once every year or every two years the above sites accept applications for teacher-leader training.

18. Trainers of teacher leaders in the United States must hold a doctorate in education and are trained only at Ohio State University, Columbus, Ohio. Additional training sites may be established on a limited, planned basis.

19. A national Reading Recovery conference is held every February to report progress, share experiences, and present the findings from relevant research. Trainers and teacher leaders keep up to date by attending this conference.

20. Trainers and teacher leaders also attend a Reading Recovery institute, held every summer, to contribute to committees that deal with administrative matters and to make policy decisions.

21. A policy-making group, composed of representatives of teacher-leader training institutions, has been established to guide the national implementation of Reading Recovery.

The point of listing all of these features is to indicate that so much that is essential lies hidden beneath the surface and is easily misunderstood or overlooked. There is more to this program than meets the eye. To overlook one part of any complex program or to make changes without a careful appraisal of the consequences is to threaten the integrity, and therefore the effectiveness, of the entire program.

IMPLEMENTATION ISSUES

Now we can turn specifically to issues of implementation and to examining some of the threats that are already beginning to appear.

HOW MUCH DOES IT COST? WHO SHOULD PAY? • Reading Recovery is introduced to a district, or region, by a trained teacher leader who teaches up to twelve Reading Recovery teachers per year. The first step then is to train a teacher leader, or make arrangements with another district to share in this training venture. Costs of implementation vary and depend upon location. Districts in Ohio enjoyed a distinct advantage until 1989 because, until then, Ohio State University was the only place in the United States where teacher leaders could be trained. Now that teacher leaders can be trained at other universities (and this number will grow steadily over the next few years), teacher-leader training will become more accessible and less expensive for school districts close to these institutions.

For the past three years, despite problems of distance and the cost of specialized training, school districts and universities outside Ohio have sent teachers and professors to Ohio State University for an academic year to become Reading Recovery teacher leaders. The costs of this training have included all or part of an annual salary, living expenses, graduate tuition, purchase of instructional materials, and miscellaneous incidental expenses for materials and travel. In other cases, individual teachers have taken a leave of absence and borne these costs themselves. For each of the last two years, two teacher leaders in training have been assisted by a small grant from the National Diffusion Network to cover some of the costs of tuition and program materials. In any case, the start-up costs are substantial, and the investment made by many individuals testifies to their strong belief in the effectiveness of Reading Recovery. Once a teacher leader is trained, the teacher-leader role is a full-time position and the teacher-leader's salary also becomes part of the cost of Reading Recovery.

The next costs to consider are those of training Reading Recovery teachers and providing instructional materials for children. For districts that are near an existing program, this is where the costs begin. The course for Reading Recovery teachers, taught by a teacher leader, usually carries graduate credit from a sponsoring university. There is a charge for the training, but, if the teacher leader is employed by the school district, no more than a standard registration cost is involved. There will also be a charge for textbooks, books for children, and supplies. The instructional materials are large quantities of carefully selected, well-illustrated, natural language books for children; a variety of miscellaneous items (magnetic letters, chalkboards, and writing supplies); and forms for record keeping. Costs for these materials are currently estimated to run from $850 to $1,200 per teacher for the first year and from $150 to $300 for subsequent years (additional books and supplies).

Other costs involve the training facility with sound system and one-way observation window, supervision during the implementation year (optional in subsequent years), and the costs of sending teacher leaders and some teachers to the annual conference and annual institute.

It is much to their credit that many school districts, without outside assistance, have carried the costs of Reading Recovery themselves. For a while, in some states, this may be the only way Reading Recovery will spread. However, a strong case can be made for state support. As Levin has argued:

> First, the states are responsible for education, and at-risk students have not been getting the education that they deserve and that will serve the states. Second, the states have much to gain from investments in at-risk students in the form of higher tax revenues and economic benefits attributable to a better trained labor force that enables the state to compete more effectively. Finally, successful educational interventions for disadvantaged populations will reduce state costs for public assistance. (1989, p. 57)

In the year following Marie Clay's introduction of Reading Recovery to the United States, the state of Ohio initiated legislation to pay the training costs. This support included tuition, travel, and instructional materials for Reading Recovery teacher training, and, most importantly, a portion of the salary of Reading Recovery teacher leaders within the state. Half of a teacher leader's time is spent in a training role that may cross district lines. This state support gives them the flexibility to serve across many school districts other than their own. More recently, the state has increased the amount of support and pays some of the continuing contact, conference, and institute costs of the project. As a result, Reading Recovery is well established in this state. Annual site reports summarized by Ohio State University report the success of the program. Large numbers of first-grade children at risk of reading failure, those in the lowest 20 percent of their class, are reading at average levels and being successful in their classrooms.

Many states have policies to assist at-risk children. In these states, school districts can make requests for specific and immediate support. While this program has already passed extensive field tests and proved its effectiveness, in each new state, trial periods should be proposed and data collected so that responsible decisions about its operation and effectiveness can be made in terms of local goals.

Whether or not school districts or universities take the initiative to introduce Reading Recovery to their states, state departments of education should become informed about the program and work collaboratively. A good beginning would be for state departments to study the kinds of support provided by the state of Ohio and more recent implementations, and form their own comprehensive plan for the kinds of support they would be willing to offer. This plan would encourage school districts and universities within the state to become involved. School districts and state departments can share the costs of training salaried teachers to teach Reading Recovery and sending teachers to train for Reading Recovery teacher-leader roles.

ARE WE TOO SMALL? TOO FAR AWAY? • Small school districts and districts that are remote from the large population centers of their state may despair that Reading Recovery is not for them. This need not be the case. Distance may present some problems, but size should not make a difference.

A Reading Recovery teacher leader can serve a total school population, K–12, of approximately 10,000 students; or, put another way, a population of 800 to 1,000 first-grade children. Most school districts in the United States are much smaller than this, but with a little administrative imagination—and cooperation—districts can combine to form consortia. In many cases, consortia already exist in the form of educational service districts. For example, Canby Elementary School District, in Clackamas County, Oregon, has fewer than 2,000 elementary school children. In school year 1990–91, they will have their own Reading Recovery teacher leader. She will spend half of her time as a Reading Recovery teacher in her own school. She will spend the other half of her time training and supervising twelve Reading Recovery teachers for other neighboring districts, many of which are smaller than her own. Through careful planning, her work will be administered jointly through her own school district and the Clackamas County Educational Service District. She will continue to receive full salary, retirement contributions, and all fringe benefits through her own district. However, an amount equivalent to half of her salary will be paid to her school district by the other districts that will receive her services as a teacher leader.

When school districts in remote areas combine to form consortia, the schools are often very far apart. The teachers may travel long distances to attend class, and the teacher leader may travel long distances to supervise their work. Clearly the teacher leaders should be located as centrally as possible. The difficulties are real, but they can be overcome.

WHY CAN'T WE GO IT ALONE? • One of the first and most obvious threats to the program is for well-intentioned people, well informed about recent developments in the theory and practice of the teaching of reading, and familiar with Marie Clay's work, to attempt to implement Reading Recovery on their own. There are good, understandable, reasons for this, but it is a mistake. Marie Clay's textbooks and procedural manual are readily available and explicit to a degree. They contain a gentle admonition that it is assumed that training would accompany any attempt to implement the program. While there may appear to be a wealth of information about the teaching of children, it is not quite enough. Instructional procedures are well explained, but some essential items are missing. For example, there are no graded passages for evaluating text reading—an essential measure of children's progress and for support of instruction. Of even greater importance are the interpretations of children's behavior and teacher's behavior that are unlikely to come without specific training and experience within the program. There are no descriptions of the teacher education program, and this is a vital part of the total program.

No serious-minded reading teacher with experience should be discouraged from studying *Reading: The Patterning of Complex Behavior* (Clay 1979), or, if the opportunity arises, from working experimentally with one or two children, systematically following the procedures outlined in *The Early Detection of Reading Difficulties* (Clay 1985). There is much to be learned. The Reading Recovery program in the Portland public schools began in such a way. A group of four teachers guided by a university consultant worked with ten low-achieving children. They made use of behind-the-glass sessions and implemented every aspect of the program as faithfully as they were able. The consultant had never before attempted a sustained implementation of the program but had used the diagnostic tests and some of the teaching procedures for several years. The program was audited by the district's research and evaluation department and the results were encouraging. Good progress was made, but the following excerpt from the final report (Dunkeld 1989) illustrates some of the difficulties that were encountered.

> We were never sure whether we had missed things that more experienced observers would have noticed, and we may easily have misunderstood some of the procedures. It is more than likely that many of our procedures resembled our previous experiences with the language experience approach, with a process approach to writing, and with invented spelling, more

closely than a strict and faithful interpretation of Reading Recovery. We had no way of knowing. We would have welcomed trained supervision . . . it is easy for even careful readers to miss parts of *The Early Detection of Reading Difficulties.*

Efficient cost-effective implementation is not likely to come quickly without experienced guidance. And experienced guidance is more readily available now than it was one year ago and is likely to increase steadily in the next few years. It should not be necessary in future to proceed without it.

It became very clear by the end of this year of exploration that it would be irresponsible to commit further resources without trained leadership and all the experience and support services offered by the Reading Recovery network.

A number of districts have sent teachers for teacher leader training. They know the value of the training and they know the value of the support services. Reports from districts in Ohio given at the National Reading Recovery Conference in February, 1989, show that when everything is properly in place and conscientiously delivered, there is good reason to believe that Reading Recovery is cost effective. These districts are enthusiastic about the efforts of the program, but they are modest in their claims. They know that it is not a panacea. They also know that it is a labor-intensive program and that it is difficult to compute cost effectiveness. It would be irresponsible to mount such a labor intensive program without taking advantage of all the available experience that has been gathered to date.

Districts wishing to implement Reading Recovery should not commit large-scale resources without the guidance of trained teacher leaders and the complete support services offered by the program. A hasty beginning may impede the future of this program.

LET'S MAKE SOME CHANGES! • There is an ever-present temptation to some administrators to take a program and adapt it to local needs, local pressures, or local budgets. Concerned about the high cost of individualized instruction, some administrators hypothesize that cost effectiveness would be improved by adapting the program for use with small groups. This is a researchable question and empirical answers suggest this is a less successful alternative (Lyons, Place, and Rinehart 1990). The following arguments must be considered.

One of the great benefits of Reading Recovery is that the program can be adjusted much more precisely than any classroom or small-group program. Anyone who has taught the program knows that the teacher can select a book for a particular child, can respond precisely to every detail of the child's behavior, can direct the child to a specific cuing system, can reinforce a specific behavior, and can sustain a child's attention. It is not possible to provide so many opportunities for children to work so intensively in a group. It is almost certainly because of these finely tuned adjustments that children learn to work independently, reach the average level of their class as quickly as they do, and sustain their gains. In any program, a group must either accelerate at the rate of the slowest child or leave some children behind. Therefore, group instruction tends to keep most children in the program longer than they really need to be there or neglects the most needy children. In the individualized instruction of Reading Recovery, we know there is a good chance of a child being discontinued in an average of twelve to fifteen weeks to the point where he or she can function independently at an average level. Though more children would be served in a group, they would almost certainly remain in the group longer, removing any short-term cost benefit.

Another adaptation designed to save money is the proposal to use aides and volunteers rather than teachers. By national policy, only successful, certified, experienced teachers are admitted to Reading Recovery training. There are very good reasons for this policy. Any attempt to staff the program with less than certified teachers would diminish the effectiveness of the program. It would show a reduced regard for a problem that demands the highest possible professional commitment. There are some aides who are superb teachers, and it would be foolish to deny that some are perfectly capable of learning Reading Recovery; however, the program requires sustained, skilled observation, and decision making based on theory. In general, aides are less familiar with theoretical issues, have had less professional training than teachers, and are not likely to do as well. Concerning volunteers: the training period is too long and the implementation far too demanding to consider seriously the use of even the most committed volunteers.

Another proposal is to adapt Reading Recovery for use with older children. It succeeds so well at grade one, why not try it at higher levels? Once again, these are researchable hypotheses that should be, and are being, investigated. Again, a number of considerations need to be kept in mind. Children who have struggled and failed for a year or more almost certainly bring with them different habits, different attitudes, and different kinds of reading and writing behaviors than children encountering difficulty for the first time right at the beginning of first grade. Some behaviors have gone "underground" and are harder to observe and interpret. Children are likely to be more discouraged. Some ineffective strategies are likely to be more firmly established and more resistant to change. Some additional procedures, as yet undeveloped, will almost certainly be needed. And, most important of all from a practical point of view, the class average has now risen, is comparatively much further away, and much harder to reach. A much longer period of time will be needed to bring low achievers to an average level after they have left grade one. Thus, a short-term, cost-saving program may not be possible. While something must be done to help older nonreaders, these considerations must make very clear that the most cost effective plan will always be the earliest possible intervention.

Any form of adaptation that distorts the Reading Recovery program, no matter how justifiable or well intentioned it may appear to be, should be given another name. Reading Recovery is a specific name for a specific program of individual help given by specially trained teachers only at the first-grade level. The good name of this program and a proper appraisal of its effectiveness depend upon every condition being met and every step being carried out with integrity.

ARE PRESENT RESOURCES SUFFICIENT TO SUSTAIN READING RECOVERY'S RECENT GROWTH? • Reading Recovery has already moved beyond the campus of the university that introduced it to this country. It has also moved well beyond the boundaries of the state of Ohio where it was so quickly recognized and so effectively supported. It has grown rapidly and there are strong indications that it will continue to grow. It now stretches from coast to coast. Two major threats to this development are that it may proceed haphazardly and that it may proceed too rapidly and outstrip the resources needed to sustain it.

At one time, applications for teacher-leader training at Ohio State University could be handled in much the same way as applications to any other program or course. Now it is time to ask whether other criteria beyond the proper qualifications of the applicant need be considered. For example, should strategic locations for regional and national development be considered? It is also appropriate to ask whether projections should be made about the total number of Reading Recovery trainers of teacher leaders that might be required nationwide in the next few years. What steps might be taken to make high-quality teacher-leader training accessible to each region of the country?

Every teacher leader trained by Ohio State University and the other regional sites needs support in terms of supervision, awareness of program development, and relevant research. As the number of trained teacher leaders increases, so do these needs. These are not the kinds of demands typically placed upon university faculty. When an innovative university offers Reading Recovery as part of its curriculum, usually as a public service, it takes on a program that generates comparatively little income in terms of tuition for student credit hours and supervision, yet places very heavy instructional, supervisory, and administrative demands upon its faculty.

At the moment, the appearances are that the faculty at Ohio State University, with a little assistance from specific grants and the National Diffusion Network, carry Reading Recovery and all of its attendant administrative and research functions as part of their normal teaching-service-research load. Reading Recovery faculty at Ohio State University do not work exclusively on Reading Recovery; they also teach other university courses. The same pattern is likely to be repeated at the regional Reading Recovery teacher-leader training institutions. It is a heavy load. This demand for services may soon be more than the present faculties can handle. It is difficult to see where the resources will come from for additional administrative and clerical staff needed to support a growing program of this scope.

In addition to these administrative costs are the costs of research. Resourceful faculty members at Ohio State University, appropriately, write grant proposals and have received some assistance from a private foundation for research. Currently research is also conducted by doctoral candidates and, of course, by any member of the research community who has an interest. While research of this kind is essential, it is again appropriate to ask whether the present arrangements are sufficiently comprehensive or systematically planned. And it is also appropriate to ask, given the ways in which faculty loads are computed, whether Reading Recovery faculty members are able to carry out all of their administrative, instructional, and supervisory responsibilities and still have sufficient time for high-quality research.

There is much current interest nationally in programs for children at risk. Levin, who cites Reading Recovery as example of a promising program, argues for "increasing investments in the education of at-risk children, because there has never been evidence of the resolve necessary to bring these students into the educational mainstream" (1989, p. 48). He describes the social costs of neglecting these children and suggests both private and public sources of funds. And Slavin has written, "What is needed is a sizable long-term commitment to the creation of effective programs for children at risk" (1987, p. 116).

Reading Recovery shows much promise of accomplishing what it was designed to do; however, it needs stable sources of support for its growing administrative and supervisory responsibilities, for evaluation, and for research. As a vehicle for studying teacher change, system intervention, and children's learning, current research has barely scratched the surface.

University faculty who offer a demanding, innovative program like Reading Recovery, take on administrative, supervisory, instructional, and research responsibilities far greater than those of typical university courses. They also provide a valuable public service. Schools of education should recognize the scope and the value of these commitments, and accordingly make adjustments in faculty loads.

Each district, each state, and the nation as a whole stand to benefit from a properly administered, properly researched program. No one gains when a program is jeopardized because personnel and resources are spread too thin. Those districts that have adopted Reading Recovery have made a considerable financial commitment. It is appropriate that state and national agencies, especially those that have made public announcements prioritizing assistance to children at risk, make strong moves to support programs like Reading Recovery. The Reading Recovery program as a whole has grown steadily, is about to expand at a faster rate, and is in danger of trying to do too much with too few resources. State and national agencies should be quick to recognize this and provide some of the needed support. This is an opportunity too valuable to be squandered by frugality, indifference, or neglect.

Reading Recovery faculty at Ohio State University and at the new regional teacher-leader training institutions should seek stable services of funds from their own institutions, and through grants from private sources, state departments, and the U.S. Office of Education, for administrative needs and comprehensive research.

If Reading Recovery lives up to the expectations its proponents cautiously hold for it, it may well become an important national resource. The annual summer Reading Recovery institute currently serves as a policy-making group and an opportunity for continued growth. An advisory group of trainers currently exists, but it might be time to consider the formation of a national policy committee, with members from the regional institutions, state departments, and the U.S. Office of Education. This group could supplement current efforts, seek resources, and guide future growth. It might also be time to seek funds for a permanent administrative position to direct the program at the national level.

The excitement that has been generated by this program is well founded. We can look forward to the benefits of a more literate society, and teachers who are prepared to explore new horizons in teaching.

REFERENCES

Allington, R. 1989. "Evaluation of the Reading Recovery Program." Luncheon address presented at the Reading Recovery Conference, February, Ohio State University, Columbus, Ohio.

Clay, M. M. 1979. *Reading: The Patterning of Complex Behavior.* 2d ed. Portsmouth, N.H.: Heinemann.

———. 1985. *The Early Detection of Reading Difficulties.* 3d ed. Portsmouth, N.H.: Heinemann.

———. 1990. "The Reading Recovery Programme, 1984–88: Coverage, Outcomes, Education Board District Figures." *New Zealand Journal of Educational Studies* 25 (1): 61–70.

DeFord, D. E., S. Tancock, & Nora White. 1990. *Teachers' Models of the Reading Process and Their Evaluations of an Individual Reader: Relationship to Success in Teaching Reading and Judged Quality of Instruction.* Technical Report. Columbus, Ohio: Ohio State University.

Dunkeld, C. 1989. *Gaining Experience with Reading Recovery: A Pilot Project Between Portland Public Schools and Portland State University.* Occasional Paper no. 891215. Portland, Oregon: Portland State University.

Levin, H. M. 1989. "Financing the Education of At-Risk Students." *Educational Evaluation and Policy Analysis* 2 (1): 47–60.

Lyons, Carol A. 1989. "Reading Recovery: A Preventative for Mislabeling Young At-Risk Learners." *Urban Education* 24 (2): 125–39.

Lyons, Carol A., W. Place, & J. Rinehart. 1990. "Factors Related to Teaching Success in the Literacy Education of Young At-Risk Children." Technical Report. Columbus, Ohio: Ohio State University.

Lyons, Carol A., & Nora White. 1990. "Belief Systems and Instructional Decisions: Comparisons Between More and Less Effective Teachers." Technical Report. Columbus, Ohio: Ohio State University.

Pinnell, G. S. 1986. "Helping Teachers Help Children at Risk: Insights from the Reading Recovery Program." *Peabody Journal* 62 (3): 70–85.

———. 1990. "Success for Low Achievers Through Reading Recovery." *Educational Leadership* 48 (1): 17–21.

Pinnell, G. S., D. DeFord, & C. Lyons. 1988. *Reading Recovery: Early Intervention for At-Risk First Graders.* Arlington, Va.: Educational Research Service.

Pinnell, G. S., M. Fried, & R. Estice. 1990. "Reading Recovery: Learning How to Make a Difference." *The Reading Teacher* 43 (4): 282–95.

Slavin, R. E. 1987. "Making Chapter 1 Make a Difference." *Phi Delta Kappan* (October): 110–19.

THREE

Reading Recovery Surprises

MARIE M. CLAY

When Maxine Greene wrote about teaching in an article called "How Do We Think About Our Craft?" her words captured for me what I believe to be some of the important achievements of Reading Recovery.

> Through our own attending and the going-out of our own energies, we are able to break the bonds of the ordinary and the taken-for-granted, to move into spaces never known before. And that is what some of us, considering our craft, want for those we teach: the opportunity and capacity to reach beyond, to move towards what is not yet. (1986, p. 23)

The Reading Recovery program aims to undercut a high proportion of literacy problems by providing children with a second chance to learn after their first year at school. The results of this early intervention program have been surprisingly good but they come into conflict with educators' expectations about children who have problems with early literacy learning. The program has been subject to continuous monitoring at several levels in New Zealand, Australia, and the United States, providing careful documentation of the findings that I will be discussing. Outcomes of the program have been evaluated at the level of individual children, or groups of children, or teaching, or outcomes for an education system. (A single source for most of the discussion in this paper is Clay 1985.[1])

In education we assume that teachers are dealing with learned behaviors in school subjects, but sometimes we fail to recognize that there are also important learned components in psychological processes, and in general ability as it is tested by intelligence tests. Classroom teaching and intervention programs can work to change the learned components of any of these behaviors. High numbers of successful Reading Recovery children in several countries imply that some important learning is occurring, which has not previously been possible for many children with reading or writing problems. To understand how these children can be successful, it is necessary to think about the following assumptions that underlie Reading Recovery instruction as you read this chapter.

Assumption 1 is that all children bring to school stores of knowledge and ways of processing information from the world and from language, and literacy instruction can build upon their prior knowledge.

This conflicts with the view that learning to read and write are new skills and can be taught to children in programs designed by adults who have analyzed the nature of these skills without reference to what children can already do.

Assumption 2 is that many things that are important for successful achievement in reading and writing are learned—oral language, visual perception, motor behavior needed for literacy behaviors (although maturational factors may set limits to the rate of learning), and even test performance on intelligence tests. If children come to school with more or less learning in each of these areas they can be helped by the classroom program to round out their foundational learning in these areas at the same time as they begin to work with reading and writing.

This conflicts with the view that children are either ready or not ready for literacy instruction, that low scores on assessments of prior learning reflect differences in abilities—not learned achievements—and that waiting for readiness to arrive and delaying opportunities for literacy experiences is the necessary first step in instruction.

Assumption 3 is that successful readers and writers show us how they use what they know in reading to help their writing and vice versa, and that therefore both must be part of an early literacy intervention program for second-chance learners.

This conflicts with common practice, which sees early reading instruction as separate and different from early writing opportunities, separating these in theory and in practice.

SOME SURPRISING OUTCOMES

For the reader who accepts those three assumptions, what happens in Reading Recovery instruction is not hard to understand. But for many educational systems with policies that conflict with such assumptions, the implementation of Reading Recovery produces many surprises, which will be discussed in this chapter. The most surprising is the ease with which low achievers can learn.

THE PROGRAM WORKS WITH DIVERSE POPULATIONS • The program is up and running in different education systems. There is a national system in New Zealand, and it operates in two Australian states. In North America, Reading Recovery teacher programs are operating in selected cities in thirteen U.S. states, and two sites in Canada. New programs are expected to begin in 1990 in Hawaii and Surrey, England, as well as other sites in the United States.

Irrespective of social problems, ethnic differences, second-language problems, low intelligence, school absence, sickness, special handicaps, or physical factors, children are given a second chance to learn what their classmates have learned easily, but they do it in one-to-one instruction and in a way that enables them to regain the ground they have lost. There is flexibility in the program for the teacher to design the instruction to suit a particular child and to weight the activities according to his or her particular needs.

✓ *THE RATE OF LEARNING ACCELERATES* • It may seem unreasonable to expect "slow-learning" children to learn at an accelerated rate. After all, this is what slow-learning children do not do. They do not keep pace with their classmates. They do not catch up with their classmates. They do not reach a level of independence in the literacy activities of their classrooms, but remain dependent on interactions with their teachers.

Yet, in Reading Recovery, the children whom teachers selected because they were slow learners, progress at faster rates for a period of time than their better-performing classmates. The acceleration is surprising. Each research study has found that children take twelve to fourteen weeks to reach the average-band performance of their classmates if they begin after a year at school (around their sixth birthday), although some take as long as twenty weeks.

INDEPENDENCE IS FOSTERED • The children leave the program not only at average levels for their class, but also with a large measure of independence over how they learn. They are not discontinued until the teacher can describe how they are problem-solving new texts in reading in satisfactory ways, self-correcting errors without prompting, and writing their own stories and messages. In other words, the child must be able to work independently with print in both reading and writing. Because busy classroom teachers will have limited time to interact with individual pupils, children need to have independent problem-solving strategies as an insurance. Then they will be able to extend their control of literacy tasks even at times when they cannot have the teacher's attention. Children who once seemed to be "slow learners" can become processors of information who teach themselves from their own efforts. They can be encouraged to be independent from their first lessons. This is not so strange, since each of these children has already learned to talk and has worked out the rules of conversation—syntactic, semantic, and social rules.

In education we have come to expect that slow learners cannot learn their school subjects in this way. Our expectations about slow learners have led to the development of a whole vocabulary of terms to describe such children and their handicaps.

CONTINUED PROGRESS IS MAINTAINED • It is a common prediction that even though such gains might be possible under some special conditions (such as the Reading Recovery program), the children will slip back to the slowest progress group when their special program ends. In fact, follow-up research studies in New Zealand and in Ohio show that children increase their achievements after they leave the program, gaining at rates that are comparable with those of average children in their classrooms. As a group, children continue to function within the average band of their classroom even three years after the program has ended.

The period when the child makes the transition from extra instruction to classroom instruction only is very important in achieving these successful outcomes. The criteria by which the children are judged ready for discontinuing are related to whether they can engage with the classroom program close to the average for their class. At first they might get a little more help than other children to maintain that progress, but following a successful transition they should be able to work within the class average like any other class member.

The program seeks to eliminate a group of children whose achievements are so limited that they really cannot engage effectively in the work of the classroom, because the instruction they need is instruction that other children learned in the first year or so of school.

A HIGH NUMBER OF CHILDREN RESPOND TO THE INTERVEN-TION • When the lowest 20 percent of the age cohort in New Zealand are given individual instruction of this kind for twelve to twenty weeks (thirty minutes each day), 19 percent have been able to learn at accelerated rates and catch up to their classmates. This presents a strong challenge to our theories about the incidence of literacy problems and their causes.

In 1984–88 there were ten Education Board areas in New Zealand. This allowed fifty tests of the percentage of children referred to specialists for further help (Clay 1990). This means that the ordinary school program and the Reading Recovery program together could have more than 99 percent of children aged six to seven years reading and writing in relatively independent ways, and the remainder identified for specialist attention and special assistance.

CHILDREN WHO NEED MORE HELP ARE IDENTIFIED • Occasionally, then, the program is not enough for a child who needs more than it offers. Perhaps any one child has multiple difficulties, or a problem that is too severe in some respect, or a problem that is too puzzling for the Reading Recovery teacher and his or her teacher leader to work out how to teach that child. At the end of an intensive program, children who have been able to "recover" control of literacy activities have been effectively distinguished from those who cannot. Then the parents and the school's Reading Recovery team can decide how referral to a specialist should be made and the carefully assembled records of the child's progress in the program kept by the teacher can be forwarded to the specialist to be used as part of his or her diagnostic evaluation of what next to do.

In these cases the program has been of assistance because some learning has taken place during the program but at a rate that makes average-band performance an unrealistic goal. The program does not harm the child; it acts diagnostically to distinguish the child who fails to accelerate from other children who are responding. The time in Reading Recovery is long enough for a fair trial and a reliable assessment, and makes it clear that a longer period of help is required from teachers with more specialized training. Without loading specialist services with massive testing and impossible discrimination decisions, an education system could plan effective programming for such different groups of children after one year of school.

SOME SURPRISING OPERATIVE CONCEPTS

The surprising outcomes discussed above lead people to assume that a selection process is used that sets aside the intractable learners and somehow selects only those with good potential. This is not so. No child in ordinary classrooms is excluded from Reading Recovery for any reason. This provides a tough test for the intervention.

PARTICIPATION IS BASED ON AN INCLUSIVE DEFINITION • The program is designed for children who are the lowest achievers in the class/age group. What is used is an inclusive definition. Principals have sometimes argued to exclude this or that category of children or to save places for children who might seem to "benefit the most," but that is not using the full power of the program. It has been one of the surprises of Reading Recovery that all kinds of children with all kinds of difficulties can be included, can learn, and can reach average-band performance for their class in both reading and writing achievement. Exceptions are not made for children of lower intelligence, for second-language children, for children with low language skills, for children with poor motor coordination, for children who seem immature, for children who score poorly on readiness measures, or for children who have already been categorized by someone else as learning disabled.

SELECTION IS MADE BY TEACHERS • A team of teachers (three or more) in a school choose the poorest performers based on low achievement relative to classmates. Class teachers can nominate the poorest performers in their classes and other teachers can check the selection with very simple observation instruments. Procedures like this reduce teachers' selection errors. There are several advantages to such an approach.

- First, nonspecialist teachers can be trained to select children on achievement criteria and other specialist assessment is not essential at this time.
- Second, it deals with the social deprivation problem that could yield a low intelligence-test score and a low achievement score as a result of poor preschool learning opportunities.
- Third, as resources are increased, more children can be taken into the program, but as those selected initially were the poorest performers and the hardest to teach, the job gets easier

as the operation gets larger. It is easier to teach the next 5 percent in an expanding program than it was to teach the first 5 percent.

- Fourth, any child who might otherwise have been labeled learning disabled ought to be caught up because their achievement is low. This gives them help that is likely to lift some (perhaps many) of them out of the learning-disabled category.

It is surprising that an inclusive definition of low achievers, not excluding anyone in ordinary classrooms for any reason, has worked in all Reading Recovery programs.

INTERVENTION TAKES PLACE EARLY • When children enter school they have had very different preschool experiences, not only because they have grown up in different homes and social groups, but also because they have selectively attended more to some aspects of their environments than others. Classroom learning is a new set of experiences and expectations, which calls for adjustments and learning how to live and work in the new environment. Most children make the transitions and begin to engage with the school program. Some do very little; others strive hard but get confused by these literacy learning activities. The idea is to give them another way of getting to grips with the classroom activities, in a second-chance program. Children are selected after one year at school if they are judged not to be engaging with the school's program—a pragmatic approach. It is not that the child has a cluster of inadequacies, but that the program is not reaching the child's level for engagement to occur.

Critics have argued that this is too soon, that the children are too young, that they will mature into reading and writing, that the second language learning children should be left longer, and that lifelong attitudes to literacy will be affected by too early instruction. Some technical arguments mounted against this age of entry must be addressed.

1. *Tests are not reliable for low-scoring children until after seven and a half years.* I would agree, but that refers to normative or standardized tests constructed on the basis of sampling the universe of reading competencies. Until a child has quite extensive learning in a new area, a sampling of that learning does not work at all well. However, a different approach is to find out what young successful learners are learning about beginning reading and writing and test the low achievers for knowledge in these areas. Reading Recovery assessments are of this kind.

2. *Discrepancies between intelligence and achievement of two years are normally expected and cannot appear until after two years at school.* This is overcome by avoiding intelligence in selection and selecting only on achievement. It is assumed that as the lessons are designed around the child's strengths any child will benefit from individual teaching that starts at his or her level of engagement with the tasks.

3. *Maturation should be allowed for and children need to be left until after seven years.* I can only point to thousands of replications and many reports of the successful responses of children under seven years to the program. Observations at the end of the first two weeks of the program indicate that young children begin to change their behaviors as early as this. During this period the teacher is not allowed to use in lessons anything the child does not already know, but must devise tasks that support the child in using what he or she can already do. During this time teachers begin to report that the child is taking control of the task.

4. *Readiness theory says that children will come to reading when they are ready.* Reading Recovery results can be explained by Vygotskyan concepts of the child's (a) being able to do with support what he or she is unable to do alone, and (b) being able to do alone tomorrow what he or she must have support for today. Reading Recovery instruction continually calls for the child to take control of all that is within his or her independent grasp. Instead of these children having to get their acts together by themselves, they will have support and help from an attentive and informed teacher. If children have not been able to learn some skill alone in their social environment, having a teacher who knows their response patterns well and can anticipate what is likely to be difficult will facilitate that learning. This is a program with little faith in maturation of anything in literacy learning, except some aspects of motor performance, and considerable confidence that the child can be supported to learn how to go about literacy learning.

THE INTERVENTION PERIOD IS BRIEF • It was never anticipated that we would find the conditions that allowed children to make such rapid progress. The first field trials suggested twelve to fifteen weeks, but we suspected these results because some of the field trial population began with somewhat higher levels of achievement than expected. (They were children from small

schools that were using their Reading Recovery teacher with children above the poorest 20 percent in literacy learning.) However,
about twelve to fifteen weeks has continued to be average for the
program and a limit of twenty weeks (interpreted liberally) has
been a cutoff point used for practical reasons in New Zealand.

EVERY CHILD'S PROGRAM IS DIFFERENT • Teachers not only
deliver individual lessons, they also design and adjust individual
programs according to the current balance of the child's needs and
strengths. It stands to reason that if children have difficulties and
if we take into the program all who are low achievers, they are
likely to have different problems, one from another.

Therefore there can be no program packages and no computer
disks. Each child's program is determined by the child's strengths
and the teacher works with what the child does well and independently. Novel demands are a result of a judgment by the teacher of
what will have the greatest payoff for this child's processing of print
at this stage. This is essential if acceleration is to be achieved. There
is no time for plodding through the steps of a sequenced program.
What the child can currently do determines the shifts that might be
made. The program gives little overt attention to practice of items
of knowledge. It is assumed that, language being what it is, the
features of a language learned today will recur and so the language,
its frequencies, and its rule-guided forms will ensure that the necessary practice will occur.

Teachers are trained to observe a particular child's reading and
writing behaviors and to make program decisions that bring these
in line with normal reading progress. They relate a particular child's
behavior to an awareness of different ways in which the acquisition
of normal reading progress can take place. Teachers get really
excited and can talk in articulate ways about what is happening,
and what are the learning needs of a particular student at a particular point in his or her progress.

LEARNING OCCURS WITHOUT A TEACHER • A particular feature of the program is that the teacher observes very closely what
the child is already able to do and designs instruction that strength-
ens established responses. For example, in the first two weeks of
lessons the teacher is not allowed to teach the child anything new.
The child finds all the tasks "doable." Feeling secure, the children
often become venturesome and discover ways of working when
previously they would not try. Confidence increases even though
the situation is new, because the children discover that everything

that has to be done can be done. One can see the children assuming some control of the learning even in these first two weeks.

Teachers find it hard not to teach new things; it seems to negate their role as teacher. But it serves to remind the teacher that she or he must design the lessons to extend outwards from what the child can already do, and that the tests and observations have only revealed some of the child's repertoire of competencies.

The teacher learns more than she or he knew about the child and the children learn that they have strengths to bring to the tasks.

CHILDREN READ WHOLE STORIES • From the beginning the child's reading is supported by a sense of story and constant checking about whether the real world or the world of books allows one to make sense of what one is reading. This is facilitated by the story being introduced to the child in its entirety, and by permission to return to stories again and again for rereading and familiar reading.

Although the storybooks have not been written with a strict control over vocabulary, there is natural word control in all language based on the frequency principle. If you read extensively, the same words keep coming up. As you gain control of the high-frequency words, attention, and more deliberate learning, goes to the next most frequently occurring words.

It is a written rule of the program that all instruction must be related to the reading of texts and the writing of texts. Things may be given separate or special attention only if those items (letters, sounds, words) are needed in order to read or to write text.

CHILDREN READ A NEW STORYBOOK EVERY DAY • These (ostensibly) slow learners of literacy can "read" a new book every day. This needs some explanation.

Reading Recovery teachers have found many "little storybooks" that provide easy reading for beginners. The New Zealand list has more than 3,000 titles in it. Some are "good literature" and others take small steps toward children's literature. The language of the most useful books is close to the language that the children speak or may have heard. Teachers avoid texts usually found in controlled vocabulary books because children cannot predict the upcoming language from the way they, the children, speak.

During the program teachers usually avoid a book that is too long for the child to read a whole story in a day. Reading the whole story allows the plot or the story pattern to assist the reading. So although first books may have very little text, they will have a clear story line (like Wildsmith's *The Cat on the Mat*).

There are three stages to the reading of the new book.

1. The introduction. First, the teacher introduces the book to the child, getting the child to anticipate the story from the pictures and discussing difficult language or concepts. New words are used and discussed, the thread of the story is worked over, the climax is talked about, and the humor appreciated.

2. The problem solving of the text. Then, having provided this support system—some knowledge of what is to come—the teacher encourages the child to work independently through the story but helps and teaches where necessary. As the child attempts the book for the first time, the teacher helps the child problem-solve the text with prompts and other teaching interactions in a way that interrupts this reading minimally.

3. Independent rereading. The next day, to test the quality of the introduction and first reading, the child reads that new book independently, with no help from the teacher who is busy taking a running record of the reading, so that the problem solving (which I also call "reading work") that the child is doing can later be analyzed.

On the rare occasions when a successful second reading does not occur, the fault is seen to be not in the child but in the teaching. If the second and independent reading is not achieved with 90 percent accuracy, the teacher assumes that the new book was too hard or that it was not introduced and taught properly during the first reading. A new book every day is highly dependent on teacher expertise for its success.

After these three steps the new book goes into the child's box of books and, as the child reads three to five books every day, the book will be sure to be selected by the teacher or the child on several more occasions before it is removed from the child's current books to make room for other books that challenge the child's reading processes.

THE VOLUME OF READING IS INCREASED • Despite a crowded thirty-minute lesson in which many things occur, Reading Recovery needs the warning that successful readers read a lot. Research shows large differences between good and poor readers in how much reading they do. During a Reading Recovery lesson a child may read three to five "little books" as well as do several rereadings of the story or sentence he or she wrote in the lesson. How is this achieved?

Children have their own box of about twenty books from which they choose familiar books to reread at the beginning of the lesson—easy reading, during which the child is practising the orchestration of the reading process, calling up decision processes to suit particular texts, and being reinforced for this by understanding and enjoying real stories. Then there is the independent reading of yesterday's new book, the introduction of today's new book in which the child participates actively, and the first reading of the new book.

The volume of reading can be viewed as the mediator through which known vocabulary is increased (a new way of achieving many repetitions without using contrived texts or tasks), opening up the way to more difficult texts. It is the means by which the lift in text difficulty comes about. The more support the child has from known vocabulary requiring little attention, the freer the child is to attend to new vocabulary without losing the benefit of understanding.

CHILDREN WRITE MESSAGES THAT THEY HAVE COMPOSED •
Children write stories every day after orally composing them. In these sentences children encounter the high-frequency words that they can already write. These they must complete on their own, and they receive all the repetition they need to bring that writing to fluency.

It is in the part of the daily lesson where the child composes a sentence or two to write that attention is directed to the "sound sequences in words." The teacher asks, "How do you think we could write that?" This means "What can you hear?" and "In what order?" and "What is a possible way of writing that?" Attention is being directed to phonological information at the subword level, and to information the child has about which letters and letter sequences might be used to represent those sounds. The learner becomes aware that there are sometimes alternative ways of representing similar sounds, rather than having a fixed association of one letter with one sound.

It does not matter if the messages they compose contain words they have not written before or "learned." There are several ways in which these can be handled, all of which develop for the child ways of getting to write new words.

1. If, in the teacher's opinion, the item is too difficult for this child at this time, the teacher will write it into the story in a deliberate fashion as if sharing the task with the child.

2. If the word is one the child could analyze for sound sequences the teacher will support such an analysis, helping the child to say the word slowly, hear the sounds within it, and discover possible ways of writing down those sounds. This is a kind of invented spelling; the child carries most of the work load, but the teacher shares the task.

3. Sometimes children show that they know where to find a word in a book, on a chart, or in some previous story they have written. Soon the child builds up a known writing vocabulary that facilitates the writing of longer "stories."

Although many people imagine that children must read words before they can write words this is not the case. In fact the business of trying to write words is very helpful for children having difficulty with reading. To write words children are forced to pay attention to visual cues; they cannot work on language only. They have to construct the word letter by letter. New words are often like old words in some part. The more familiar children are with written words, the more examples the learner has to use as building blocks for other words. Children are adept at getting to new instances by analogy with old instances; and if they are not, they can quickly learn how this can be done.

MANY SOURCES OF INFORMATION IN PRINT ARE ATTENDED TO • It is surprising to many that a program for children who have found literacy learning difficult does not have an apparent emphasis on skill training and practice. The children do learn skills, but there appears to be little traditional skill training going on.

The theory behind the procedures assumes that the big discovery task for the young reader is to find out what kinds of information exist in texts and what the reader has to attend to in order to extract that information (Clay 1990b). Skill in using such sources of information can follow only after learning about such information sources. Here the word *information* is being used in two ways: (a) in the everyday sense, and (b) in the technical sense, as in information theory. So the beginning reader has to learn to get meaning (another word for information) from texts; to discover how his or her oral language knowledge relates to texts; to work out how available syntactic awareness is relevant to reading tasks; to learn that existing phonological awareness can be applied to reading; to find out how visual information provides cues and facilitates processing of letters, clusters, words, phrases, and various print conventions, including tracking information, spacings, and punctuation; and to discover how many other things about books and the way they are presented help the reader. Child and teacher work on interesting texts, gradually uncovering new features of print that provide information to the reader. The child is learning to pick up and use information while problem-solving new texts and in the process is reading quantities of texts that allow commonly occurring words to become part of a controlled vocabulary of "known words."

Any detail attended to must arise out of reading or writing texts; having received attention, it is then embedded back into the text activity. It is assumed that two or three examples are enough for the child to see an analogy or begin to form a primitive rule, that for the moment further practice is unnecessary, and that new learning on two or three examples will be encountered in a new context on another day. The children will gradually round out the rule system as they do more reading and writing because of the rule-guided nature of language.

ORDINARY CLASSROOM TEACHERS ARE USED • Another surprising thing about the program is that the selection and the instruction is carried out by ordinary classroom teachers.

A widespread prevention program operating in every school could not expect to have highly trained specialists making the decisions; that would be too costly. Teachers have been trained in New Zealand in an inservice course, in school time, once every two weeks for half a day throughout a school year.

TEACHERS THINK ABOUT THEIR TEACHING • In Reading Recovery training, teachers begin to look at child behaviors and the teaching behavior of their peers, and begin to talk about the relationships between these. Clearly their discussion, the explanations and the comments, emerges from their present view of literacy learning, the practice and assumptions with which they currently work.

Two kinds of conflict occur in this situation. The more obvious one is conflict between what they see the child doing (or having difficulty with) and the teaching moves the teacher they are observing is making. When teachers see such mismatches, they begin to articulate what they think should have been done and open all the assumptions about teaching interactions and literacy learning for public consideration by other trainees who are their peers.

The less obvious conflict, and yet a more significant source of change, is when a trainee teacher notices a mismatch between what the child is doing and the teacher's own rationales. This is a mis-match between what is observed and how the observer is explain-ing it. The behavior being observed cannot be denied, and it is the teacher's own assumptions that must be called into question. The teacher knows that the explanation has to shift to account for what is really occurring. Teachers learn to check on their own assump-tions about teaching and to shift those assumptions in the face of clear data. They learn to check assumptions against behaviors. They learn to articulate in discussions with peers what the conflict and possible shifts in their ideas could be. Their teaching interac-tions become finely tuned as a result of observing, articulating, reviewing, and gradually changing their theories of the task.

Throughout one year's apprenticeship training, teachers shift in what they do (their practices), and in their understanding of learning to read and write. They become more articulate about reading and writing processes and many become very astute as they question their colleagues. They pick up an issue related to learning and reason it through, bringing it into relationship with bodies of knowledge they have or are reading about. Teacher lead-ers are expected to work in this way, but many teachers are just as thoughtful about their work. So Reading Recovery training of teachers improves teaching as well as children's learning.

THE PROGRAM IS DESIGNED FOR EXPANSION • The program is a hierarchical or tiered system of expertise, sometimes likened, unkindly, to pyramid selling. Highly trained teacher leaders nego-tiate with administrators above them and train classroom teachers. One trained leader can train one or two groups of twelve teachers in a year. If a program has only one leader then it can expand to 12 or 24 new schools each year. However, if a program trains twelve tutors (teacher leaders) in any one year, then in the following year the education system could have 144 or 288 new schools having teachers trained.

Canberra, the Australian Federal Territory, provides an exam-ple of system coverage. It began with an exploratory study of chil-dren having difficulty a year after entry to school. Then it had two leaders trained. After those preliminaries, and despite funding problems, in four years it expanded throughout all the schools in the district (about 60). One teacher leader sought promotion to another job and a further one was sent for training. All schools in the district that wanted the program now have at least one Reading Recovery teacher and the next goal is to increase this number in selected schools that have a heavier weighing of low achievers.

Surprisingly (that word again), the training system has proved adaptable in three countries and it can spread the program fast enough to demonstrate a return for money or effort spent.

SOME CHALLENGES FOR THE PROGRAM

Education and communication are key words in Reading Recovery. Because the program breaks with many traditions and popular assumptions, teacher leaders are encouraged to regard misconceptions about the program as opportunities to educate. They have to enlist the help of educators and so need to explain and help others to understand what the program is trying to do.

Because the program is surprising and different in so many ways, there is a continuing need to communicate clearly about it because otherwise what it is trying to do is misunderstood. The one-way screen provides a window on the program and parents, administrators, psychologists, and politicians have watched the process of learning to read and write going on before their very eyes. Observers are impressed with the intensity of the interactions they observe and by the competence the children display on the tasks set. Even without knowing the intricacies of the theory or procedures, two first-time observers (both academic researchers from the United States but one observing in New Zealand and another in Columbus, Ohio, in 1989) made these comments:

> Next she (the teacher) spent several minutes going over the entire story with the child, page by page, picture by picture, making sure to use key words and phrases in the text, such as "little bean" and "big stalk." She prompted the child to participate in constructing the story with her by asking him questions and encouraging his comments and observations. "If you know what the story's about it helps you read it," she told him, and she demonstrated this to him (and to us) by having him read key passages. He then read with much more fluency sentences such as "The little bean grew into a big stalk." It was a remarkable and tangible demonstration of . . . the complex and subtle interplay between acquiring the skills of literacy while focusing on the meaning for which literacy is a vehicle. (Goldenberg 1989)

> I visited Ohio State last Monday and had a wonderful time observing Reading Recovery. I was very impressed with both the teaching and the interaction between one of the teachers and a child, just how much effort it takes for some children to attend to print. This particular child, I believe, could have spent

years in a classroom without learning much. In the Reading Recovery program, he was rapidly becoming a reader. (Elfrieda Hiebert, pers. com. 1989)

THERE IS NO ROOM FOR COMPLACENCY • I like the challenges of the Reading Recovery program because they show that many children we had given up on can become active constructors of their own knowledge. More than that, the program provides teachers with ways in which they can construct their own understanding of literacy processes. A program full of surprises keeps those involved in it thinking about new possibilities for children. When a different set of circumstances allows children to show us that they are capable of doing well what we labeled them as being unable to do, we question our old expectations. We should discuss the assumptions we make about children and test out what child-behavior types or categories are a result of our instructional positions and organizations rather than a significant limitation in the child. A quite different approach may produce different results.

The primary assumption of Reading Recovery is that when we take the poorest achievers in any school they will all be different rather than grouped in three or four categories. They will be having difficulty for different reasons. If their teachers become observers, who start where the child is, and go with the child, and adapt to the child's strengths in learning, and waste no learning time unnecessarily, the program should be flexible enough to work with almost any child in an unhurried yet accelerative way.

THE INTERVENTION WORKS IN MANY SETTINGS • Experience across three countries shows that the intervention works with almost any children, with all kinds of teachers, with teacher leaders trained in different courses, and in many different settings. The program is not a cure-all for or excuse for bad programs, but, should a child find beginning literacy instruction too hard a challenge in a classroom setting, then, whatever the prior experience of that child, a quality Reading Recovery program ought to be able to get that child back into the mainstream of classroom instruction.

In New Zealand it is a national program and so it has to work with many different cultural groups in that country, but particularly Maori children who are not in immersion Maori programs, and all the different groups of children who come from the islands of the South Pacific, ten or so different languages and cultures.

In the state of Victoria in Australia, it has to work with many Greek and Italian children of immigrant parents as well as some Australian aboriginal children. In Columbus, Ohio, it works with black children and children from the Appalachian region of the United States. There must be something important happening here, because in the early days of the program people predicted that it would not work with different children, with different teachers, in different education districts, and in different countries. Now that we know it does, we have to acknowledge that we are all part of a very challenging change that is occurring in what we may expect of children who have difficulty learning; that leaves us with two big surprises for the future. How widely can we offer this new success story to children who might otherwise fail? Are there messages from the success of Reading Recovery that might be applied to other areas where anyone has difficulty learning?

THE LONG-TERM EFFECTS OF THE PROGRAM MUST BE MONITORED • A recent researcher visiting New Zealand junior school programs described the efforts at the turn of the decade in this way.

> New Zealand is interested in improving the quality of literacy education for all children, and while they already have good average results by international standards they are fine-tuning their system to lift the performance levels of the population even higher given the need for populations to be highly educated in this information age. They are paying special attention to early intervention in literacy problems. (Goldenberg 1989)

I hope that we will be able to show the effects on a national scale. We have one education system for the whole country and we work on a small scale compared with state education in Australia or the United States. We already have seven years of extensive delivery of the program and in another four years we might begin to see the achievement levels in the elementary school changing for the better, as Reading Recovery graduates move up the school as average achievers. It takes a great deal to change the levels of achievement in an age cohort because these are very stable measures, so it will be the ultimate surprise if this should occur.

THE RESULTS BELIE SOME TRADITIONAL CONCEPTS • Research in psychology and education earlier in this century has encouraged us to believe things about children that do not seem to be true any longer, especially for those of us who have watched children succeed in the Reading Recovery program. Among the challenges implied in this account of surprises are a questioning of the ways in which concepts of maturation and readiness have been used to the disadvantage of learners; of many beliefs about learning to read and what is helpful, necessary, or confusing; of the divided curriculum, which places reading, writing, and spelling in separate curriculum slots and does not encourage cross-referencing of knowledge across the boundaries; and of the inevitability of slow learning as a characteristic of children rather than a function of the group or class instruction we deliver. Maxine Greene's quotation, which began this chapter, leads us back to thinking about the professional value to teachers of being surprised by what their children can do and also by what teachers can learn. Her message continues:

> I think of . . . Wallace Stevens' man with the blue guitar who would not play things as they are. I think of numerous figures in literature, yes, and in history who overcame their own pow-erlessness through "shocks of awareness". . . . These are images of transcendence, images of resistance. Thinking about our craft, thinking about what it might mean to release the newcomers, the diverse young, to learn how to learn, we can think of ourselves as empowering. And the desired end-in-view? To enable persons to reach beyond, to seek in distinctiveness and membership for what is not yet! (1986, p. 23)

ENDNOTE

1. The responses of each child in his or her daily lessons are recorded because they are the basis of the teacher's responses in subsequent lessons, contributing to the quality of the instruction. Those who train the teachers maintain contact with them, fostering networks of support, communication, and peer evaluation. Education systems monitor the expansion and operation of the program for organizational, resource, and effectiveness reasons to inform policy. Research reports have evaluated individual child progress, teacher training, program delivery, and the positive effects of the intervention on the education system. Studies of the first year of operation have been mounted in New Zealand (Clay 1985), Central Victoria, Australia (Wheeler 1984), and Ohio, U.S.A. (Pinnell, DeFord, and Lyons 1988). Follow-up studies of the children after one year and three years are available for Ohio (Pinnell et al. 1988) and New Zealand (Clay 1985). A discussion paper of how an education system can adapt to such an innovation has been published (Clay 1987) and two major expansions of the program have been documented, to national implementation in New Zealand (Clay 1990) and state level in Ohio (Pinnell et al. 1988).

REFERENCES

Clay, M. M. 1985. *The Early Detection of Reading Difficulties.* 3d ed. Portsmouth, N.H.: Heinemann.

———. 1987. "Reading Recovery: Systemic Adaptations to an Educational Innovation." *New Zealand Journal of Educational Studies* 22 (1): 35–58.

———. 1990. "The Reading Recovery Programme, 1984–1988: Coverage, Outcomes and Education Board District Figures." *New Zealand Journal of Educational Studies* 25 (1): 61–70.

———. 1991. *Becoming Literate: The Construction of Inner Control.* Rev. ed. of *Reading: The Patterning of Complex Behavior.* Portsmouth, N,H.: Heinemann.

Goldenberg, C. 1989. "Learning to Read in New Zealand: Some Observations and Possible Lessons for American Educators." Dept. of Psychiatry and Behavioral Sciences, UCLA. Typescript.

Greene, M. 1986. "How Do We Think About Our Craft?" In A. Lieberman, ed., *Rethinking School Improvement: Research, Craft and Concept.* New York: Teachers College Press, Columbia University.

Pinnell, G. S., D. E. DeFord, and C. A. Lyons. 1988. *Reading Recovery: Early Intervention For At-Risk First Graders.* Arlington, Va.: Educational Research Service.

Wheeler, H. 1984. *Reading Recovery: Central Victorian Field Trials.* Bendigo, Australia: Bendigo College of Advanced Education.

2

On Reading and Readers

● ● ● ● ● ● ● ● ● ● ● ● ●

This section examines aspects of learning to read: how classrooms support the reader; how an integrated use of reading and writing facilitates children's literacy learning; how to select books for young readers; and how to encourage literacy in the home.

"The most important lesson children learn by becoming literate is that they can learn, *in the way that school endorses learning. Then they join the school society of young learners who use their literacy as currency, as the medium of communication, as tools of thought and the means of deep symbolic play. The bond between the teacher and the taught is strengthened; exploration, discovery, ambition and achievement expand and flourish. The few children (and their number is not large, nor is it growing as many believe) who cannot read and write worry us, because they are exiles from the society of child learners in school and are threatened, by parents, teachers and other adults, with exclusion from the wider social world outside school if they fail to become literate."*
Margaret Meek

FOUR

·················

Using Reading and Writing to Support the Reader

DIANE E. DEFORD

·····························   ·····························

*P*arents are a child's first teach-
ers. This teaching and learning occurs many times throughout the
day in a variety of settings as parents and children explore their
world. The parent often structures the environment and activities
to provide support for learning. The child, in turn, actively explores
within the comfort of these bounds. Bedtime stories are a good
example of how parents teach and children learn.

Dottie King made a tape of her reading a picture book (Krahn
1980) with her four-year-old son, Matthew. In the following
excerpt, Dottie helps Matthew use illustrations, personal experiences, and language as he learns to read:

DOTTIE: This is a book. What do you think it is about?
MATTHEW: Ah . . . I think it is about a gorilla.
DOTTIE: What does this say here? (*She points to the front of the book.*)
MATTHEW: See the great gorilla. (*They both examine the next picture
            page, then turn to the title page.*) What does this say?
DOTTIE: *The Great Ape* being the version of the famous saga of
            adventure and friendship newly discovered by Fernando
            Krahn—I think . . . I don't know how to say that word.
            (*They then turn to the first two continuous pictures.*) O.K.
            Read me this story.
MATTHEW: A long time ago there was a ship. And on that ship was
            a little girl. People were seeing . . . *There aren't any words!*

DOTTIE: Just pretend there are words. What would this say if there were words?

MATTHEW: A long time ago, there was people on a ship. And people were seeing . . . There was a little girl and a man on it.

Part of the world a parent helps to define is this realm of literacy. The bounds of literate behavior are first established in the home through the experiences parents and children have around their own culturally based literate traditions (Heath 1983). Literacy is defined by Scribner and Cole (1981) as a set of socially organized practices that make use of a symbol system and a technology for producing and disseminating it. They go on to say that literacy is not simply knowing how to read and write a particular script, but applying this knowledge for specific purposes in specific contexts of use (p. 236). The story Matthew and Dottie read is an example of a literate tradition. Other family rituals may center around cooking, food buying, or household chores. In these instances, the reading of recipes, the making of lists, or the reading of do-it-yourself manuals becomes the vehicle through which literacy is explored in the home.

The events that help to define literacy in the home, however, may not prepare children for the specific contexts of literacy found in the schools. When there is a difference in the patterns of language socialization between the home and school, children may be at risk of failure. Heath (1983) suggests that the kind of talk that surrounds adult/child interactions and the nature of the literacy events occurring in the home are most important for a successful beginning to literacy. If the patterns of language use and the literacy events found in the home have not provided a rich context for helping the child read and write, the experience in school must provide the context.

This chapter describes the contexts for reading and writing that provide at-risk children with rich literacy experiences, which pave the way for success. Children who are at risk in school settings may not have had experiences with books and writing in the home, and so have not explored the "how to" of reading and writing. Children who have had rich literacy experiences in the home usually have some well-defined notions about how print is organized and used to convey meaning. They have concepts such as where to begin reading, which direction print flows on the page to read and write, how organizational structures such as "Once upon a time" and "There once was . . . " are used to get stories started and keep stories going. They have a repertoire of books they know well, and have begun to use writing in the home to write messages, make signs, and so on. Typical classrooms have come to expect this as the "average" background.

For the young child who has yet to sort out some of the basic foundational information about reading and writing, the first year of school can be a mystery. They need to learn how to hold the book, how pictures and print work together but are used in different ways when you read, how stories are similar and different, how letters and words work in general and in detail, and how to organize and use all this information in an orchestrated process in large-group instructional settings. Therefore, the instructional program must be fashioned to create talk about books and writing that is reminiscent of early parent/child literacy experiences in the home. Reading and writing must occur throughout the day as the child reads books, writes, and rereads stories. The teacher and child build a special language context around books and written stories, each reading offering the learner an opportunity to bring language and meaning together. In this way, the child grows into new understandings about books and print and what it means to be a reader at the same time.

LEARNING THROUGH READING

An example from a transcribed Reading Recovery lesson will demonstrate this web of language and how it influences the reading experience for a child determined to be at risk in his school setting. The teacher, Bill, is from New Zealand. He is working with Jake, a Maori child. They are talking about a book, *Our Teacher, Miss Pool* (Cowley 1983).

BILL: Have you seen this book before?

JAKE: Yes, in my room.

BILL: Yes, it's all about *Our Teacher, Miss Pool.* Here she is. Anyway, in this story, Miss Pool's car breaks down.

JAKE: And she rides everything.

BILL: Does she ride everything? Here, let's have a look. *Our Teacher, Miss Pool.* Look what happens! Miss Pool's car broke down. What's she wondering? (*Pause*) She's wondering, "How will I get to school?" What would *how* start with? You tell me, what would *how* start with?

JAKE: *H.*

BILL: Can you find it? Where is *how?*

JAKE: (*Points to* how *on the page.*)

BILL: Look how she went on Monday. What did she go by? (*Jake points to the picture of Miss Pool in a hang glider.*) She went by hang glider. That was Monday. Let's see what she does on Tuesday. Look what she went by on Tuesday.

JAKE: Motor bike.

BILL: And what did she go by on Wednesday?

JAKE: Balloon.

BILL: Wednesday she went by balloon. What about Thursday?

JAKE: She went by roller skates.

BILL: What about Friday?

JAKE: She went by elephant.

BILL: Gosh—what do you think she's going to do on Saturday?

JAKE: Ride a cow? (*Jake is puzzled; he doesn't remember what came next in the book.*)

BILL: Ride a cow. (*Bill rephrases his question.*) What do you think she is going to do with her car?

JAKE: Fix it.

BILL: On Saturday she fixed her car. "Now I can drive to school."

The teacher seeks to draw the child into the book, its pictures, and the language the author has used to tell the story. When Jake reads the story on his own, the careful discussion of the book has built a web of meaning and language that he can draw upon as he begins to deal with the printed message. The teacher supports Jake; he helps him keep from focusing too heavily on the print and thereby excluding what he knows about the sense and language he has already explored through the pictures. Bill's running record of Jake's first reading of the story is shown in Figure 4–1.

In early encounters with new books, the teacher works with individual children or in groups, using big books as described by Holdaway (1979). The power of books, however, is that they can be read again and again. The young child at home who asks for *that book* for the tenth time is demonstrating an important concept for us. Some books are important enough for children that they must be read many times, and each child has to tell us which books are the important ones, because the ones that are requested time after time are teaching something the child wants to learn (Meek 1988).

For the teacher who is carefully observing the child during reading, multiple readings of the same text offer an opportunity to view shifts in a child's use of meaning, language structure, and visual information. As Jake reads the book *Our Teacher, Miss Pool* for a second time, it is evident he is integrating meaning and structural and visual information in an effective manner (see the running

First Reading of "Our Teacher Miss Pool"

Text: Miss Pool's Car broke down.

"How will I go to school?"

Text: On Monday

she went by hang glider.

Text: On Tuesday

she went by motor bike.

Text: On Wednesday

she went by balloon

Text: On Thursday

she went by roller skates.

Text: On Friday

she went by elephant.

Text: On Saturday

she fixed her car.

Text: "Now I can drive to school,"

said Miss Pool.

SC = self correction	
Pooly / Pool	= Substitution
T = Told	
- / hang	= Omission

Second Reading

Text: Miss Pool's car broke down.   *[broke = broked above]*

"How will I go to school?"

Text: On MOnday   *[Wednesday ✓ written above, with *]*   /SC   *No!

she went by hang glider.   *[gun gliders written above]*   /SC

Text: On Tuesday   /R

she went by motor bike.

Text: On Wednesday

she went by balloon

Text: On Thursday   )R

she went by roller skates.

Text: On Friday   *[F-|Monday|F- written above ✓]*   /SC

she went by elephant.

Text: On Saturday   *[Tuesday written above]*

she fixed her car.   *[✓)R above she]*

Text: "Now I can drive to school,"

said Miss Pool.

record shown in Figure 4–2). This is different from his first reading where he paid more attention to the print than to meaning and language cues. He was more able to use predicting to keep the flow of reading moving forward—he was reading for meaning.

After this reading, the teacher noted that the days of the week were not working as a helpful device, so together they talked about the days of the week. They quickly leafed back through some of the pages, talking about what day of the week it was when Miss Pool did each thing. This helped make the days of the week a more predictable element of stories, so that Jake could use this information in other book readings, as in *The Very Hungry Caterpillar* (Carle 1981).

As readers select favorite books to be read again, they learn more about the text and its structure, but they also explore new understandings of characterization and subtleties of plot and theme (Beaver 1982; Pappas & Brown 1987). One reader involved in Reading Recovery lessons had recurring love affairs with *Dear Zoo* (Campbell 1982), *Where's Spot?* (Hill 1980), *Rosie's Walk* (Hutchins 1968), and *Spot's Birthday Party* (Hill 1982). Some of these were read as many as eight or nine times without any loss of enjoyment. Ryan enjoyed the anticipation of which animal was behind closed doors and elaborated on the characters—their actions and motives. The same pauses, the same inflections, and the same comments would be part of the shared book experience. In trying to work out what was really happening in *Spot's Birthday Party*, he made comments like "I think the bear must be telling Spot where everyone else is hiding." And finally, "No, the bear isn't telling Spot anything, he's just hiding . . . and Spot is just being a good detective!" Ryan worked out this particular puzzle across three separate readings of *Where's Spot?*

Multiple readings allow and encourage the building of links between books. Readers comment on how one book is like others— books that were read weeks before. *Dear Zoo* and *Where's Spot?* were alike because they had doors, or held surprises, or they both had nice animals. These links between and across books build comprehension—the bridges between the new and the known (Pearson and Johnson 1978). The connections children make between books and their own experiences often come out in their writing. Sarah, after reading *Dear Zoo*, pretended to receive a letter from and then wrote a letter to Jack Hanna, the director of the Columbus Zoo (see Figure 4–3).

In more complex story writing, children borrow from and improvise upon the variety of texts they have read and loved (DeFord 1986). In the following story, Laura used devices, or char-

FIGURE 4–3 SARAH'S ZOO LETTERS

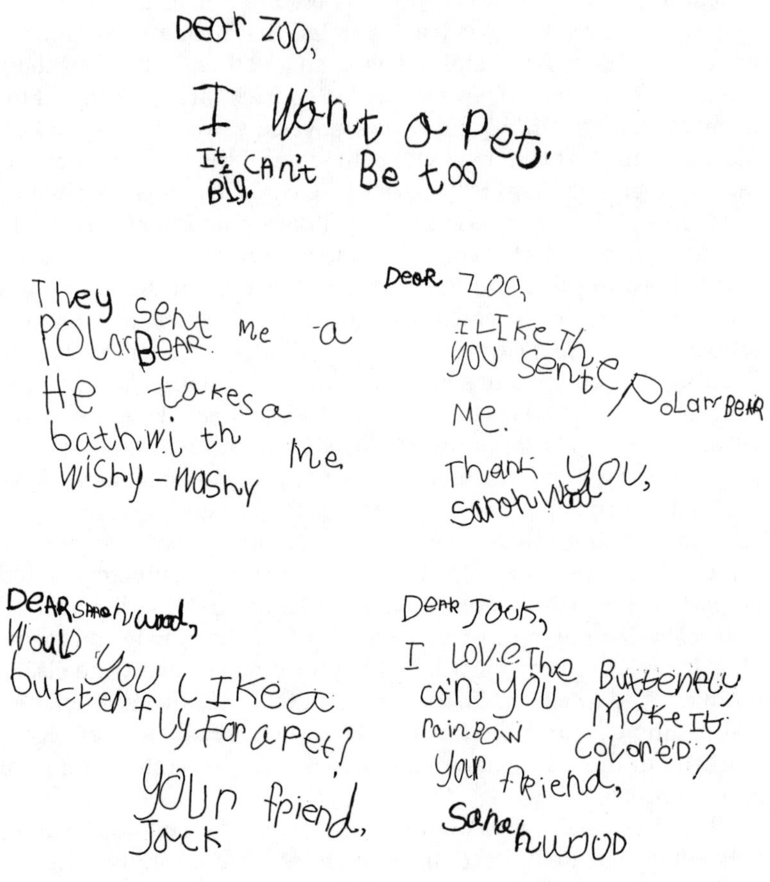

DEor ZOO,

I Wont a Pet.
It CAn't Be too
Big.

They sent me a
POLorBeAR.
He takes a
bathwith me
wishy-washy

DeoR ZOO,
I LIKE Th
You sent ePoLar BeAR
Me.
Thank you,
sarahWood,

DeAR SarahWood,
Would you LIKe a
butterfly For a Pet?
your friend,
Jack

DeAR Jack,
I LOVe The Butterfly
can you Make It
rainbow Colored?
your friend,
Sarah Wood

acters, from four separate books in writing her own story (see Figure 4–4). She had read *Horace* (Cowley 1982b), *Dear Zoo* (Campbell 1982), *The Chick and the Duckling* (Ginsburg 1972), and *Grumpy Elephant* (Cowley 1982a). She added her own counting sequence ("I kept him for a day; I kept her for two days") and her own experiences to have the animals coming from the pound.

Favorite books read and savored again through shared reading and writing experiences are as important to children's continued learning in the classroom as bedtime stories, signs, and grocery lists are to the very young child in the home. Beaver (1982),

FIGURE 4–4   LAURA'S STORY

I got a new DoG named Horace. I kept Him For a day.

I Sent Him back to the Pound. They sent me two Siamese Cats. They were Big trouble makers! I Sent Them back.

They Sent me a Parrot. She bit me on The arm And Said Naughty Things. I Kept her for two days.

I Sent Her back to the Pound. they sent me a baby Chick She was Just right. I kept Her.

Schickedanz (1978), and Pappas and Brown (1987) report on the necessity of multiple encounters with stories in classroom settings. As children experience books again and again, they begin to own the language, the story, the experience, and the reading and writing processes.

There are four important areas in which a teacher can observe growth as children read in ongoing literacy experiences. First, a teacher can observe shifts in strategies across readings. Shifts in the reader's focus of attention between print, illustrations, and story meanings are natural, and important events in the learning-to-read process. These shifts help the child build bridges among books and personal experiences, and develop flexibility. A child who continues to focus only on print will not develop a self-improving system (Clay 1985) or be able to learn to read through reading (Smith 1988; Goodman 1986).

In order to learn to read through reading, children must begin to orchestrate strategies. Records of reading across time will provide a means of analyzing how the readers are using such strategies. When readers come to something they don't know, they have to be able to search for new information, predict, cross-check cue sources against each other, and reread if necessary to build momentum and reestablish a comprehending pace. They have to be independent in this process.

As readers become independent, they must also be flexible in utilizing available cues from the text and their own knowledge base. If they do not balance the use of visual, structural, and meaning cues as they focus in and out of print, illustrations, and personal experiences, the reading process may break down. So the final area readers must develop is an awareness of the judgment calls they have to make. The judgments independent readers make to continue reading are complex. Do I continue reading, reread, search forward or back for information, put in something that makes sense, look at the pictures, look at the print more closely, look somewhere else for the information, put the book down and take another book for the moment, ask someone else to help? Any one of the above choices made to the exclusion of others across reading events is a sign of inflexibility.

LEARNING THROUGH WRITING

Writing is too often seen as an end in itself—children learn the mechanics of forming letters and words, and learn the conventions of print. The last two decades have shown us the narrowness of this view (Graves 1983; Calkins 1983; Pearson and Tierney 1984; Shanklin 1982). Reading and writing are reciprocal processes (Clay 1985). In other words, as readers and writers engage in one of the processes, they learn about the other as well. It is this process of learning about and through language to which children are so well adapted.

When young children write, the reading/writing process is conveniently slowed down; to form messages and print, children must work on a variety of levels. They have to think about what they want to say, what they hear and how to represent it, what they expect to see if they can't hear it and it doesn't look right, where they are in their message, and how they can make their message clear to other readers.

That is why too many artificial copying tasks or isolated practice activities fail in the very purposes for which they were designed; they do not allow the children to think about what they do and use their own language with real communication the intent. Consequently, in copying, children merely seek to "get the letters"

FIGURE 4–5   EXAMPLE OF AN ARTIFICIAL COPYING TASK

down on paper, and having focused on minute aspects of language, they can get off track. They have nothing to check against; no meaning, no purpose other than to fill the page (see Figure 4–5). In fill-in-the-blank or other isolated practice activities, getting the right answer may be the child's purpose instead of trying to understand the language relationships the teacher thinks are readily apparent (see Figure 4–6).

Because young children must learn to balance the act of writing (a very slow process) and the conventions of print with their thoughts and intentions (which are very rapid), teachers must constantly help the beginning writer focus inward (learning how print operates) and outward (how stories and messages work and will be

FIGURE 4–6   EXAMPLE OF AN ISOLATED PRACTICE ACTIVITY

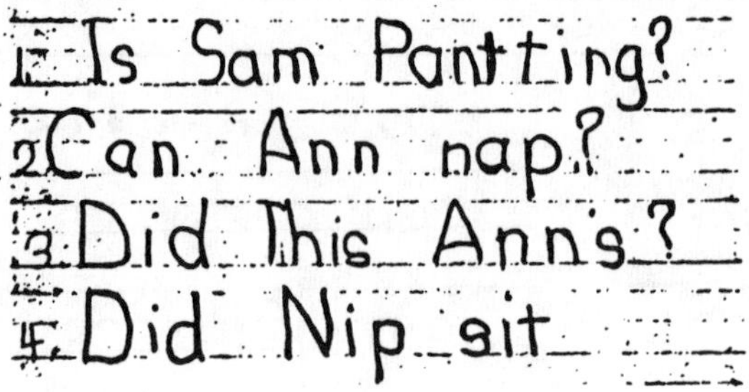

1. Is Sam Pantting?
2. Can Ann nap?
3. Did This Anns?
4. Did Nip sit

received). The only way to accomplish this is to make the writing events purposeful, shared, and used over time. In this way, writing is an integral part of the reading program as well as a communication process children learn about as they write (DeFord 1986).

As young writers focus in on smaller or physical aspects of writing, they learn certain principles about print formation, letter/ sound relationships, spelling patterns, and the meaning of certain morphological forms (-s, -ing, -ed, -est, and so on). As they focus outside of the act or representation of their written message, they must keep their place in the writing and reconsider their message, so they learn to reread and check on what they have done. It is at this point that they may consider punctuation, information they may have left out, or the formation of the rest of their message. In the example documented in Figure 4–7, a young first grader is busy putting this all together with her friends while she forms her own rendition of *The Three Bears*.

Brenda uses a variety of sources as she writes. Her friends, print around the room, her teacher, and her own knowledge serve her well. The children had constructed their own story of *The Three Bears*, and Brenda referred to this at times. She conferred with her friends on choices of words and found books (*Rosie's Walk*, Hutchins 1968) to help her as well. But most of all, Brenda was thinking about the meaning she wanted to communicate, how to represent it, and how to keep on going. She reread her writing as she was working and at different points shared her work with others. This helped her not only to keep her place, but also to get responses from others and ideas to keep going. She knew how to find or generate what she needed to write, and she could conduct this complex process independently.

FIGURE 4–7   RUNNING RECORD OF BRENDA'S VERSION OF
THE THREE BEARS

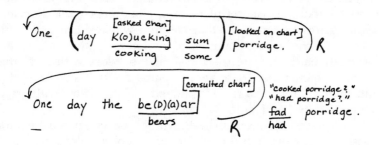

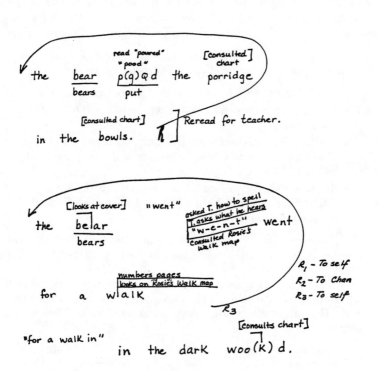

DEVELOPING INDEPENDENT READERS AND WRITERS

Independence grows out of knowing the "how to" of reading and writing as one reads and writes with others. This volume has presented important aspects of reading aloud, book selection and teaching for the strategies that children will need to use. Little books, big books, and examples of invitations, letters, signs, and informational books are the tools children work with in shared reading experiences. These are presented carefully by the teacher and children, read and reread, savored each new time with growing familiarity (see Figures 4–8 and 4–9).

McKenzie suggests "shared writing" be integrated into the classroom day through the writing of school events, stories children know, messages, songs, poems, games, class topics, school activities; through extending favorite stories; and through creating new ones. McKenzie explains the concept of shared writing thus:

> As the teachers on courses discussed the range of work they were sharing, they found themselves focusing on:
>
> - the different procedures they use in producing such texts;
> - the kinds of stories and events that seem to lead to joint text production;
> - exactly what children were learning about literacy as they worked together to create texts to read themselves and to be read by others;
> - the way "shared" or collaborative writing fits into, and differs from, all the other writing that occurs in an effective learning environment.
>
> Since these experiences grew out of what we called SHARED READING, we called this new phase of our work, SHARED WRITING.
>
> Shared writing is *one* part of the range of opportunities open to children in a language effective classroom for composing written text. The range of writing going on is summarised below and includes:
>
> - children's individual writing, from their first preliterate attempt at messages to writing with real control over written language;
> - teachers writing at children's dictation as in the language experience approach to reading;
> - curriculum related writing needed to carry on the business of the classroom, or writing growing out of children's play,

FIGURE 4–8   VIMALA'S LETTER TO DR. DEFORD

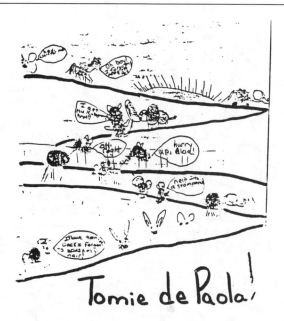

Tomie de Paola!

Dear Dr. Deford,

Our school is having Tomie de Paola come. Tomie de Paola is a writer of children's books. We would be very happy if you will come to school on Feb. 8, 1994. P.s. I am in the dance and choir.

Yours truly,

Vimala Paruppati

Mrs. Kaufmann's class.

FIGURE 4–9   DARCY'S "WHEN I'M ALONE"

e.g. menus for cafe, rules for feeding animals, charts for keeping track of "hospital" patients, etc;

• writing and making story books. (1985, p. 4)

As children compose and write, and as the teacher transcribes aspects of language children need help with, children take on the process for themselves. Individual writing and group writing can revolve around the work of the classroom and bring in science, math, and social studies to extend what children learn (see Figures 4–10a and 4–10b).

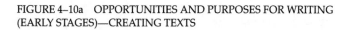

FIGURE 4–10a   OPPORTUNITIES AND PURPOSES FOR WRITING
(EARLY STAGES)—CREATING TEXTS

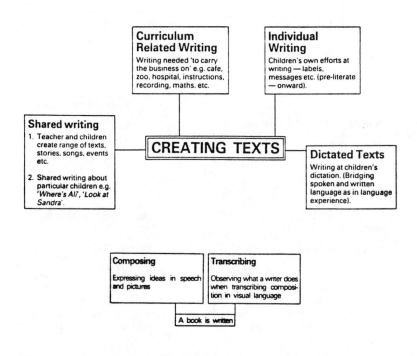

A classroom that revolves around the use of reading and writing offers invitations (DeFord 1981; Harste, Short, & Burke 1988) for children to become apprentices with their peers and their teachers. Young children who may not have had a wealth of experiences benefit most from these invitations. They learn the personal strategies they need to use to continue to develop as readers and writers, how to solve their own problems, and what a store of information and personal joy books can provide.

What Meek said of learning to read can also be said of learning to write. She suggests that a reader (and writer) has to discover that every story, every book, has its own voice—what she calls "the tune on the page." The learner has to learn that the stories in books bring pleasure and delight, a way of looking at the world. All else in literacy will follow because the learner will want to be part of the process so as to prolong what he or she enjoys (1982, pp. 22–23).

• •

FIGURE 4–10b   OPPORTUNITIES AND PURPOSES FOR WRITING
(EARLY STAGES)—SHARED WRITING

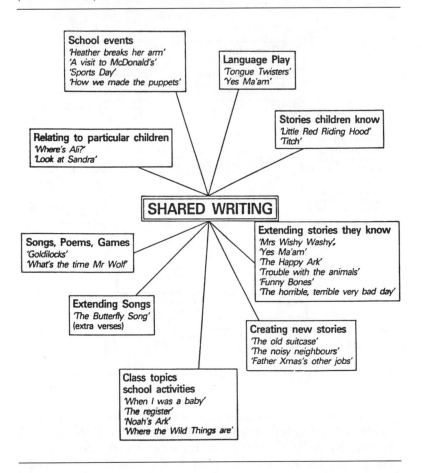

She also offers us, the world of teachers, a message we can learn by:
Good teachers never underestimate the ability of children to learn,
nor overestimate the part we play in the process. This is especially
true of learning to read (and write) (1982, p. 28).

REFERENCES

Beaver, J. 1982. "Say It! Over and Over." *Language Arts* 59 (2): 143–48.
Calkins, L. 1983. *Lessons from a Child*. Portsmouth, N.H.: Heinemann.
Campbell, R. 1982. *Dear Zoo*. New York: Four Winds Press.
Carle, E. 1981. *The Very Hungry Caterpillar*. New York: Putnam.

Clay, M. 1985. *The Early Detection of Reading Difficulties.* 3d ed. Portsmouth, N.H.: Heinemann.
Cowley, J. 1982a. *Grumpy Elephant.* San Diego, Cal.: Wright Group.
———. 1982b. *Horace.* Auckland, New Zealand: Shortland Publications.
———. 1983. *Our Teacher, Miss Pool.* Wellington: New Zealand Department of Education.
DeFord, D. E. 1981. "Literacy: Reading, Writing and Other Essentials." *Language Arts* 58 (1): 652–58.
———. 1986. "Children Write to Read and Read to Write." In D. Tovey & J. Kerber, eds., *Roles in Literacy Learning: A New Perspective,* 79–93. Newark, Del.: International Reading Association.
Graves, D. 1983. *Writing: Teachers & Children at Work.* Portsmouth, N.H.: Heinemann.
Ginsburg, M. 1972. *The Chick and the Duckling.* New York: Macmillan.
Goodman, K. 1982. *Language and Literacy.* 2 vols. Boston: Routledge & Kegan Paul.
———. 1986. *What's Whole in Whole Language.* Ontario, Canada: Scholastic.
Harste, J., K. Short, with C. Burke. 1988. *Creating Classrooms for Authors: The Reading Writing Connection.* Portsmouth, N.H.: Heinemann.
Heath, S. B. 1983. *Ways With Words.* New York: Cambridge University Press.
Hill, E. 1980. *Where's Spot?* New York: Putnam.
———. 1982. *Spot's Birthday Party.* New York: Putnam.
Holdaway, D. 1979. *The Foundations of Literacy.* Sydney, Australia: Ashton Scholastic.
Hutchins, P. 1968. *Rosie's Walk.* New York: Macmillan.
Krahn, F. 1980. *The Great Ape.* New York: Penguin.
McKenzie, M. 1985. "Shared Writing." *Language Matters* (Inner London Education Authority, Center for Language in Primary Education) Nos. 1 & 2: 1–33.
Meek, M. 1982. *Learning to Read.* London: Bodley Head.
———. 1988. *How Texts Teach What Readers Learn.* Lockwood, England: Thimble Press.
Pappas, C., & E. Brown. 1987. "Young Children Learning Story Discourse: Three Case Studies." *Elementary School Journal* 87 (4): 455–66.
Pearson, P. D., & D. Johnson. 1978. *Teaching Reading Comprehension.* New York: Holt, Rinehart and Winston.
———. 1984. "Toward a Composing Model of Reading." In J. Jensen, ed., *Composing and Comprehending,* 33–46. Urbana, Ill.: ERIC Clearinghouse on Reading and Communication Skills and the National Conference on Research in English.
Rhodes, L. K. "I Can Read! Predictable Books as Resources for Reading and Writing Instruction." *Reading Teacher* 34 (5): 511–18.
Schickedanz, J. 1978. "Please Read That Story Again!" *Young Children* (July): 48–55.
Scribner, S. and M. Cole. 1981. *The Psychology of Literacy.* Cambridge, Mass.: Harvard University Press.
Shanklin, N. 1982. "Relating Reading and Writing. Developing a Transactional Theory of the Writing Process." *Monographs in Language and Reading,* 79–93. Newark, Del.: International Reading Association.
Smith, F. 1988. *Understanding Reading.* Hillsdale: Erlbaum.

FIVE

....

Literacy Environments That Support Strategic Readers

KATHY GNAGEY SHORT

....

I n recent years, there has been a growing recognition that reading is an active thinking process in which the reader makes efficient use of strategies to construct meaning from print (Clay 1985; Goodman 1983; Harste 1985; Smith 1978). This emphasis on reading as an active thinking process has focused the attention of educators on creating supportive literacy environments that facilitate the learning of strategies (Baker & Brown 1984; Clay 1985; Deschler & Schumaker 1986). Teaching and learning are coming to be viewed as collaborative ventures between teachers and students. Instead of characterizing the teacher's role as primarily the imparting of specific bits of knowledge about reading skills, the emphasis is on guiding and facilitating the learning of reading strategies (Goodman & Burke 1980).

Deschler and Schumaker define learning strategies as "the techniques, principles, or rules that enable a student to learn, to solve problems, and to complete tasks independently" (1986, p. 583). The focus of learning strategies is on teaching students *how* to learn.

Reading strategies are general cognitive and social processes that readers use to help them search for and construct meaning from text. As readers become strategic and independent learners, they are able to monitor their own learning. They develop "self-improving systems" (Clay 1985), which allow them to learn more about reading every time they read, independent of instruction.

These readers are thus able both to act and to come to know through their actions. Teachers support this growth toward independence by creating learning environments that allow learners to explore and develop a wide range of learning strategies. This chapter explores the literacy environment that one particular program, Reading Recovery, creates for learning reading strategies and the implications of this environment for other classroom settings.

SUPPORTING THE LEARNING OF STRATEGIES

Baker and Brown (1984), in their review of research on metacognitive strategies, provide insights into some of the characteristics of learning environments that have successfully supported the learning of strategies. They point out three major factors that distinguish recent instructional research on comprehension and study strategies from previous research. The first factor is a current focus on programs that pay attention to learners' awareness of why they are learning something and to learners' ability to regulate their own learning activities. The second factor is teaching for strategies within the context of actual reading activities, where a student's attention is focused on the understanding of text rather than on separate skills or items. The third characteristic of recent instructional studies is an emphasis on the interactions between the teacher and student.

This interest in dynamic learning situations is influenced by the Vygotskian notion of a "zone of proximal development" (Vygotsky 1978). Vygotsky's zone consists of the distance between the thinking that a learner can do independently and the thinking that a learner is capable of with the support of an adult. Interactions with a supportive, knowledgeable adult are seen as allowing students to go to the limits of their own understanding (Cazden 1988). This type of interaction assumes that the teacher monitors each student's individual learning needs and strategies. Other recent studies by Harste, Woodward, and Burke (1984), Rowe (1986), and Short (1986) have argued that these supportive interactions are not limited to teacher/student interactions but occur whenever two learners collaboratively interact and offer learning demonstrations to each other.

Reading Recovery is based on characteristics similar to those found by Baker and Brown in their review of research. Marie Clay (1985) began developing Reading Recovery when her review of remedial programs indicated that the majority of students never left remediation and developed dependency behaviors that resulted in little or no growth if they did leave. As noted in earlier chapters, Clay developed an early intervention program for young readers "at risk" of failure, which focused on reading strategies and the development of independent, self-monitoring readers.

Clay (1985) defines reading strategies as the mental activities that a learner initiates to construct meaning from text. Strategies are "in-the-head" problem-solving processes, which cannot be directly observed but about which inferences can be made by closely observing learners as they are reading. When readers are engaged in reading, their theories of the world and of written language form the basis for the strategies they use to make predictions and to solve any problems they encounter during reading. These strategies are general processes such as self-monitoring and searching for cues, which readers use to help construct meaning.

In Reading Recovery, strategies are developed through supportive teacher/student interactions as learners are engaged in the processes of reading and writing whole texts. The reader's focus is on constructing messages from meaningful texts rather than on practicing separate, isolated skills. The program is aimed at helping students become independent readers who are able to monitor their reading. Teachers' interactions with students are based on careful monitoring of the strategies that students are and are not using, so that teachers can support students' growth in developing independent, self-generating systems of learning.

General strategies such as self-monitoring and searching for cues are encouraged in Reading Recovery lessons by comments that help readers grow to understand their use across multiple reading experiences. In conversations about reading, the teacher and the student might notice the visual features of words, such as first-letter cues, identify particular sentence patterns and language structures, focus on whether the text is making sense, use the pictures to establish a meaning focus, make connections to past experiences and other texts, or discuss how to use several information sources at once (e.g., using the context of the story plus the first letter of a word).

The teacher might also encourage particular reading behaviors, such as rereading to get another running start on a section of text, looking through the text and pictures to get a frame for the story and to make predictions about the story content before reading, using the cover of the book to review the story briefly before rereading, talking with others about a story, reading or glancing ahead to the end of a sentence or section, reading together to gain momentum and fluency, and making connections between reading and writing experiences.

The goal of instruction in Reading Recovery is to help students develop a variety of reading strategies. Instead of the teacher working to drill several skills to "mastery," readers experience the use of a wide range of strategies from which they can choose when they encounter difficulty during reading. These strategies differ radically from most "scope and sequence" lists of skills, which contain specific items to memorize such as certain letter sounds or vowel rules. Teaching for strategies focuses at a more general level on the processes that use these specific items. Students still often learn many of these more specific skills, but they do so as they actually read and write rather than through direct, isolated instruction. The students' attention is focused on strategies they can use to construct meaning, especially when they run into difficulty, instead of on specific items of knowledge, which have much more limited utility. When students are taught specific items, they become dependent on teachers to give them the next item to learn. They have not developed independent strategies that will allow them to continue learning through reading and reflecting. Teaching for strategies puts the emphasis on reading for meaning and on becoming an independent reader.

By examining the literacy environment created within Reading Recovery lessons, classroom teachers can gain insights into teacher/student interactions they can use to support the teaching and learning of strategies in regular classroom settings. To create a supportive context for strategy development in the classroom, three major characteristics of the learning environment will be considered in this chapter: (1) the continuous monitoring of a student's strategy development; (2) a curricular structure that provides a variety of literacy settings with differing amounts of support for readers; and (3) teacher/student interactions before, during, and after the reading of whole texts. Examples from Reading Recovery lessons will be used to describe the kinds of interactions and curricular structures teachers can consider as they work to build strong literacy environments in their classrooms. These examples come primarily from videotapes of myself and Sue Hundley, a Reading Recovery teacher in Columbus, Ohio, working with children in daily lessons. (I wish to thank Sue for allowing me to observe her sessions.) These videotapes provided the opportunity to observe Reading Recovery teachers and students more closely as they work at strategy development.

CONTINUOUS MONITORING OF READING STRATEGIES

Clay (1985) refers to teaching as a conversation in which you carefully listen to the speaker before you reply. Teachers can support their students by attentively listening and responding during actual learning situations. In order to do this, teachers must have a thorough understanding about what each student knows. This knowledge is gained by observing students in the process of reading and writing and in their daily activities in the classroom. This form of evaluation plays an essential role in helping teachers make decisions based upon students' strengths. Close observation gives teachers the ability to construct a curriculum that fits the learners' strengths. Careful record keeping of these observations is equally important in decision making and in documenting children's progress.

During observations of a student's reading in Reading Recovery, a daily record of oral reading miscues is taken so that the teacher can analyze the strategies and cues used by that reader. The running records developed by Clay (1985) require only a blank sheet of paper and a pencil. As the child reads an entire book aloud, the teacher records any changes in the text that the student makes. The running records are then analyzed to determine whether the student was using meaning, structure, and/or visual cues in the substitutions and self-corrections. This analysis provides an important source of information for making inferences about the kinds of strategies and cue systems that students are using in their reading.

The example of a running record shown in Figure 5–1 indicates cues that Mntambo was using in his reading. He expected the text to make sense and sound like language, but was only beginning to integrate visual information into his reading (note the circles around meaning (m) and structure (s), with one self-correction (sc) under one rereading (r)). This information was then used by his Reading Recovery teacher to make decisions about how to interact with him during subsequent lessons.

Unless teachers develop some way of systematically gathering observations of students as they actually engage in reading and writing, much of this information is lost and unavailable to teachers as they make decisions about instruction. In addition to recording and analyzing oral reading samples, teachers can record anecdotal comments about student behaviors during reading and writing. These anecdotal comments should reflect the reading behaviors of students across a variety of texts and situations. Through systematically gathering observations on students, teachers can make more

FIGURE 5–1 RUNNING RECORD FOR MNTAMBO, GRADE ONE

SUMMARY OF RUNNING RECORD

Name: Mntambo Date: 12-19 D. of B. ______ Age: ____ yrs. ____ mths

School: ______ Recorder: ______

SUMMARY OF RUNNING RECORD TEXT TITLES	RUNNING WORDS ERROR	ERROR RATE	ACCURACY	SELF-CORRECTION RATE
1. Easy		1:	%	1:
2. Instructional		1:	%	1:
3. Hard Tree House (2)	31/7	1: 4	75%	1: 8

Directional Movement ______

ANALYSIS OF ERRORS Cues used and cues neglected

Easy ______

Instructional ______

Hard Reliance on structure & meaning cues, little use of visual. Problems if can't get the pattern. Problems with

CROSS CHECKING ON CUES literary language + unusual sentence construction.

Page	The Tree House	E	SC	CUES USED E	CUES USED SC
	Here/A/SC ✓ ✓ ✓		1	(m)(s)v	m(s)(v)
	up / Here ✓ up ✓ ✓	1		(m)(s)v	
	up / Here ✓ R ✓ ✓ / up	1		(m)(s)v	
	✓ ✓ ✓ ✓				
	✓ ✓ ✓ ✓				
	✓ ✓ ✓ ✓				
	They all fall down / Down came the treehouse	4		(m)(s) v	

informed decisions about the classroom learning environment and their own minute-by-minute interactions with readers.

While the example of an anecdotal record shown in Figure 5–2 is based on a form used in a Reading Recovery lesson, classroom teachers will want to develop their own forms to meet their needs.

FIGURE 5–2   LESSON RECORD SHEET FOR TONJA, GRADE ONE

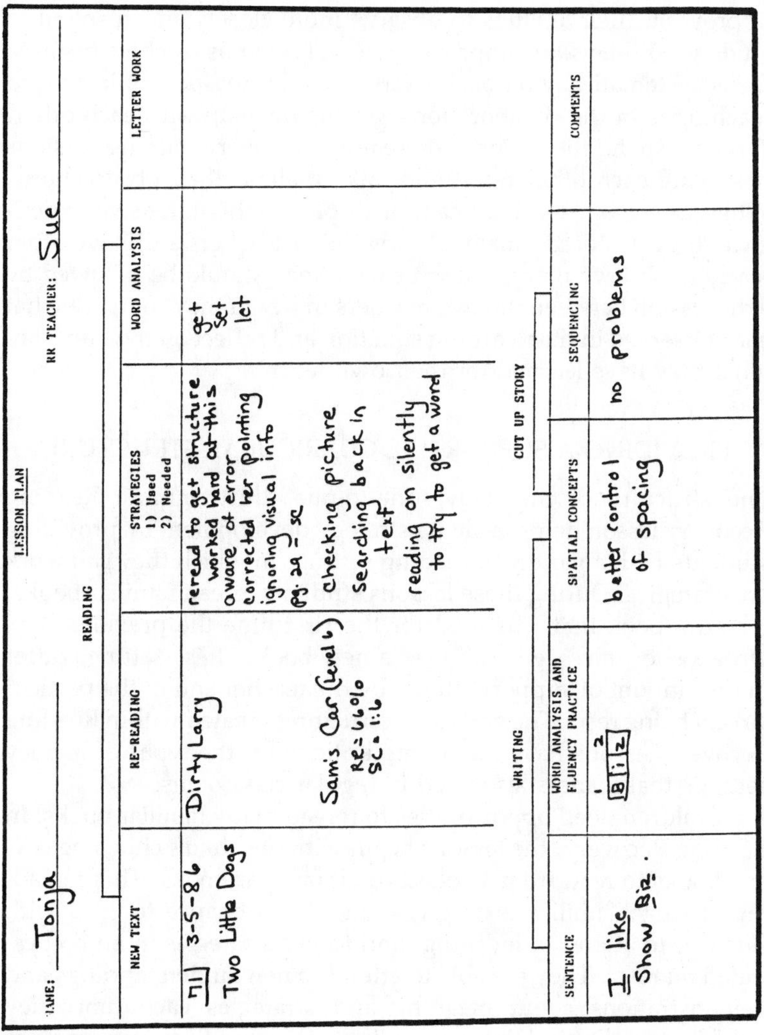

NAME: Tonja

RR TEACHER: Sue

LESSON PLAN

READING

NEW TEXT	RE-READING	STRATEGIES 1) Used 2) Needed	WORD ANALYSIS	LETTER WORK
① 3-5-86 Two Little Dogs	Dirty Larry	reread to get structure worked hard at this aware of error corrected her pointing ignoring visual info pg. 2a ≃ x	get set let	
	Sam's Car (level 6) RE=66% SC=1:6	checking picture searching back in text reading on silently to try to get a word		

WRITING

CUT UP STORY

SENTENCE	WORD ANALYSIS AND FLUENCY PRACTICE	SPATIAL CONCEPTS	SEQUENCING	COMMENTS
I like Show Biz.	Ⓑ[li]z	better control of spacing	no problems	

In this example, Tonja's teacher, Sue Hundley, used the form to note information about strategies Tonja was using across texts.

As teachers observe and record what they see, they will improve in their abilities to observe more closely and respond to students. While some improvement will occur as teachers begin to focus systematically on observations, a critical aspect of improved teaching is in the collaboration teachers develop with each other. Teachers spend the majority of Reading Recovery training sessions observing each other teach and talking about their observations. While classroom teachers cannot duplicate this intensive experience, they can occasionally observe other teachers and have other teachers observe them. These observations should be followed by a discussion between the two teachers in which they compare what each observed in that learning situation and reflect on the impact of what they have learned for their own teaching.

PROVIDING A SUPPORTIVE CURRICULAR STRUCTURE

The structure of the daily, one-to-one, thirty-minute Reading Recovery lesson helps facilitate strategy development by providing students with a variety of reading settings in which they can work on strategies. During these lessons students reread familiar books, reread a book that was read for the first time the previous day, write a short message, and read a new book. These settings differ in the amount of support offered by the teacher and in the particular text being read. The curricular structures created within Reading Recovery lessons have many implications for the types of literacy settings that readers also need in regular classrooms.

Children need opportunities to reread many familiar books. In Reading Recovery, the lessons begin with the child's choosing several books to read from a collection of familiar books. This rereading of easy, familiar texts gives students a chance to read with fluency, to attend to meaning, and to use strategies in an orchestrated manner. They are able to attend to new understandings and demonstrations about meaning and strategies each time they reread a text. During these rereadings, Reading Recovery teachers interact minimally with students, allowing students to work at developing their own self-monitoring systems and moving away from teacher dependency.

While other students are involved with familiar reading, teachers can be free to listen to individual children as they read independently from a book. This independent reading provides an opportunity for teachers to take a running record of a student's oral reading. In Reading Recovery, during the reading of familiar books, the teacher interacts with the student to create a web of meaning and enjoyment. The focus is on what students are able to do without support from the teacher, including the kinds of cue systems and strategies students use on their own without any prompting from the teacher. Instances when readers monitor and use cues on their own during reading are carefully noted.

The book used for the running record in Reading Recovery is always a story that the child had read for the first time the previous day. Within classroom settings, however, teachers can take running records as students read from both familiar and unfamiliar books and note their strategies across different kinds of texts and reading situations.

Another aspect of reading instruction is the writing students do in the classroom. Writing is not only an important way to think and communicate but it also allows students to take a different perspective on the reading process. They focus more closely on the visual features of written language as they write and develop strategies related to these visual features within the frame of a meaningful message. Writing also allows them to use both structural and meaning cues as they construct messages. Often this writing is based on the language structures and content of the stories they are reading during other parts of the school day. If teachers are available as children write, they can support them and record anecdotal information about their writing processes.

Each day, students should encounter new, challenging texts as well as the easy, familiar texts that they can read with fluency. In Reading Recovery, when a book is read for the first time, the teacher and student look through the new book together before the students read it. As they look through the book, they talk about the pictures, make predictions about the story, and read segments of text to build a framework of meaning and language that will help the reader in future readings. They then read the new book, working on new strategies and focusing on problem solving with supportive teaching during and after that reading. Big books are well suited to this purpose when introducing a new book to a group. Students can then read the new book individually or in small groups with support from the teacher or from other readers.

The choice of the new book, how it is introduced to readers, and the interactions during the introduction and reading of the book all affect strategy development. Readers need to encounter books regularly that challenge them so their use of strategies is stretched.

The difference in the amount of support given by teachers across reading events is part of the process of building independence in reading. During familiar readings in Reading Recovery, the teacher is less directly involved with the student, indicating the student's independence from the teacher. During the book introductions, however, the teacher usually is closely involved in a warm, supportive manner as the teacher and student interact with the new book.

All teachers need to establish a variety of literacy settings in their classrooms, in which students experience different levels of support by the teacher or other readers and by the text. Students need to have opportunities continuously to read and reread familiar as well as challenging texts and to write their own texts. They need opportunities to read independently as well as to read with support from the teacher or other readers in the classroom. Shared reading experiences—in which two students informally share the reading of a book, or in which the teacher reads a big book aloud, inviting students to read/recite as much of the text they know or can predict—can be used in the classroom to support readers.

SUPPORTING STRATEGIES THROUGH
TEACHER/STUDENT INTERACTIONS

In addition to monitoring reading behaviors and providing a variety of literacy settings, the interactions between the teacher and student before, during, and after reading can support strategy development. These interactions focus students' attention on strategies they are using during reading and introduce them to new strategies.

During Reading Recovery lessons, teachers support learners as they actually use strategies in reading and writing whole texts. The most powerful teacher/student interactions occur when students operate within their "zones of proximal development" (Vygotsky 1978). As students read whole texts and interact with a knowledgeable and supportive adult, they are pushed beyond what they could understand on their own. The student and the Reading Recovery teacher are initially mutually responsible for getting the task done, but, as the student develops more strategies and begins to self-monitor, the adult steps back.

INTERACTIONS BEFORE THE READING OF A TEXT • Two types of interactions often occur between Reading Recovery teachers and students before the reading of a text. One highly supportive interaction comes before the reading of a new book. The second, less supportive interaction occurs before the rereading of familiar books. Both interactions focus the readers' attention on meaning.

The teacher/student interactions surrounding the choice and introduction of a new book can have a major impact on strategy development. The type of book that the teacher chooses and the comments and questions made during the introduction of the book focus the student on the meaning of the story and on certain cue systems, strategies, and aspects of the text. Teachers adjust their introductions to fit the needs of particular students and in response to characteristics of the text that will be read. The goal of the introduction is to provide a framework for the story that will support that student in successfully reading and being challenged by the new book. The following examples from actual Reading Recovery lessons illustrate how book introductions can vary with the child and the text.

> Jerry is leaving off the inflectional endings of words as he reads. His teacher, Sue, therefore begins choosing books that use endings naturally in their texts, such as *The Great Big Enormous Turnip* (Tolstoy 1971) and *The Record Player* (Schaub 1976). As Sue and Jerry look through the pictures and make predictions about these books, Sue makes sure she uses words with endings in her oral language and that she asks Jerry questions that encourage him to reply using words with inflectional endings before reading the book.

> Tonja needs books that have structural support but not high structural predictability. Sue begins moving away from books like *My Home* (Melser 1981) to stories such as *Two Little Dogs* (Melser 1982) and *Sam's Car* (Lindgren n.d.), which still have strong structures but are not so highly predictable. In her introductions, Sue uses language and asks questions that focus Tonja's attention on how to use the structure that is there. This helps support Tonja, who is finding the move away from high structural predictability difficult.

> Dorothy seldom makes use of pictures as she reads. I choose a book called *Dirty Larry* (Hamsa 1983), which highlights the use of pictures to support the reading of the text. As we discuss which part of Larry was dirty on each page, I draw Dorothy's attention to the pictures to help her successfully read the text.

The choice of the book and how it is introduced highlights cues and strategies the student needs to attend to without specific item teaching. The teacher's questions and comments affect the student's focus during the first reading of the book. These introductions also provide the opportunity for teachers to help students draw connections from the new book to other literature, their writing, or their lives. Talking about these connections helps readers develop the general strategy of searching for connections with past experiences to understand current experiences.

The major emphasis in new book introductions is on meaning. Language structures and unusual terminology are naturally included in the conversations around new books before the child begins to read instead of being taught in isolation. The interactions between teachers and children around new books can encourage children to use a variety of strategies within the meaning and language frame established.

How much support is offered by the Reading Recovery teacher during the introduction of a new book varies according to a number of factors. In the above examples, Sue provided a great deal of support through comments and questions as she and the student looked through the first part of the book. However, she asked only a few questions during the rest of the book. The introductions also varied by child. With Tonja, who was at a standstill in her reading, Sue did a fairly thorough introduction, but with Jerry, who was reading more independently, she discussed the first page or two and then suggested he page through the rest of the book on his own to see what happened before he began reading.

The highly supportive interactions that often occur before reading new books do not usually occur when children reread familiar books. In the classroom, there may be little interaction with the teacher during these rereadings. During Reading Recovery lessons, teachers often establish a meaning focus by talking briefly with the student before the student rereads a book. Usually only a comment or two is made before the student begins reading a text unless the text has caused difficulty in an earlier reading. The following interactions occurred before the rereading of books during Reading Recovery lessons.

> Jerry picks up his running record book for the day, *The Record Player* (Schaub 1976). "His mom and dad and sister can't sleep," he tells Sue as he opens the book to read. "That record player is just too loud," responds Sue.

> Tonja is going to read *The Red Rose* (Cowley 1983c) for the second time. She has had difficulty reading the book the previous day. Before she begins reading, Sue and Tonja reconstruct the plot line and the names of the animals. Sue primarily asks

questions but also fills in parts of the story that Tonja does not remember. Sue then asks Tonja what word each animal says during the second part of the story. "Gone," replies Tonja. "That's right," replies Sue, "and then each one went back home."

Dorothy has chosen to reread *My Home* (Melser 1981). "That book is about animals' homes," I say as she picks up the book. Dorothy looks at the book and then points to the inside of the pig pen saying, "What's this?" "It's mud," I reply. "Why do pigs live in mud?" she asks. "I think it keeps them cool," I explain. Dorothy shrugs her shoulders and opens the book to begin reading.

These interactions before rereading a familiar text were brief and emphasized meaning. In contrast, interactions before the reading of a new book emphasize both meaning and strategy development.

INTERACTIONS DURING AND AFTER READING • A few well-placed questions or comments during and after reading can benefit strategy development. Comments during reading are made judiciously so as not interrupt the student's reading. Comments and questions are most productive following the reading of a story when the teacher and student can return to certain parts of the text to focus on the student's strategies and use of cue systems.

There are four major questions that Clay (1985) recommends teachers use to teach the child how to search for cues:

1. Does it make sense?
2. Does that look right?
3. Can we say it that way?
4. What would you expect to see?

The choice of questions depends on the kinds of cue systems that the teacher observes the student using or not using and on the particular segment of text involved. The main purpose of the questions is to teach readers how to use what they know to solve new problems.

Teacher comments during reading are kept to a minimum to maintain the forward momentum of students as they construct meaning from the story. During reading, their focus needs to be on meaning and on making and testing out their own predictions. Readers who read for meaning are likely to self-correct as they monitor their own reading. If the teacher immediately steps in whenever readers encounter difficulty, the readers learn to depend on the teacher rather than on their own problem-solving abilities.

There are, however, other types of interactions that occur occasionally during the reading of texts in Reading Recovery. These interactions tend to occur when the student runs into difficulty in a particular section and becomes confused or when the student stops and will not continue reading. If the student gets more and more confused in a particular section of text, the teacher might simply say, "Try that again," hoping that another running start at that section will help.

If a student runs into trouble and stops reading, the teacher's first response is usually to sit and wait. Sue was especially good at waiting for long periods of time to let students work on an area of difficulty and to decide for themselves whether to continue reading or to work at the section until they had figured it out. After a period of time, if the student was still sitting silently, Sue would say "What are you thinking about?" or "What are you checking to figure it out?" The student's response gave her insight into what the student was doing and allowed her to know how to support that student better.

An example of this type of interaction occurred when Tonja was reading *Grumpy Elephant* (Cowley 1982).

> In the middle of the story, Tonja comes to a portion of text that reads "Louder louder louder!" She stops and sits there for a long period of time just staring at the book. When Sue finally asks her what she is doing, Tonja replies, "Checking the word." Sue wants Tonja to use more meaning cues and so decides to provide a frame for Tonja to consider the strategy of using the broader story context. Sue says, "Let's think about what is happening. The parrot is singing. The monkey is playing. The giraffe is dancing. All at the same time. How did they get?" "Noisy," replies Tonja. "That's right," says Sue. "There is noise and it is getting . . . " Sue points to the word on the page as she makes this comment and Tonja immediately says, "Louder," and continues reading.

Another response used by teachers if a student is stuck is to say, "Skip it and read on." The teacher and student can then come back and talk about that section after the student finishes reading the book. Occasionally teachers tell the student the word or phrase causing difficulty. In Reading Recovery, this is done through asking a question such as "Could it be 'surprise'?"

or "Would you say 'surprise' or 'goodbye'?" rather than just giving the word.

After the student has finished reading, the Reading Recovery teacher and student go back and discuss particular parts of the text where the student has had difficulty or has done some particularly good reading work on substitutions or self-corrections. The decision of which sections in the book to discuss following reading is sometimes a teacher decision and sometimes a student decision.

An effective technique to get students involved in decision making is for the teacher to say, "Find a place where you did some good reading work. How did you figure that part out?" or "Find a part where you had some trouble. What did you have problems with? How did you know you were wrong? What did you try to do? What else could have you done?" Another more general question is for the teacher simply to ask, "How did you do today on this book? Why?"

There are several advantages to using this type of questioning with students. One is that it actively involves students in decision making and encourages them to monitor their own reading rather than to expect the teacher to do it. Another is that, in many readings, the student will make multiple miscues; discussion of all of these miscues is usually overwhelming. Allowing the student to have some choice in which one or two miscues or sections of texts to discuss often leads to more productive discussions.

Allowing students to choose the sections to be discussed following reading is based on the assumption that learners usually attend to and learn best from their newest language discoveries (Harste, Woodward, & Burke 1984). By having the student choose, there is a greater chance that the discussion will be supportive to the student's strategy development rather than focusing on information not useful to the student at that time.

During the reading of the book *Little Brother* (Cowley 1983a), Dorothy makes a number of substitutions. Near the end of the story, she substitutes the word "boy" for "baby" in the sentence "Mother had a baby." After making this substitution, she stops and puzzles a bit, and then reads on to the end of the story. When I ask her to find a part that gave her trouble, Dorothy immediately goes back to the sentence about the baby and points to the word "boy." "What do you think the word might be," I ask. Dorothy responds by rereading the page again, substituting the word "boy" for "baby" with uncertainty. When I ask her what else the word might be, she replies "baby." We talk about how both words make sense and then look at the two words visually to see which one the author used.

Dorothy chose a substitution that I would not have chosen to discuss because the substitution made sense in the story. It bothered her, however, and her choice of that substitution gave us the opportunity to work on the strategy of using both context and the visual features of words. Dorothy was becoming aware that she could use several cue systems at once in reading.

The discussions following reading can focus on areas of the text that the reader has dealt with successfully as well as areas the reader was unable to figure out. Following reading, the Reading Recovery teacher and student often talk about the strategies the student used to read a section of text successfully that initially caused difficulty.

> Dorothy reads *Our Teacher, Miss Pool* (Cowley 1983b) for the second time. On the last page of the book, she does extensive reading work on the sentence, "On Saturday, she fixed her car. 'Now I can drive to school,' says Miss Pool." Dorothy rereads this entire passage three different times making different substitutions and self-corrections until finally she reads the passage with only a minor change in the text. When Dorothy finishes reading, I ask her to find a place where she did some good reading work. She proudly goes back to the last page of the book. When asked how she figured it out, she replies, "I just kept trying."

Dorothy was a "swivel-head" child who constantly looked at me for confirmation as she read. Her various attempts at reading this passage were a major breakthrough for her. This experience allowed us to discuss how getting another running start and going back to reread a section of text was a useful technique that she could use when she got into trouble instead of looking at the teacher.

During Reading Recovery lessons, teachers as well as students make decisions about which sections of text to discuss following the reading of a book. The interactions following reading involve constantly working at achieving a balance between the teacher and student in deciding on the focus of their discussions about the reading. In order for teachers to make effective decisions about teaching points, they must be closely observing their students. They can then use these observations to choose parts of the text that will support a productive discussion with the student. Self-corrections or substitutions allow the teacher and child to discuss cue systems and strategies the student may have used or those they can begin to use during reading.

Reading Recovery teachers also make comments such as "I liked the way you checked the picture on the page" or "Why don't we check the picture and see if something there would help you figure out this part?" These comments help students become more aware of information they are using and direct their attention to new information. When students are unable to verbalize the information they are using, the teacher might say, "It looked like you were using the first letter" or "It looked like you were seeing if it made sense. That's a good strategy to use."

There is a balance between teachers and students in decision making and discussion when the focus is on real communication. Instead of the teacher's simply imposing information onto the student, the teacher and student talk *with* each other. The teacher asks "real" questions—questions to which the teacher may not already have an answer. The interaction resembles a conversation between two people rather than a quiz in which the student has to feed the correct answer back to the teacher. All participants listen carefully and respond actively to others' actions and words.

THE ROLE OF ANOMALIES IN INTERACTIVE DISCUSSIONS • Anomalies play a major role in the teacher and student's discussions about reading. The reader predicted one thing and another thing occurred. Most of the time readers read along not consciously thinking about their reading process or puzzling over the meaning they are constructing until they encounter something that surprises them in the text. These anomalies are unexpected responses that cause readers to rethink the story or to go back and use other strategies to try and solve the problem. The reader's attention is shifted to process.

The parts of texts where anomalies occur are the most productive to discuss, because these are the points where readers are most likely to be aware of the cue systems or strategies they used. Even though they may not be aware of which specific cues they used, they know that something was not quite right at that point in the text. Anomalies thus provide a point of awareness that is more productive for strategy development. The presence of anomalies as students read is usually indicated by long pauses, rereading, making self-corrections, a look of puzzlement, running a finger under a word, or questions.

When students make substitutions or some other change in the text which does not produce an anomaly for them, they keep on reading without awareness of that change. Since the change has not caused an anomaly, the student is usually not aware of or concerned about the change and so that section of text is not as productive to discuss. This focus on anomalies allows both students and teachers to see miscues and unexpected responses as a natural part of learning rather than as errors that are wrong and need to be immediately corrected.

THE IMPORTANCE OF AWARENESS OR REFLECTION IN TEACHING FOR STRATEGIES

Two assumptions underlie the notion of teaching for strategies. The first is that strategies involve choice; readers develop a range of options from which they can choose when they encounter difficulty. Readers need to develop both a repertoire of strategies and a knowledge of how to orchestrate these cues in different settings to develop flexibility during reading. To do this, they must experience a wide variety of strategies as they read whole texts, rather than being drilled on several to achieve "mastery."

The second assumption is that becoming a strategic reader involves some degree of reflection or awareness about these strategies. It is not enough for students just to engage in a number of strategies; they need to be aware of these strategies as options that they and other readers can use in many different reading situations. Margaret Meek (1983) found that special education students who experienced a wide range of strategies in their special education classroom did not carry these over into the regular classroom because they were not aware of them. They did not realize that they could use these strategies in many situations and that these strategies were the same ones used by proficient readers. Baker and Brown (1984) argue that self-awareness is a prerequisite for self-regulation, the ability of learners to monitor their own cognitive abilities during reading.

When a student is using new strategies or techniques, reflection is needed before they become part of that student's repertoire of strategies. This assumption about teaching for strategies is a crucial factor in learning about reading processes. While awareness of some type is considered to be important during the learning of new strategies or techniques, it is not assumed that students consciously think through their options whenever they encounter difficulty while reading. This processing, especially as readers gain experience and become more proficient, occurs rapidly and often unconsciously.

Several other qualifications must be made about the importance of reflection or awareness to the teaching of strategies. One

qualification is that this awareness is not of isolated bits of knowledge but of broad strategies developed in the context of real
language use on whole texts. The second qualification is that, as
Carolyn Burke (pers. com. 1985) says, "A little goes a long way."
While some awareness of the new strategies employed by a reader
is important to allow for the use of those strategies in new situations, teachers need to recognize that too much awareness para-
lyzes the reader and takes the focus away from meaning.

The reader must be intent on the construction of meaning
during reading, not on the learning of strategies. When the focus
on meaning is lost in the interactions between teacher and students, students begin to lose their focus on reading as making
meaning and become too aware of what they are doing as they
read.

In the examples given earlier from Reading Recovery lessons of
interactions between teachers and students were brief comments
about strategies, not long drawn-out analyses. The teacher's concern was not to have students name isolated rules or procedures
but to make them aware of alternative cue systems and strategies
that could be used during reading. Students were also learning
about strategies as they actually engaged in reading and in monitoring their own learning. Teachers did not assume that strategy
development occurred only in their discussions with students.

A third qualification is that awareness is not equated with meta-
linguistic expression. When teachers ask students to speak about
their strategies of reading, they cannot assume that students do not
have strategies if they cannot express them verbally. The social interaction between teachers and students gives students the opportunity to share their learning experiences. The teacher serves as a
sounding board against which students can try out ideas and gradually come to the point of being able to put their ideas into words.

Students learn strategies by engaging in reading and by reflecting on their reading processes. They also learn through observing
the demonstrations of other readers. Frank Smith (1981), Halliday
(1975), and Harste, Woodward, and Burke (1984), among others,
have argued that what students learn from the demonstrations that
other language users provide is crucial to language learning.
Demonstrations from other readers help students develop a range
of reading strategies, both cognitive and social. Even though teachers and students can develop strong social relationships when the
teacher takes the role of both a monitor and a demonstrator, students still need multiple demonstrations from other readers. Since
reading is a social process (Bloom & Green 1984; Halliday 1978), it

is important that teaching for strategies should stress both psychological and social strategies.

Within a regular classroom setting, teachers can create a learning environment that encourages students to engage in reading, to observe the demonstrations of other readers, and to reflect on their own reading. Engagements, demonstrations, and reflection are all essential components in supporting learners as they become proficient readers. Much of what students know about reading will develop from their many experiences in reading widely and in interacting with other readers. While reflection, highlighted in this chapter, certainly does play a major role in reading, it must always take place in this context of engaging in reading and interacting with other readers.

Readers can be encouraged to reflect on their reading processes by their interactions with teachers and other readers. Instead of fragmenting and isolating parts of the reading process, the learning environment should allow readers to discuss their strategies in real reading situations. Although these interactions are more intense and frequent in Reading Recovery than would be necessary or possible in a regular classroom, classroom teachers can still use their interactions with students to help them become more aware of the strategies available to them as readers.

LEARNING ENVIRONMENTS FOR STRATEGIC READERS

All learners, including students at risk of failure, need to develop a broad repertoire of strategies that they can use to successfully engage in constructing meaning from text. These strategies are the same ones proficient readers use to monitor their reading. Students learn these strategies as they engage in reading and writing whole texts for meaning, see the demonstrations of others engaged in reading and writing, and reflect on these engagements and demonstrations (Harste 1985).

Interactions between readers, whether they be teachers or students, about reading and writing can support literacy and communicate to students that reading involves searching, discovering, and problem solving. Reading is an active search for meaning in which readers monitor the meaning they are constructing and draw from their repertoire of strategies when they encounter difficulties. Supporting the reader through interactions focused on strategies and meaning gives readers the chance to become independent learners who can continue to grow and learn from text. When teachers develop learning environments for strategic readers, they support students in becoming independent readers who have a broad range of cognitive and social strategies that can be used to construct meaning in many literacy contexts.

REFERENCES

Baker, L., & A. Brown. 1984. "Metacognitive Skills and Reading." In P. D. Pearson, ed., *Handbook of Reading Research*, 353–94. New York: Longman.

Bloom, D., & J. Green. 1984. "Directions in the Sociolinguistic Study of Reading." In P. D. Pearson, ed., *Handbook of Reading Research*, 395–422. New York: Longman.

Cazden, C. 1988. *Classroom Discourse*. Portsmouth, N.H.: Heinemann.

Clay, M. 1985. *The Early Detection of Reading Difficulties*. 3d ed. Portsmouth, N.H.: Heinemann.

Cowley, J. 1982. *Grumpy Elephant*. San Diego, Cal.: Wright Group.

———.1983a. *Little Brother*. San Diego, Cal.: Wright Group.

———.1983b. *Our Teacher, Miss Pool*. Wellington: New Zealand Department of Education.

———.1983c. *The Red Rose*. San Diego, Cal.: Wright Group.

Deshler, D., & J. Schumaker. 1986. "Learning Strategies: An Instructional Alternative for Low-Achieving Adolescents." *Exceptional Children* 52 (6): 583–90.

Goodman, K. S. 1984. "Unity in Reading." In A. C. Purves & O. Niles, eds., *Becoming Readers in a Complex Society* 79–114. Chicago: University of Chicago Press.

Goodman, Y., & C. Burke. 1980. *Reading Strategies: Focus on Comprehension*. New York: Holt, Rinehart, & Winston.

Halliday, M. K. 1975. *Learning How to Mean*. London: Arnold.

———.1978. *Language as a Social Semiotic: The Social Interpretation of Language and Meaning*. Baltimore, Md.: University Park Press.

Hamsa, B. 1983. *Dirty Larry*. Rookie Reader. Chicago: Children's Press.

Harste, J. 1985. "Portrait of a New Paradigm: Reading Comprehension Research." In A. Crismore, ed., *Landscapes: A State-of-the-Art Assessment of Reading Comprehension Research, 1974–1984*. Bloomington, Ind.: Language Education Department, Indiana University.

Harste, J., V. Woodward, & C. Burke. 1984. *Language Stories and Literacy Lessons*. Portsmouth, N.H.: Heinemann.

Lindgren, B. N.d. *Sam's Car*. New York: Morrow.

Meek, M. 1983. *Achieving Literacy: Longitudinal Studies of Adolescents Learning to Read*. London: Routledge & Kegan Paul.

Melser, J. 1981. *My Home*. San Diego, Cal.: Wright Group.

———.1982. *Two Little Dogs*. San Diego, Cal.: Wright Group.

Rowe, D. 1986. "Literacy in the Child's World: Preschoolers' Exploration of Alternate Sign Systems." Ph.D. diss., Indiana University, Bloomington, Ind.

Schaub, P. 1976. *The Record Player*. London: Bowmar.

Short, K. G. 1986. "Literacy as a Collaborative Experience." Ph.D. diss., Indiana University, Bloomington, Ind.

Smith, F. 1978. *Reading Without Nonsense.* New York: Teachers College Press, Columbia University.

————.1981. "Demonstrations, Engagements, and Sensitivity: A Revised Approach to Language Learning." *Language Arts* 58: 103–12.

Tolstoy, A. 1971. *The Great Big Enormous Turnip.* Glenview, Ill.: Scott Foresman.

Vygotsky, L. 1978. *Mind in Society.* Cambridge, Mass.: Harvard University Press.

SIX

··········

Selecting Books for Beginning Readers

BARBARA PETERSON

······················· *A* ·····························
ccording to custom in the
United States, first grade is the year in which children learn how to
read. Each child brings to the task approximately six years of language and life experiences. Some enter first grade with so little
reading experience that they may not realize that print conveys the
message; a few others easily read books such as *Charlotte's Web*
(White 1952). Most children could be placed somewhere on that
continuum.

More than one mother has shared with me the story of a child
who seemed to make no progress in learning to read in the classroom reading series but who could blithely wander through a
beloved dinosaur book pointing out all the tough words like
stegosaurus, triceratops, and *pterodactyl.* Tutoring Reading Recovery
students has given me an opportunity to observe similar responses
of beginning readers as they worked with many different kinds of
texts. My adult perceptions of what constitutes "easy" or "difficult"
passages were constantly challenged by the actual reading behaviors of young students. Teachers who love reading and value the
wealth of literature available for children realize that much of it is
too difficult for beginners to read on their own. At the same time,
they are aware that many of the supposedly "easy" textbook passages are in fact quite tricky for some children.

The purpose of this chapter is first to look at ways in which the
physical designs of books and the texts of their stories can support

the changing needs of beginning readers. Second, a way of evaluating this support will be presented. Most of the books used in Reading Recovery are narratives in story form, and thus the word *story* is used interchangeably with the word *book*. With one exception, all of the books discussed in this chapter are children's literature trade books currently available from libraries and bookstores. Because the process of evaluation can only be internalized by examining books, it is recommended that readers refer to them while reading this chapter.

While many fine series of "little books" are currently available for use in kindergarten and first-grade classrooms and can be purchased in multiple copies at relatively modest prices, none can offer the rich variety of story, language, and illustration of the many talented writers and illustrators in publishing today. On the other hand, the "little book" series are valuable in that they provide simple, repetitive texts that quickly engage beginners in the process of reading.

Studies of children's response to literature in kindergarten and first-grade classrooms (Hickman 1980; Beaver 1982; Kiefer 1988) document the values of providing beginning readers with many different kinds of books and classroom reading experiences. As Margaret Meek has noted, "The most important single lesson that children learn from texts is *the nature and variety of written discourse,* the different ways that language lets a writer tell, and the many and different ways a reader reads" (1988, p. 21).

READABILITY, PREDICTION, AND BEGINNING READERS

Historically, attempts to assign levels of difficulty to texts have been grouped together under the term "readability." Although the goals of readability research have been to investigate a wide range of characteristics that make a text easy or difficult to read and to use that knowledge to effectively match readers and texts (Chall 1984), the best-known aspect of that research has been a series of formulas designed to predict quickly the grade level of a text (Klare 1984). Readability formulas are statistical tools that can take into account only a limited number of text features such as word difficulty, word frequency, word length, and sentence length. These formulas were not designed to account for factors such as reader interest and prior knowledge, classroom instruction, or text layout and illustration.

Furthermore, many publishers have misused readability formulas to produce textbooks that match a specified grade level. This practice has often led authors to write texts to conform to the specifications of a formula, resulting in short, choppy sentences and the avoidance of rich, interesting language (Cullinan & Fitzgerald 1984). First-grade teachers familiar with the "preprimer" books of many graded series of reading textbooks will have encountered examples of formulaic writing that simultaneously confuse and bore beginning readers.

A concern for the particular reading needs of first-grade students led several researchers (Rhodes 1979; Gourley 1984; Bussis et al. 1985) to observe beginning readers and closely examine features of texts that supported readers. Comparisons were made between students' readings of children's literature storybooks and of selections from instructional reading texts with controlled vocabularies. Although readability levels were lower for the instructional texts, a striking result from each of the studies was that students were able to read and comprehend the literature stories with greater success. The researchers concluded that factors such as the familiarity with the story, the match between the illustrations and text, and the predictability of language patterns and story episodes influenced the quality of the readings in ways not accounted for by readability formulas.

According to Smith (1982) and Clay (1985), beginning readers are engaged in a task that is very similar to what more experienced readers are doing when they read. Proficient readers expect a text to make sense and, consequently, draw on a variety of personal and textual resources to support the reading and understanding of the author's message. Beginning readers also can draw on valuable stores of prior knowledge that will support their reading of new texts. In a longitudinal study of early reading behaviors, Clay (1982) observed that when children substituted one word for another while reading a story, the majority of the substitutions were grammatically acceptable. Furthermore, the children often noticed when their reading did not make sense, and they would then work to correct their miscues. One conclusion drawn from this study was that children have more opportunity to develop useful reading strategies when they read from texts that reflect the language they speak fluently.

Ample evidence from research indicates that children from birth undergo a multitude of language and life experiences that serve as foundations for learning to read (Goodman 1986; Teale 1986). From infancy, children learn to employ the resources of language to communicate information about themselves and to learn about the people and places close to them (Halliday 1975; Wells 1986). During their preschool years, children from print-oriented cultures are immersed in an environment of printed messages. Street signs, names of favorite toys, and labels on cereal boxes are just a few examples of print young children are likely to encounter regularly. They may also observe family members reading newspapers, magazines, books, and other printed materials.

Preschool children develop a "sense of story." They learn to tell stories about the events in their lives (Moffett 1983), incorporate the language of story books into their play (White 1984; Butler 1980), and develop expectations that characters such as witches and fairies will act in predictable ways (Applebee 1978). Through familiarity with written stories, "children learn literary discourse in much the same way they learn to talk" (King and McKenzie 1988). In other words, they learn to "talk like a book" (Clay 1979). Recent research demonstrates that when "prereading" preschool and kindergarten children are asked to read familiar stories they actively work at constructing the message of the author and illustrator (McKenzie 1977; Holdaway 1979; Cook-Gumperz and Green 1984; Sulzby 1985; Pappas 1987).

Predictability is a useful concept for considering how early learning experiences assist children in learning to read. In his essay "Going Beyond the Information Given," Bruner (1973) argues that in order to make sense of the enormous amount of information present in the environment, human beings make inferences and predictions about the present and future based on expectations derived from past experiences. Prediction is, according to Smith (1982), a continuous, dynamic process routinely engaged in by beginners as well as by mature readers.

The task at hand, then, is to derive a way to select books for beginning readers that will take into account their unique needs at different times. Predictability helps us in considering similarities and differences among texts, but as Rhodes points out, it is also a complex concept that encompasses many factors:

> Clearly, the notion of predictability should be considered as residing on a continuum dependent on both the reader and the text. For first graders, factors like repetition of large chunks of language and episodes, familiarity of story lines, story sequences, or concepts appear to encourage more effective reading. However, these factors and others vary uniquely and to different degrees from text to text and from reader to reader. (1979, p. 129)

THE ROLE OF BOOKS IN READING RECOVERY LESSONS

Students read many books during each half-hour Reading Recovery lesson. At the beginning of the lesson, they "warm up" by rereading two or more books from previous lessons. The lesson closes with the teacher's introduction of a new book and the student's first reading of the new book. The teacher has carefully selected the new book to support the reader's present knowledge and, at the same time, to provide some new challenge and opportunity for engaging in "reading work" (Clay 1985; see the DeFord and Short chapters for more thorough discussions of the use of books during Reading Recovery lessons). The following day, after the rereading of the familiar books, the Reading Recovery teacher takes a running record of the student's first independent reading of the new book.

Reading Recovery teachers learn to analyze and select books along a continuum of difficulty. They know that children just beginning their lessons need books with predictable features such as commonly used spoken language structures, repetition of phrases, content that describes familiar experiences, illustrations that clearly depict the message in the written text, and print laid out in a consistent location. Reading Recovery teachers also understand that their students must gradually shift to reading longer, more complex stories with less patterned language and more varied vocabulary. Important, too, is that each book bring pleasure to its reader.

ORGANIZING BOOKS INTO LEVELS OF DIFFICULTY

Sources of books include many "little" books from reading series, as well as many children's literature trade books. Books selected are approximately 20–400 words in length. They are organized into twenty reading levels to guide teachers in introducing children gradually to a variety of stories and features of print. The hierarchy of levels was developed in New Zealand based on teachers' observations of their students' progression through the Ready to Read books, a graded series of little books read by all beginning readers designed to reflect the experiences of children growing up in New Zealand. Thus, these books came to serve as bench marks for comparison in assessing levels for new books.

Levels are only approximations of gradients of difficulty. They serve as a guide and are not an inflexible sequence. Levels of individual books may be changed on the recommendations of Reading Recovery teachers who have used the books with children. Level 1 books are usually built on one sentence pattern organized around a theme familiar to most children, such as babies, families, or animals. The complexity of level 20 material roughly corresponds to that found in typical basal reading programs for children at the end of the first-grade year. There is no formula that can be used to assign levels because factors such as the reader's background of experience, the match between pictures and text, language patterning and vocabulary, and episodic structure are all major considerations.

A particular book may be appropriate for one child at one level but inappropriate for another child who reads at the same level. This situation often happens with the very familiar stories such as *The Three Little Pigs*. On the one hand, a child who knows the refrains and sequence of events from memory has very usable expectations as to what the text is going to say, so that the reading becomes a kind of checking of the meaning of the story, the structure of the language, and the print on the page. On the other hand, a child for whom this is a new story must make sense of an unusual set of events as well as some nonsense language. "Not by the hair of my chinny-chin-chin" can be a substantial intrusion into a story reading for someone who has never heard those words put together in quite that way. Thus, it is essential to keep "the reader" in mind, and to consider the possible range of experiences, knowledge, and expectations that might influence the first reading of a book, subsequent readings of the same book, and the reading of other books.

AN EXAMINATION OF PREDICTABLE FEATURES OF BOOKS

Just as there is no formula that can determine a book's level, there are no specific criteria for each level. Yet, a close examination of a selection of books from each level reveals a continuum of patterns that seems to be useful in describing how texts become progressively more complex (Peterson 1988). Several factors interact to influence the choice of a level for a particular book, including content in relation to children's personal experiences, language patterns, vocabulary, illustration support for the meaning of the text, and narrative style. Making a decision about the appropriate level for a book is a process of examining the relationship of such features within the context of an entire book. The process of assigning a book to a level is also made easier by making comparisons to other books with similar characteristics.

An example of a level 1 book that is attractive to children and supportive of their learning to read is *Baby*, a Price Milburn Instant Reader (McMillan 1979). Photographs on the left hand pages show "baby" in a variety of poses: drinking, eating, laughing, crying, sitting, crawling, and sleeping. The text on an otherwise blank right-hand page repeats the same language pattern and describes the pictures. For example:

Page	Text
2	Baby can drink.
4	Baby can eat.
6	Baby can laugh.

This text supports the beginning reader by making explicit the many links connecting the message of the story, the structures of the English language, and the visual features of the print that signal specific words. First, the theme of "baby" is one that has meaning for most first graders, thus making it easy for them to predict the message of this text from their own experiences and expectations for what babies can do. Second, the clear photographs with no distracting features provide another source for predicting the meaning of the text. They unambiguously illustrate what is happening. Third, the language pattern "Baby can . . . " is an oral language structure that is naturally used by young children and represents another source of prediction. Fourth, the repetition of this phrase gives the reader many opportunities to confirm that the print conveys a specific message.

An example of a book that is slightly more difficult to read than *Baby*, but that still provides the beginning reader with the support of repeated language patterns and predictable events, is the level 3 book *All Fall Down* (Wildsmith 1983). Through pictures and language, Wildsmith's story vividly mimics a familiar childhood play of stacking one block upon another and another and so on until the whole tower tumbles down. However, instead of blocks, the characters are a ball, a seal, a rabbit, a bird, a butterfly, and a bee. Predictably, they "all fall down."

Like the pictures in *Baby*, the illustrations in *All Fall Down* clearly depict the characters and events of the story. The language patterns, too, reflect language familiar to a young child.

I see a bee.

I see a bee and a butterfly.

Even the concluding sentence, "all fall down" has been elicited easily from Reading Recovery children when asked what they would say if their block towers fell down.

Thus, within *All Fall Down* are many sources of prediction to support young readers. This book also provides new challenges. Each time a character is added to the stack the sentence increases in length, challenging the reader to monitor carefully up to three lines of print.

> I see a bee and a butterfly and
> a bird and a rabbit and a seal
> and a ball.

Where's Spot? by Eric Hill (1980) is an example of a book at level 8 that is more difficult than *Baby* or *All Fall Down*, but that still provides the beginning reader with the support of repeated language patterns and predictable events. The theme of the book reflects another common childhood experience, that of playing a game of "hide and seek." In this book Spot's mother looks for him in several places. On the left-hand page a question is asked about Spot's possible hiding place, such as "Is he behind the door?" To find out if Spot is behind the door the reader lifts a flap on the right-hand page. Under the flap, a bear says "No."

> That Spot! He hasn't eaten his supper. Where can he be?
>
> Is he behind the door?   No.
> Is he inside the clock?   No.
> Is he under the bed?   No.

Predictable features of this book include the familiar "hide and seek" game, the repetition of the question format "is he," the "no" response, and illustrations that clearly depict the possible hiding place. Some features that make this more difficult than *Baby* and *All Fall Down* are language structures closer to those found in "book language" than childrens' oral language, and a change in the question pattern on each page.

Unlike *Baby* and *All Fall Down*, however, where a good memory for pattern can carry a reader through the printed message in the text, the reader of *Where's Spot?* is forced to pay close attention to the visual aspects of print. For example, the substitution of the word *in* for *inside* while reading the sentence, "Is he inside the clock?" would not interfere with the meaning or syntactic structure of the text. However, a substitution of *in* for *behind* or *under* in other sentences would change the meaning and would probably encourage the reader to check predictions against the print.

Along the gradient of levels, texts become more complex and challenging in a variety of ways within the context of a complete story. A higher-level story may have many characters acting in a string of episodes. While pictures may enhance the story and contribute to the overall meaning, they seldom correspond in a totally consistent way with the words in the text. Sentences may become longer and have dependent clauses, or may be so short as to require the reader to infer precise meaning from one's knowledge outside the text.

To understand the gist of *Titch* by Pat Hutchins (1971) (level 12), one would need to have some experience or empathy with the youngest child in the family who always gets the short end of things, but who triumphs regally in the end. Readers of folktales would quickly recognize that theme!

Titch is more complicated than *Where's Spot?* because there are three characters to keep track of and each one (Pete, Mary, and Titch) owns several items. Some objects may be unfamiliar to young readers, such as pinwheels, trumpets, and little wooden whistles. The language pattern is repeated on several pages ("Pete had . . . "; "Mary had . . . "; "And Titch had . . . "), but the syntax is much more literary—or booklike—than the language in books at earlier levels. The predictable elements of meaning in the story are found in cycles of threes across a series of events. The reader knows that Pete will always have the biggest of whatever object is owned; Mary will have something big; and Titch will always have something small.

> Pete had a kite that flew high above the trees.
> Mary had a kite that flew high above the houses.
> And Titch had a pinwheel that he held in his hand.

Books such as *Titch* provide students with opportunities to read stories with longer stretches of discourse that are less dependent on the repetition of language patterns and vocabulary than are found in books discussed previously. They help prepare students to manage books with longer stories with well-developed episodes. One example is "The Story," from *Frog and Toad Are Friends* by Arnold Lobel (1972). Four times as long as *Titch*, "The Story" is only one of several stories in the book. While there are only two characters to follow, Frog and Toad, the story is made more complex by the greater amount of description that surrounds each event.

> One day in summer Frog was not feeling well.
> Toad said, "Frog, you are looking quite green."
> "But I always look green," said Frog. "I am a frog."
> "Today you look very green even for a frog," said Toad.

This is a story within a story, because Toad tries so hard to think up a story to entertain Frog that he falls ill. Next it is Frog's turn to cheer up Toad, so he tells a story that in fact is a retelling of the sequence of events that has occurred to that time. The second story is predictable for the reader because it is almost a repeat performance. At the same time, the change in point of view challenges the reader to follow the shift in predicament.

Contributing to the story, though not essential to its enjoyment, are the different personalities of Frog and Toad and the subtle bursts of humor that are part of all of their adventures. Frog and Toad stories could stand on their own without Lobel's endearing illustrations (though this is not suggested!). Thus, in order to read the story successfully, the reader must be able to interpret the printed text. Pictures cannot be relied on to supply most of the meaning of the story as was possible in *Baby, All Fall Down,* and *Where's Spot?*

A GUIDE FOR EVALUATING DIFFICULTY LEVELS OF TEXTS

The first section of this chapter described a few characteristics of several books that both support and challenge readers. Because texts were selected from those written as stories and not according to "formula," all characteristics may not occur in linear order. A text may be generally appropriate at one level, but also have some characteristics of texts at another level. Thus, while the designation of levels is a useful way to indicate roughly a progression of difficulty for books used during Reading Recovery lessons, such a system may not be suitable for other settings.

For teachers, parents, librarians, and others who work with beginning readers, the key to selecting appropriate materials is learning how to think about the relationship between various features of texts and the experiences of individual readers. These relationships are most easily understood by adults who enjoy reading, who have read widely from children's literature, and who have closely observed children learning how to read.

The purpose of this section of the chapter will be to provide guidelines for examining and sorting books along a continuum, from easier to more complex. Since it is difficult, if not impossible, to define precisely the qualities of books at each level (Peterson 1988), typical features of each of five groups of levels will be described. Five books having a similar "all fall down" theme will illustrate some of the shifts that take place across the continuum of levels.

Levels	Book
1–4	*All Fall Down* (Brian Wildsmith)
5–8	*Sam's Lamp* (Barbro Lindgren)

9–12   *"Pardon?" Said the Giraffe* (Colin West)
13–15   *The Great Big Enormous Turnip* (Alexei Tolstoy)
16–20   *Mr Gumpy's Outing* (John Burningham)

LEVELS 1–4 • Books in levels 1–4 have memorable, repetitive language patterns. The illustrations strongly support most of the text because objects and actions are clearly portrayed without much clutter or extraneous detail. Each book presents a complete message or story that is likely to reflect the experiences or knowledge common to many beginning readers. The language of books at these levels reflects primarily the syntax and organization of young children's speech. Sentences and books themselves are comparatively short. The print of the text is carefully laid out so that it consistently appears on the same place on the page throughout each book.

Thus, the sources of support and prediction for readers at these levels are many. While reading these books, the child can easily learn that while there is a precise message conveyed in the printed text, many other sources of information assist the reader in using the reading process. When encountering an unknown word, the child learns to search for information in the illustrations, in the overall meaning of the book, and in the language patterns of the sentences, as well as in the cues within the word itself.

All Fall Down (level 3) (Wildsmith 1983), a simply told story described earlier in this chapter, presents a "bare-bones" sequence of events in which both words and illustrations carry the message. Once a child can read the repeated phrase "I see" and understands that the objects are linked by "and," the identity of the rest of the words can be checked directly with the pictures. Although the concluding phrase "all fall down" seems like an abrupt departure from the repeated language pattern, children who can read to that page quickly understand the ending of the story. Furthermore, they recognize "all fall down" as an expression they have heard or used many times.

LEVELS 5–8 • Books in levels 5–8 continue to have memorable, repetitive language patterns, but the same pattern does not dominate the entire text. When a pattern is repeated through most or part of a level 5–8 book, it is with more variation than the one or two word changes found in levels 1–4. Some books in levels 5–8 do not have consistent sentence patterns that are repeated. Instead, phrases or groups of words may appear to express different meanings through a slightly different sentence structure. By level 8, most books have some syntax that is more typical of written than oral language. One example is the opening page of *Where's Spot?* (Hill 1980): "That Spot! He hasn't eaten his supper. Where can he be?" Because the text cannot be illustrated precisely, readers must gradually decrease their dependence on pictures.

Sam's Lamp (level 6) (Lindgren 1983) is the story of Sam who climbs up on a stool, a chair, and then a table to reach his lamp that hangs from the ceiling. Predictably, he falls down, Mommy comes, puts on a bandage, and then Sam is happy. Like *All Fall Down*, *Sam's Lamp* consists of a simple sequence of events. The story of Sam may be easier for a child to understand because most children have experienced similar tumbles.

The language patterns in *Sam's Lamp* are more varied, however, than those in *All Fall Down*. For example,

> Look, there's Sam.
>
> The lamp is pretty.
>
> Sam climbs up on the stool.

At the same time, the reader receives support through the repetition of some phrases.

> Look, there's Sam.
>
> Look, there's Sam's lamp.
>
> ***
>
> Sam climbs up on the stool.
>
> Sam climbs up on the chair.
>
> Sam climbs up on the table.

Many pictures, like those in *All Fall Down*, clearly illustrate the meaning of the story language. For example, when Mommy puts a bandage on Sam's knee, the picture shows the child in her lap and her hand touching the edge of the bandage. On the other hand, the precise language of the story will not be found in other illustrations. For example, one picture shows Sam leaning on his stool. One arm is reaching toward the lamp and his eyes gaze upward, and the accompanying sentence says, "The lamp is pretty." The concept of "pretty" is less easily portrayed than an object such as a bandage, so while the reader can check the picture for help, the word "pretty" must also be read.

LEVELS 9–12 • In levels 9–12 most of the books exhibit a great deal of variation in sentence pattern. Some books contain repeated language patterns, but the sentences are longer than those at earlier levels or they serve as refrains rather than as primary carriers of meaning. A written style of language becomes more prominent as well as the use of some verb forms not often used by young children in oral settings. One example is the closing of *Titch*, in which his tiny seed "grew and grew and grew."

Sentence lengths increase in levels 9–12, and the longest is approximately double that found in levels 5–8. At the same time, there are books in levels 9–12 with many short sentences, made more difficult because they contain unfamiliar or idiomatic expressions. For example, the mouse in *Whose Mouse Are You?* (Kraus 1970) explains that he is his father's mouse "from head to toe" and his baby brother is "brand new." At lower levels, sentences of similar length would typically express concrete, more easily illustrated ideas.

In contrast to books at earlier levels which usually have events completed in a single sentence on one page of text, many books in levels 9–12 have a single event that continues over several pages. One example is *Titch*, described earlier in this chapter. Another is *The Carrot Seed* (Krauss 1945), in which a little boy plants a seed, and the skeptical members of his family insist that "it won't come up." One event continues over four pages.

> Every day the little boy pulled up the weeds around the seed and sprinkled the ground with water.
>
> But nothing came up.
>
> And nothing came up.
>
> Everyone kept saying it wouldn't come up.

"Pardon?" Said the Giraffe (level 9) (West 1986) tells of a frog who hops first on the ground, then on the lion, the elephant, and the giraffe. The giraffe sneezes, the frog falls back to the ground. The story is carried forward by an exchange between the frog and giraffe.

"What's it like up there?" asks the frog as he hops on increasingly taller animals. Each time the frog hops on a different animal, the repeated and thus predictable response is, " 'Pardon?' said the giraffe." These two language patterns alternate for most of the text in a seemingly simple format. However, one of the sentences incorporates dialogue, an independent clause, and a dependent clause.

Thus, the reader must be able to read and comprehend longer stretches of more complex language structures that cannot be easily illustrated. The illustrations in books from levels 9 to 12 provide moderate support to the meaning of the stories.

LEVELS 13–15 • Books in levels 13–15 do not differ markedly from many of the books in levels 9–12. Variation in sentence pattern continues, with less dependence on the repetition of the same words or groups of words. Many books at these levels use a greater variety of words or a more specialized vocabulary. Illustrations usually contain many details and thus provide support for the overall meaning of the story but cannot be used by the reader to interpret the precise message in the printed text.

The Great Big Enormous Turnip (level 14) (Tolstoy 1968) is similar to an "all fall down" story, but in reverse. The old man attempts to pull a turnip out of the ground, but no matter how much he pulled, "he could not pull it up." One by one he called the old woman, the granddaughter, the dog, the cat, and the mouse until "up came the turnip at last." In contrast to books at earlier levels, this tale opens and closes like a traditional story.

> Once upon a time an old man planted a little turnip and said, "Grow, grow, little turnip, grow sweet. Grow, grow, little turnip, grow strong."
>
> ***
>
> They pulled and pulled again, and up came the turnip at last.

LEVELS 16–20 • Most of the books at levels 16–20 are longer stories or sequences of events. The events in these narratives are often developed more fully than individual books at lower levels. The vocabulary is rich and varied, and there is no effort to repeat words solely to serve as signposts for novice readers. Words used often are those that would be high-frequency words in the natural context of the language. Written language forms are more common than oral language forms. Illustrations help to create and portray the atmosphere of each story, but they do not specifically depict the content of the text. A major challenge to readers at these levels is to follow a text layout that might have full pages of print. At these levels, single episodes are often longer than entire books at the lower levels.

Mr Gumpy's Outing (level 19) (Burningham 1970) is a fanciful adventure that begins when Mr Gumpy decides to go out in his boat and a number of children and animals ask to come along. For a little while, all goes well. Then, pandemonium erupts and they "all fall down" into the water. The story contains many expressions that might be unfamiliar to beginning readers. In the sequence of actions that lead to the upset of the boat, each of the verbs is synonymous for the commotion created by each character.

For a little while they all went along happily but then . . .
The goat kicked
The calf trampled
The chickens flapped
The sheep bleated
The pig mucked about
The dog teased the cat
The cat chased the rabbit
The rabbit hopped
The children squabbled
The boat tipped . . .

ONE BOOK, MANY LEVELS • A story such as *The Chick and the Duckling* by Mirra Ginsburg (1972) offers opportunities for beginners reading with different degrees of independence. Although placed at a Reading Recovery level of 6, a teacher and student could share the book at a much earlier level. In the story, the chick mimics every action taken by the duckling.

"I am taking a walk," said the Duckling.
"Me too," said the Chick.

One child just learning to identify one or two words in a repeated pattern could chime in with "me too" after the teacher has read the duckling's longer lines. Another child may be able to read the entire phrase fluently. A third child may be able to do that, as well as read the variations of that pattern.

"Me too," cried the Chick.
"Not me," said the Chick.

Another child will fluently read the entire story. The first child who reads "me too" establishes an anchor that will enable him to stretch that bit to " 'Me too,' said the Chick." The second child will be able to stretch to the variations in that pattern. The third child firmly in control of all of the chick's words will probably extend his reading to the entire story. And the fourth child will be ready to move to another book that challenges him further.

SUMMARY

The intent of this chapter has been to propose a framework for evaluating and sorting books along a gradient of difficulty for the purpose of helping teachers to select appropriate instructional materials for beginning readers. Books used in the Reading Recovery program are organized into twenty levels, ranging from texts of brief descriptive phrases to stories with episodes of several paragraphs each. Levels are intended only as guidelines, and books may be assigned new levels based on the recommendations of Reading Recovery teachers. Some books may have different levels to accommodate regional and cultural differences. For example, a book about rain or the seashore may need a higher level for children living in a desert climate than for those residing in a coastal state.

There is no formula or simple method for assigning a book to a level. Essential to this process is close and continued observation of young readers and an intimate knowledge of many, many books for children. By knowing children, one can consider the range of their life experiences and the language they speak. By knowing books, one can be attuned to physical features such as print size and placement, clarity of illustrations, and repetition of language patterns. Books that have been successfully enjoyed and read by many children at different points in the instructional program can serve as bench marks for estimating a level for a newly acquired book.

Describing the characteristics of books at each level is virtually an impossible task. One reason is that the best books are creative works, so there are many variations in style within a level. However, it is possible, as well as more useful to describe shifts along a continuum. (Figure 6–1 provides a summary of predictable features of books for each group of levels.) Books from levels 1 to 4 are suitable for readers learning to control directional movement and word-by-word matching in print because they provide stories about familiar experiences in children's spoken language. Phrases are often repeated throughout the text with variation in one or two words, and the illustrations clearly describe the message in the printed text.

Gradually, readers must come to read longer sentences in language that is more "booklike." While a spoken style of language predominates in books from levels 5 to 8, sentences are longer with more variation in vocabulary than in lower levels. Repetition of phrases is present in many books from these levels. However, two

• •

FIGURE 6–1   SOURCES OF PREDICTABILITY IN GROUPS OF LEVELS

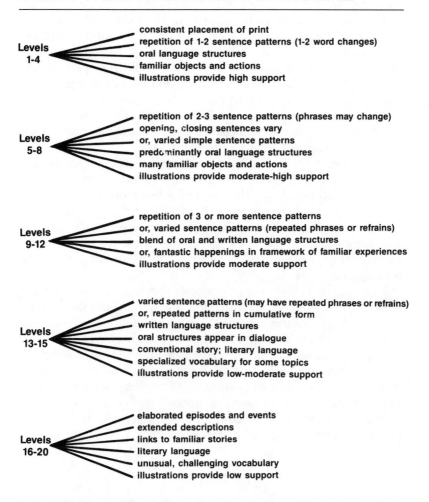

Levels 1-4
- consistent placement of print
- repetition of 1-2 sentence patterns (1-2 word changes)
- oral language structures
- familiar objects and actions
- illustrations provide high support

Levels 5-8
- repetition of 2-3 sentence patterns (phrases may change)
- opening, closing sentences vary
- or, varied simple sentence patterns
- predominantly oral language structures
- many familiar objects and actions
- illustrations provide moderate-high support

Levels 9-12
- repetition of 3 or more sentence patterns
- or, varied sentence patterns (repeated phrases or refrains)
- blend of oral and written language structures
- or, fantastic happenings in framework of familiar experiences
- illustrations provide moderate support

Levels 13-15
- varied sentence patterns (may have repeated phrases or refrains)
- or, repeated patterns in cumulative form
- written language structures
- oral structures appear in dialogue
- conventional story; literary language
- specialized vocabulary for some topics
- illustrations provide low-moderate support

Levels 16-20
- elaborated episodes and events
- extended descriptions
- links to familiar stories
- literary language
- unusual, challenging vocabulary
- illustrations provide low support

© Barbara Peterson. *Characteristics of Texts That Support Beginning Readers.* The Ohio State University. 1988.

or three phrase patterns cycle through the text, and the introductory and closing sentences usually depart from the repeated patterns. Illustrations provide moderate to high support for the meaning.

Books from levels 9 to 12 and 13 to 15 function as bridges between lower-level, patterned texts and the books at the highest group of levels. By level 9, the student must have well-developed strategies for analyzing written text and be less dependent on illustrations and repeated sentence patterns. Repetition of entire sentences is seldom seen above level 9, except in the form of refrains. The details of one event may be extended over several pages, a feature that prepares students for reading well-developed ideas in paragraph form. Many sentences are grammatically complex, consisting of independent and dependent clauses. Stories may be more fanciful and less closely linked to personal experiences, and the vocabulary more varied and challenging. Illustrations provide low to moderate support for the printed message.

Books from levels 16 to 20 provide texts similar to those found in the first-grade reader of many reading programs. Stories usually have well-developed episodes and characters more distinctive personalities than in books at lower levels. While themes may reflect common experiences, the actual events are more imaginary than real. Illustrations enhance the story and contribute to the overall enjoyment of reading, but do not provide major support for the reading of the text.

This chapter closes with two points of caution. First, assigning a book to a level is no guarantee that the writing and illustrations are of high quality and worthy of a reader's attention. Good books must delight as well as instruct, inviting the reader to visit again and again. Second, beginning readers are interested in and capable of understanding books that are far more challenging than those they are able to read independently. Charlotte Huck and Gay Su Pinnell's chapter on literature addresses the broader context of creating a supportive classroom for beginning readers; and Kathy Short's chapter also addresses this point.

REFERENCES

Applebee, A. 1978. *The Child's Concept of Story: Ages Two to Seventeen.* Chicago: University of Chicago Press.

Beaver, J. M. 1982. "Say It! Over and Over." *Language Arts* 59 (2): 143–48.

Bruner, J. S. 1973. "Going Beyond the Information Given." In J. S. Bruner & J. M. Anglin, eds., *Beyond the Information Given*, 218–38. New York: Norton.

Burningham, J. 1970. *Mr Gumpy's Outing.* New York: Holt, Rinehart and Winston.

Bussis, A. M., E. A. Chittenden, M. Amarel & E. Klausner. 1985. *Inquiry into Meaning: An Investigation of Learning to Read.* Hillsdale, N.J.: Erlbaum.

Butler, D. 1980. *Cushla and Her Books.* Boston: Horn Book.

Chall, J. S. 1984. "Readability and Prose Comprehension." In J. Flood, ed., *Understanding Reading Comprehension*, 233–46. Newark, Del: International Reading Association.

Clay, M. M. 1979. *Reading: The Patterning of Complex Behaviour.* 2d ed. Portsmouth, N.H.: Heinemann.

———. 1982. *Observing Young Readers.* Portsmouth, N.H.: Heinemann.

———. 1985. *The Early Detection of Reading Difficulties.* 3d ed. Portsmouth, N.H.: Heinemann.

Cook-Gumperz, J., & J. L. Green. 1984. "A Sense of Story: Influences on Children's Storytelling Ability." In D. Tannen, ed., *Coherence in Spoken and Written Discourse*, 201–18. Norwood, N.J.: Ablex.

Cullinan, B., & S. Fitzgerald. 1984. *"Background Information Bulletin on the Use of Readability Formulae."* Notice distributed by the International Reading Association (Newark, Del.) and the National Council of Teachers of English (Urbana, Ill.).

Ginsburg, M. 1972. *The Chick and the Duckling.* Illus. by Jose & Ariane Aruego. New York: Macmillan.

Goodman, Y. 1986. "Children Coming to Know Literacy." In W. H. Teale & E. Sulzby, eds., *Emergent Literacy: Writing and Reading*, 1–14. Norwood, N.J.: Ablex.

Gourley, J. W. 1984. "Discourse Structure: Expectations of Beginning Readers and Readability of Text." *Journal of Reading Behavior* 16 (3): 169–88.

Halliday, M. A. K. 1975. *Learning How to Mean: Explorations in the Development of Language.* London: Edward Arnold.

Hickman, J. 1980. "Children's Response to Literature: What Happens in the Classroom." *Language Arts* 57 (5): 524–29.

Hill, E. 1980. *Where's Spot?* New York: Putnam.

Holdaway, D. 1979. *The Foundations of Literacy.* Sydney, Australia: Ashton Scholastic.

Hutchins, P. 1971. *Titch.* New York: Macmillan.

Kiefer, B. Z. 1988. "Picture Books as Contexts for Literary, Aesthetic, and Real World Understandings." *Language Arts* 65 (3): 260–71.

King, M. L. & M. G. McKenzie. 1988. "Literary Discourse from the Child's Perspective." *Language Arts* 65 (3): 304–14.

Klare, G. 1984. "Readability." In P.D. Pearson, ed., *Handbook of Reading Research*, 681–744. New York: Longman.

Kraus, Robert. 1970. *Whose Mouse Are You?* Illus. by Jose Aruego. New York: Macmillan.

Krauss, Ruth. 1945. *The Carrot Seed.* Illus. by Crockett Johnson. New York: Harper & Row.

Lindgren, B. 1983. *Sam's Lamp.* Illus. by Eva Eriksson. New York: Morrow.

Lobel, A. 1972. *Frog and Toad Are Friends.* New York: Harper & Row.

McMillan, D. 1978. *Baby.* Photos by Ian Hulse. Wellington, New Zealand: Price Milburn.

McKenzie, M. G. 1977. "The Beginnings of Literacy. *Theory into Practice* 26 (5): 315–24.

Meek, M. 1988. *How Texts Teach What Readers Learn.* Lockwood, England: Thimble Press.

Moffett, J. 1983. *Teaching the Universe of Discourse.* Boston: Houghton Mifflin.

Pappas, C. C. & E. Brown. 1987. "Young Children Learning Story Discourse: Three Case Studies." *Elementary School Journal* 87 (4): 455–66.

Peterson, B. L. 1988. "Characteristics of Texts That Support Beginning Readers." Ph.D. diss., Ohio State University, Columbus.

Rhodes, L. 1979. "Comprehension and Predictability: An Analysis of Beginning Reading Materials." *Monographs in Language and Reading Studies No. 3 (New Perspectives on Comprehension, J. C. Harste & R. F. Carey, eds.):* 100–131.

Smith, F. 1982. *Understanding Reading.* New York: Holt, Rhinehart and Winston.

Sulzby, E. 1985. "Children's Emergent Reading of Favorite Storybooks: A Developmental Study." *Reading Research Quarterly* 20 (4): 458–81.

Teale, W. H. 1986. "Home Background and Young Children's Literacy Development." In W. H. Teale & E. Sulzby, eds., *Emergent Literacy: Writing and Reading,* 173–206. Norwood, N.J.: Ablex.

Tolstoy, A. 1968. *The Great Big Enormous Turnip,* Illus. by Helen Oxenbury. New York: Watts.

Wells, G. 1986. *The Meaning Makers: Children Learning Language and Using Language to Learn.* Portsmouth, N.H.: Heinemann.

West, C. 1986. *"Pardon?" Said the Giraffe.* New York: Harper & Row.

White, D. 1984. *Books Before Five.* Portsmouth, N.H.: Heinemann.

White, E. B. 1952. *Charlotte's Web.* Illus. by Garth Williams. New York: Harper & Row.

Wildsmith, B. 1983. *All Fall Down.* New York: Oxford University Press.

CHILDREN'S LITERATURE FOR YOUNG READERS: A BIBLIOGRAPHY

This list includes just a sampling of the many hundreds of wonderfully exciting books for beginning readers that can be found in public and school library collections. Level designations are only *approximations,* since text difficulty can most effectively be evaluated with real readers in the context of authentic classroom and teaching situations. Books at higher levels can be introduced early in the school year for shared reading or as read-alouds.

Savor the language, explore the illustrations, and return again and again to favorite stories. Link books of similar themes, such as *Rosie's Walk* (Pat Hutchins 1968), *Across the Stream* (Mirra Ginsburg 1982), *Hattie and the Fox* (Mem Fox 1987), in which the hungry fox just can't seem to catch the tasty hen. Read aloud books too difficult for independent reading, such as Patricia McKissack's *Flossie & the Fox* (illus. by Rachel Isadora, New York: Dial Books, 1986), the story of a young girl who outwits a wily fox. Browse through library and bookstore collections to make other discoveries!

Books in levels 1–4 provide strong links to experiences of young children who are learning to read through the use of familiar concepts and vocabulary, commonly used oral-language patterns, repetition of those patterns, and illustrations that closely portray the meaning and language of the story.

LEVEL 1 •

Hoban, Tana. 1972. *Count and See*. New York: Greenwillow.
Hutchins, Pat. 1982. *1 Hunter*. New York: Greenwillow.
Maris, Ron. 1983. *My Book*. New York: Viking Penguin.
McMillan, Bruce. 1988. *Growing Colors*. New York: Lothrop, Lee & Shepard.

LEVEL 2 •

Carle, Eric. 1987. *Have You Seen My Cat?* Natick, Mass: Picture Book Studio.
Gomi, Taro. 1977. *Where's the Fish?* New York: Morrow.
Tafuri, Nancy. 1984. *Have You Seen My Duckling?* New York: Greenwillow.
Wildsmith, Brian. 1982. *Cat on the Mat*. New York: Oxford University Press.
Ziefert, Harriet, and Simms Taback. 1984a. *Where Is My Dinner?* New York: Grossett & Dunlap.
———. 1984b. *Where Is My Friend?* New York: Grossett & Dunlap.

LEVEL 3 •

Jonas, Ann. 1986. *Now We Can Go*. New York: Greenwillow.
Minarik, Else Holmelund. 1989. *It's Spring!* Illus. by Margaret Bloy Graham. New York: Greenwillow.
Sawicki, Norma Jean. 1989. *The Little Red House*. Illus. by Toni Goffe. New York: Lothrop, Lee & Shepard.
Tafuri, Nancy. 1986. *Who's Counting?* New York: Greenwillow.
Wildsmith, Brian. 1983. *All Fall Down*. New York: Oxford University Press.
———. 1984. *Toot, Toot*. New York: Oxford University Press.
Willaims, Sue. 1990. *I Went Walking*. Illus. by Julie Vivas. San Diego: Harcourt Brace Jovanovich.

LEVEL 4 •

Kalan, Robert. 1978. *Rain*. Illus. by Donald Crews. New York: Greenwillow.
Martin, Bill. 1984. *Brown Bear, Brown Bear, What Do You See?* Illus. by Eric Carle. New York: Holt, Rinehart and Winston.
Peek, Merle. 1981. *Roll Over*. New York: Clarion.
Tafuri, Nancy. 1988. *Spots, Feathers, and Curly Tails*. New York: Greenwillow.

Books in levels 5–8, like those in the first four levels, provide support for young children's experiences using familiar vocabulary and language patterns. Gradually, however, language patterns become less repetitive, and some literary language is introduced. Illustrations provide strong support for the meaning of stories through levels 6 and 7. Around level 8, as sentences become longer and less descriptive of concrete objects and actions, illustrations provide moderate support. Picture-book versions of familiar songs often fit within this group of levels.

LEVEL 5 •

Raffi. 1989. *Five Little Ducks*. Illus. by Jose Aruego and Ariane Dewey. New York: Crown.
Stobbs, William. 1984. *One, Two, Buckle My Shoe*. London: Bodley Head.
Tafuri, Nancy. 1989. *The Ball Bounced*. New York: Greenwillow.

LEVEL 6 •

Browne, Anthony. 1988. *I Like Books*. New York: Knopf.
——. 1989. *Things I Like*. New York: Knopf.
Burningham, John. 1974. *The School*. New York: Crowell.
Carter, David. 1988. *How Many Bugs in a Box*. New York: Simon & Schuster.
Ginsburg, Mirra. 1972. *The Chick and the Duckling*. Illus. by Jose Aruego. New York: Macmillan.
Hellard, Susan. 1989. *This Little Piggy*. New York: Putnam.
Jones, Carol. 1989. *Old MacDonald Had a Farm*. New York: Houghton Mifflin.
Lindgren, Barbro. 1982a. *Sam's Cookie*. Illus. by Eva Eriksson. New York: Morrow.
——. 1982b. *Sam's Teddy Bear*. Illus. by Eva Eriksson. New York: Morrow.
——. 1983a. *Sam's Ball*. Illus. by Eva Eriksson. New York: Morrow.
——. 1983b. *Sam's Lamp*. Illus. by Eva Eriksson. New York: Morrow.
——. 1986. *Sam's Wagon*. Illus. by Eva Eriksson. New York: Morrow.
Peek, Merle. 1985. *Mary Wore Her Red Dress*. New York: Clarion.
Rounds, Glen. 1989. *Old MacDonald Had a Farm*. New York: Holiday House.

LEVEL 7 •

Crews, Donald. 1986. *Flying*. New York: Greenwillow.
Parkinson, Kathy. 1988. *The Farmer in the Dell*. Niles, Ill.: Whitman.
Shaw, Charles. 1988. *It Looked Like Spilt Milk*. New York: Harper & Row.

LEVEL 8 •

Burningham, John. 1975. *The Blanket*. New York: Crowell.
Campbell, Rod. 1984. *Henry's Busy Day*. New York: Viking.
Christelow, Eileen. 1989. *Five Little Monkeys Jumping on the Bed*. New York: Clarion.
Hill, Eric. 1980. *Where's Spot?* New York: Putnam.
Jonas, Ann. 1986. *Where Can It Be?* New York: Greenwillow.
Kraus, Robert. 1974. *Herman the Helper*. Illus. by Jose Areugo and Ariane Dewey. New York: Windmill.
Langstaff, John. 1974. *Oh, A-Hunting We Will Go*. Illus. by Nancy Winslow Parker. New York: Atheneum.
Roffey, Maureen. 1982. *Home Sweet Home*. London: Bodley Head.

Many books in levels 9–12 have more expanded stories, with sequences of episodes in which each new event is a result of the previous action. Repetition often occurs in the form of refrains, and illustrations provide moderate support for the meaning of the written text.

LEVEL 9 •

Asch, Frank. 1981. *Just Like Daddy*. Englewood Cliffs, N.J.: Prentice-Hall.
Campbell, Rod. 1982. *Dear Zoo*. New York: Four Winds.
Galdone, Paul. 1988. *Cat Goes Fiddle-i-fee*. New York: Clarion.
Henkes, Kevin. 1989. *SHHHH*. New York: Greenwillow.
Hutchins, Pat. 1968. *Rosie's Walk*. New York: Macmillan.

Lloyd, David. 1985. *Grandma and the Pirate*. Illus. by Gill Tomblin. New York: Crown.

Maris, Ron. 1984. *Is Anyone Home?* New York: Greenwillow.

———. 1985. *Are You There Bear?* New York: Greenwillow.

Stobbs, William. 1987. *Gregory's Garden*. New York: Oxford University Press.

West, Colin. 1986a. *Have You Seen the Crocodile?* New York: Harper & Row.

———. 1986b. *"Pardon?" Said the Giraffe*. New York: Harper & Row.

LEVEL 10 •

Bang, Molly. 1983. *Ten, Nine, Eight*. New York: Greenwillow.

Brown, Ruth. 1981. *A Dark Dark Tale*. New York: Dial.

De Regniers, Beatrice Schenk. 1961. *Going For a Walk*. New York: Harper & Row.

Gerstein, Mordicai. 1984. *Roll Over!* New York: Crown.

———. 1985. *William, Where Are You?* New York: Crown.

Ginsburg, Mirra. 1982. *Across the Stream*. Illus. by Nancy Tafuri. New York: Greenwillow.

Goor, Ron, and Nancy Goor. 1983. *Signs*. New York: Crowell.

Rockwell, Anne. 1984. *Cars*. New York: Dutton.

Rockwell, Harlow. 1980. *My Kitchen*. New York: Greenwillow.

Stadler, John. 1984. *Hooray For Snail!* New York: Harper & Row.

Ward, Cindy. 1988. *Cookie's Week*. Illus. by Tomie de Paola. New York: Putnam.

Watanabe, Shigeo. 1982. *I'm King of the Castle!* Illus. by Yasuo Ohtomo. New York: Philomel.

Wheeler, Cindy. 1982. *Marmalade's Nap*. New York: Knopf.

———. 1983. *Marmalade's Snowy Day*. New York: Knopf.

———. 1985. *Rose*. New York: Knopf.

Ziefert, Harriet. 1988. *Thank You, Nicky!* Illus. by Richard Brown. New York: Viking Penguin.

LEVEL 11 •

Ahlberg, Janet, and Allan Ahlberg. 1978. *Each Peach Pear Plum*. New York: Viking.

Barton, Byron. 1989. *Dinosaurs, Dinosaurs*. New York: Crowell.

Gelman, Rita. 1977. *More Spaghetti, I Say!* Illus. by Jack Kent. New York: Scholastic.

Hellen, Nancy. 1988. *The Bus Stop*. New York: Orchard Books.

Hennessy, B. G. 1989. *The Missing Tarts*. Illus. by Tracey Campbell Pearson. New York: Viking Kestrel.

Kraus, Robert. 1970. *Whose Mouse Are You?* Illus. by Jose Aruego. New York: Macmillan.

Mack, Stan. 1974. *Ten Bears in My Bed*. New York: Pantheon.

Rockwell, Anne. 1982. *Boats*. New York: Dutton.

Stadler, John. 1985. *Snail Saves the Day*. New York: Harper & Row.

Testa, Fulvio. 1982. *If You Take a Paintbrush*. New York: Dial.

LEVEL 12 •

Bonsall, Crosby. 1972. *The Day I Had to Play With My Sister*. New York: Harper & Row.

Burningham, John. 1974. *The Snow*. New York: Crowell.

————. 1975a. *The Baby*. New York: Crowell.

————. 1975b. *The Cupboard*. New York: Crowell.

————. 1975c. *The Dog*. New York: Crowell.

————. 1975d. *The Friend*. New York: Crowell.

Crews, Donald. 1986. *Ten Black Dots*. New York: Greenwillow.

Ginsburg, Mirra. 1973. *Three Kittens*. Illus. by Giulio Maestro. New York: Crown.

Hutchins, Pat. 1971. *Titch*. New York: Macmillan.

Keller, Holly. 1983. *Ten Sleepy Sheep*. New York: Greenwillow.

Kline, Suzy. 1984. *Shhhh!* Illus. by Dora Leder. Niles, Ill.: Whitman.

Krauss, Ruth. 1945. *The Carrot Seed*. Illus. by Crockett Johnson. New York: Harper & Row.

Long, Earlene. 1984. *Gone Fishing*. Illus. by Richard Brown. New York: Houghton Mifflin.

Shulevitz, Uri. 1967. *One Monday Morning*. New York: Scribner.

Stadler, John. 1987. *Three Cheers for Hippo*. New York: Crowell.

Taylor, Judy. 1987. *My Dog*. New York: Macmillan.

Van Laan, Nancy. 1987. *The Big Fat Worm*. Illus. by Marisabina Russo. New York: Knopf.

Watson, Wendy. 1976. *Lollipop*. New York: Crowell.

Wescott, Nadine Bernard. 1987. *Peanut Butter and Jelly*. New York: Dutton.

West, Colin. 1987. *"Not Me," Said the Monkey*. New York: Harper & Row.

The language in books from levels 13–15 becomes more descriptive through the use of less familiar and more varied vocabulary, and events are more fully elaborated in longer, more complex sentences.

LEVEL 13 •

Barton, Byron. 1973. *Buzz Buzz Buzz*. New York: Macmillan.

Campbell, Rod. 1985. *Misty's Mischief*. New York: Viking.

Goenell, Heidi. 1989. *If I Were a Penguin*. Boston: Little, Brown.

Jonas, Ann. 1982a. *Two Bear Cubs*. New York: Greenwillow.

————. 1982b. *When You Were a Baby*. New York: Greenwillow.

Rockwell, Anne. 1973. *The Awful Mess*. New York: Four Winds.

Rockwell, Anne, and Harlow Rockwell. 1971. *The Tool Box*. New York. Macmillan.

Stinson, Kathy. 1982. *Red is Best*. Illus. by Robin Baird Lewis. Toronto: Annick Press.

Tolstoy, Alexei. 1968. *The Great Big Enormous Turnip*. Illus. by Helen Oxenbury. New York: Watts.

LEVEL 14 •

Barchas, Sarah. 1975. *I Was Walking Down the Road*. New York: Scholastic.

Barton, Byron. 1981. *Building a House*. New York: Greenwillow.

Brown, Margaret Wise. 1974. *Goodnight Moon*. New York: Harper & Row.

Butler, Dorothy. 1989. *My Brown Bear Barney*. Illus. by Elizabeth Fuller. New York: Greenwillow.

Hutchins, Pat. 1983. *You'll Soon Grow Into Them, Titch*. New York: Greenwillow.

Kraus, Robert. 1986. *Where Are You Going, Little Mouse?* Illus. by Jose Aruego and Ariane Dewey. New York: Greenwillow.

————. 1987. *Come Out and Play, Little Mouse.* Illus. by Jose Aruego and Ariane Dewey. New York: Greenwillow.

Robart, Rose. 1986. *The Cake That Mack Ate.* Illus. by Maryann Kovalski. Boston: Little, Brown.

Spier, Peter. 1978. *Bored—Nothing to Do!* New York: Doubleday.

Taylor, Judy. 1987. *My Cat.* New York: Macmillan.

LEVEL 15 •

Ehlert, Lois. 1987. *Planting a Rainbow.* San Diego: Harcourt Brace Jovanovich.

Fox, Mem. 1987. *Hattie and the Fox.* Illus. by Patricia Mullins. New York: Bradbury.

Guilfoile, Elizabeth. 1957. *Nobody Listens to Andrew.* Illus. by Mary Stevens. Cleveland: Modern Curriculum Press.

Hayes, Sarah, and Helen Craig. 1986. *This is the Bear.* New York: Harper & Row.

Kline, Suzy. 1985. *Don't Touch!* Illus. by Dora Leder. Niles, Ill.: Whitman.

McPhail, David. 1984. *Fix-it.* New York: Dutton.

Nodset, Joan. 1936. *Who Took the Farmer's Hat?* Illus. by Fritz Siebel. New York: Harper & Row.

Rosen, Michael. 1989. *We're Going on a Bear Hunt.* Illus. by Helen Oxenbury. New York: Macmillan.

Serfozo, Mary. 1989. *Who Wants One?* Illus. by Keiko Narahashi. New York: Macmillan.

Seuss, Dr. 1960. *Green Eggs and Ham.* New York: Random House.

————. 1963. *Hop on Pop.* New York: Random House.

Wood, Audrey. 1984. *The Napping House.* Illus. by Don Wood. San Diego: Harcourt Brace Jovanovich.

Many books in levels 16–20 feature sequences of episodes that extend over several pages or are organized into paragraphs. The language is literary and illustrations enhance the story but seldom provide clues to specific words in the text. While themes may be closely related to personal experiences, the characters are fictional personalities and episodes develop around fanciful, imaginative events. Falling into this range of levels are many poetry collections, picture-book versions of familiar folk tales such as *The Three Little Pigs,* and special publishers' series designed for young readers, such as "An I Can Read Book: (Harper & Row) or "Ready-to-Read" (Macmillan).

LEVEL 16 •

Alexander, Martha. 1969. *Blackboard Bear.* New York: Dial.

————. 1980. *We're in Big Trouble, Blackboard Bear.* New York: Dial.

Barton, Byron. 1975. *Hester.* New York: Greenwillow.

Bennett, Jill. 1986. *Teeny Tiny.* Illus. by Tomie de Paola. New York: Putnam.

Bonsall, Crosby. 1974. *And I Mean It, Stanley.* New York: Harper & Row.

Carle, Eric. 1984. *The Very Busy Spider.* New York: Philomel.

Charlip, Remy. 1964. *Fortunately.* New York: Macmillan.

Hutchins, Pat. 1973. *Goodnight Owl*. Viking Penguin.
———. 1978. *Happy Birthday Sam*. Viking Penguin.
Jonas, Ann. 1984. *The Quilt*. New York: Greenwillow.
Kalan, Robert. 1981. *Jump, Frog, Jump!* Illus. by Byron Barton. New York: Greenwillow.
Kent, Jack. 1971. *The Fat Cat*. New York: Scholastic.
Kovalski, Maryann. 1987. *The Wheels on the Bus*. Boston: Little, Brown.
Kuskin, Karla. 1959. *Just Like Everyone Else*. New York: Harper & Row.
Kraus, Robert. 1971. *Leo the Late Bloomer*. Illus. by Jose Aruego. New York: Windmill.
Mayer, Mercer. 1968. *There's a Nightmare in My Closet*. New York: Dial.
McLeod, Emilie. 1975. *The Bear's Bicycle*. Illus. by David McPhail. Boston: Little, Brown.
Minarik, Else Holmelund. 1968. *A Kiss for Little Bear*. Illus. by Maurice Sendak. New York: Harper & Row.
Ormerod, Jan. 1985. *The Story of Chicken Licken*. New York: Lothrop, Lee & Shepard.
Rice, Eve. 1981. *Benny Bakes a Cake*. New York: Greenwillow.
Riddell, Chris. 1986. *Ben and the Bear*. New York: Harper & Row.
Seuling, Barbara. 1976. *The Teeny Tiny Woman*. New York: Viking.
Testa, Fulvio. 1982. *If You Take a Pencil*. New York: Dial.
Wells, Rosemary. 1973. *Noisy Nora*. New York: Dial.

LEVEL 17 •

Ahlberg, Janet, and Allan Ahlberg. 1980. *Funnybones*. New York: Morrow.
Adoff, Arnold. 1988. *Greens*. Illus. by Betsy Lewin. New York: Lothrop, Lee & Shepard. (Poems).
Bridwell, Norman. 1985. *Clifford the Big Red Dog*. New York: Scholastic.
Clifton, Lucille. 1970. *Some of the Days of Everett Anderson*. Illus. by Evaline Ness. New York: Holt. (Poems).
Flack, Marjorie. 1960. *Ask Mr. Bear*. New York: Macmillan.
Galdone, Paul. 1968. *Henny Penny*. New York: Clarion.
———. 1972. *The Three Bears*. New York: Clarion.
———. 1973. *The Little Red Hen*. New York: Clarion.
Hurd, Edith Thacher. 1985. *Johnny Lion's Book*. Illus. by Clement Hurd. New York: Harper & Row.
Hutchins, Pat. 1986. *The Doorbell Rang*. New York: Greenwillow.
Isadora, Rachel. 1976. *Max*. New York: Macmillan.
Johnson, Crockett. 1955. *Harold and the Purple Crayon*. New York: Harper & Row.
Lobel, Arnold. 1972. *Mouse Soup*. New York: Harper & Row.
Mayer, Mercer. 1987. *There's an Alligator Under My Bed*. New York: Dial.
———. 1988. *There's Something in My Attic*. New York: Dial.
Nicoll, Helen. 1976. *Meg and Mog*. Illus. by Jan Pienkowski. New York: Viking Penguin. (There are several books about Meg and Mog.)
Peppe, Rodney. 1970. *The House That Jack Built*. New York: Delacorte.
Roy, Ron. 1979. *Three Ducks Went Walking*. Illus. by Paul Galdone. New York: Scholastic.
Shulevitz, Uri. 1969. *Rain Rain Rivers*. New York: Farrar, Straus & Giroux.

Udry, Janice May. 1970. *Let's Be Enemies*. Illus. by Maurice Sendak. New York: Harper & Row.

Vipont, Elfrida. 1969. *The Elephant and the Bad Baby*. Illus. by Raymond Briggs. New York: Coward.

LEVEL 18 •

Asch, Frank. 1980. *The Last Puppy*. Englewood Cliffs, N.J.: Prentice-Hall.

Carle, Eric. 1970. *The Very Hungry Caterpillar*. New York: Philomel.

Cummings, Pat. 1985. *Jimmy Lee Did It*. New York: Lothrop, Lee & Shepard.

Dabcovich, Lydia. 1985. *Mrs. Huggins and Her Hen Hannah*. New York: Dutton.

De Paola, Tomie. 1973. *"Charlie Needs a Cloak"*. Englewood Cliffs, N.J.: Prentice-Hall.

Emberley, Barbara. 1967. *Drummer Hoff*. Illus. by Ed Emberley. Englewood Cliffs, N.J.: Prentice-Hall.

Jonas, Ann. 1985. *The Trek*. New York: Greenwillow.

Joyce, William. 1985. *George Shrinks*. New York: Harper & Row.

Keats, Ezra Jack. 1962. *The Snowy Day*. New York: Viking.

Knight, Joan. 1989. *Tickle-Toe Rhymes*. Illus. by John Wallner. New York: Orchard Books/Watts.

Krasilovsky, Phyllis. 1950. *The Man Who Didn't Do His Dishes*. Illus. by Barbara Cooney. New York: Doubleday.

Lionni, Leo. 1959. *Little Blue and Little Yellow*. New York: Astor Honor.

Marshall, Edward. 1981. *Three By the Sea*. Illus. by James Marshall. New York: Dial.

Martin, Bill, and John Archambault. 1989. *Chicka Chicka Boom Boom*. Illus. by Lois Ehlert. New York: Simon & Schuster.

Sendak, Maurice. 1963. *Where the Wild Things Are*. New York: Harper & Row.

Suess, Dr. 1967. *The Cat in the Hat*. New York: Random House.

LEVEL 19 •

Brown, Ruth. 1985. *The Big Sneeze*. New York: Lothrop, Lee & Shepard.

Browne, Anthony. 1989. *Bear Goes to Town*. New York: Doubleday.

Burningham, John. 1970. *Mr Gumpy's Outing*. New York: Holt, Rinehart & Winston.

———. 1976. *Mr Gumpy's Motor Car*. New York: Crowell.

Carle, Eric. 1977. *The Grouchy Ladybug*. New York: Crowell.

Galdone, Paul. 1975. *The Gingerbread Boy*. New York: Clarion.

Hennessy, B. G. 1990. *Jake Baked the Cake*. Illus. by Mary Morgan. New York: Viking.

Hutchins, Pat. 1969. *The Surprise Party*. New York: Macmillan.

Lobel, Arnold. 1970. *Frog and Toad Are Friends*. New York: Harper & Row.

———. 1971. *Frog and Toad Together*. New York: Harper & Row.

McGovern, Ann. 1968. *Stone Soup*. Illus. by Nola Langer. New York: Scholastic.

Murphy, Jill. 1984. *What Next Baby Bear?* New York: Dial.

Oppenheim, Joanne. 1986. *You Can't Catch Me*. Illus. by Andrew Shachat. New York: Houghton Mifflin.

Rice, Eve. 1977. *Sam Who Never Forgets*. New York: Greenwillow.

Rylant, Cynthia. 1989. *Henry and Mudge and the Forever Sea*. Illus. by Sucie Stevenson. New York: Bradbury. (There are several other books about Henry and Mudge.)

Stevens, Janet. 1987. *The Three Billy Goats Gruff*. San Diego: Harcourt Brace Jovanovich.

LEVEL 20 •

Allen, Pam. 1982. *Who Sank the Boat?* New York: Coward-McCann.

Bang, Molly Garrett. 1976. *Wiley and the Hairy Man*. New York: Macmillan.

Bennett, Jill, collector. 1987. *Noisy Poems*. Illus. by Nick Sharratt. New York: Oxford University Press.

Carle, Eric. 1989. *Eric Carle's ANIMALS ANIMALS*. 1989. New York: Philomel. (Poems).

Crowe, Robert L. 1980. *Tyler Toad the Thunder*. Illus. by Kay Chorao. New York: Dutton.

De Paola, Tomie. 1989. *The Art Lesson*. New York: Putnam.

Fisher, Aileen. 1986. *When It Comes to Bugs*. Illus. by Chris & Bruce Degen. New York: Harper & Row. (Poems).

———. 1988. *The House of a Mouse*. Illus. by Joan Sandin. New York: Harper & Row.

Galdone, Paul. 1976. *The Magic Porridge Pot*. New York: Clarion.

Heine, Helme. 1983. *The Most Wonderful Egg in the World*. New York: Atheneum.

Hoberman, Mary Ann. 1978. *A House is a House for Me*. Illus. by Betty Fraser. New York: Viking.

———. 1981. *Yellow Butter Purple Jelly Red Jam Black Bread*. Illus. by Chaya Burstein. New York: Viking. (Poems).

Hogrogian, Nonny. 1971. *One Fine Day*. New York: Macmillan.

Hopkins, Lee Bennett, selector. 1984. *Surprises*. Illus. by Megan Lloyd. New York: Harper & Row.

———. 1990. *Good Books, Good Times!* New York: Harper & Row.

Hutchins, Pat. 1974. *The Wind Blew*. New York: Viking.

———. 1985. *The Very Worst Monster*. New York: Greenwillow.

———. 1988. *Where's the Baby?* New York: Greenwillow.

Jonas, Ann. 1983. *Round Trip*. New York: Greenwillow.

Kasza, Keiko. 1987. *The Wolf's Chicken Stew*. New York: Putnam.

Kuskin, Karla. 1980. *Dogs & Dragons, Trees & Dreams*. New York: Harper & Row. (Poems).

Livingston, Myra Cohn. 1984. *A Song I Sang to You*. Illus. by Margot Tomes. San Diego: Harcourt Brace Jovanovich.

Merriam, Eve. 1985. *Blackberry Ink*. Illus. by Hans Wilhelm. New York: Morrow. (Poems).

———. 1989. *A Poem for a Pickle—Funnybone Verses*. Illus. by Sheila Hamanaka. New York: Morrow.

Preston, Edna Mitchell. 1974. *Squawk to the Moon, Little Goose*. Illus. by Barbara Cooney. New York: Viking.

Reinl, Edda. 1983. *The Three Little Pigs*. Natick, Mass.: Picture Book Studio.

Rice, Eve. 1989. *Peter's Pockets*. Illus. by Nancy Winslow Parker. New York: Greenwillow.

Sendak, Maurice. *Chicken Soup With Rice*. New York: Harper & Row.

Slobodkina, Esphyr. 1968. *Caps for Sale*. New York: Harper & Row.

Stevenson, James. 1977. *"Could Be Worse!"* New York: Greenwillow.

Tresselt, Alvin. 1964. *The Mitten*. Illus. by Yaroslava. New York: Lothrop, Lee & Shepard.

Zemach, Margot. 1987. *The Little Red Hen*. New York: Farrar, Straus & Giroux.

Zolotow, Charlotte. 1984. *I Know a Lady*. Illus. by James Stevenson. New York: Greenwillow.

SEVEN

·················

Bringing Home and School Literacy Together Through the Reading Recovery Program

KATHLEEN E. HOLLAND

·····························   ·····························

*H*ome literacy experiences, prior to school entry, are critically important in later school success (see Durkin 1966; Clark 1976; Heath 1983; Wells 1986). Teachers often mention children's home environments as immutable forces, limiting what the school can do to foster student achievement. It is also common for parents to express frustration, bewilderment, and powerlessness in the face of the power of schools and teachers. The ambassadors from one world to another are children. Their experiences at home undoubtedly influence what they do at school. Is the opposite true? Can school experiences and school-home communications influence the home environment? How can teachers play a positive role in making that happen? Those questions are especially critical for children who are having difficulty succeeding in the school literacy environment.

Few teachers or researchers have taken a close look at how school literacy programs impact family literacy contexts. The Reading Recovery program provided a chance to examine the home literacy experience of a group of children who were having trouble in classroom literacy programs. These first-grade children were being given special help in reading and writing outside the classroom for thirty minutes daily with a specially trained Reading Recovery teacher. I began to wonder what kinds of family literacy occurred in the everyday lives of Reading Recovery children and if it could be funneled into the Reading Recovery Program. I wondered what was happening within the family literacy contexts as a result of the children's participation in Reading Recovery and their bringing home natural language books to read. How did Reading Recovery affect parents and home literacy contexts? I therefore decided to study the families and homes of thirteen first graders involved in Reading Recovery (Holland 1987). Results of the study suggested some ways of connecting home and school literacy contexts and activities.

The purpose of my research was first to explore and describe characteristics of and changes in the family literacy contexts of children who participated in an intensive early intervention program (i.e., Reading Recovery) to improve their reading. Second, I examined the impact of the Reading Recovery program on children's family literacy environments. Third, I investigated, described, and compared home-school communication patterns between Reading Recovery teachers and parents of the children they served, with attention to parents' and teachers' views of each other as literacy supports for children.

For one school year, I studied the family literacy experiences of thirteen children from three different Columbus city public elementary schools who participated in the Ohio Reading Recovery program. I visited a total of thirty-five families at their homes. Parents of these children were invited to participate in a parent research project that would seek to obtain their opinions about Reading Recovery and its effects on their children's literacy development, family literacy activities, and parent-teacher communication experiences. I set two ground rules for entry into this parent research project: (1) parents would take at least one day to talk with other family members before making up their minds, and (2) a refusal to participate would be accepted respectfully without argument.

At my first meeting with all families, parents had received a formal school letter notifying them that their children had been placed in the Reading Recovery program. None of the parents knew what the Reading Recovery program was and it was not explained in the letter. They did not know their children had been selected through individual assessment by Reading Recovery teachers, an assessment that covered reading and writing abilities. They did not know that their children were going to begin intensive daily one-to-one tutoring outside the classroom from a specially trained Reading Recovery teacher for at least half of the school year. They did not know that their children would be reading natural language children's books and writing messages each day with their Reading Recovery teacher in addition to the regular classroom reading program. They did not even know who the Reading Recovery teacher would be for their children. They did not know their children would be tutored by a Reading Recovery teacher until they reached the average level of literacy in their children's first-grade classroom.

Seventeen parents agreed to be interviewed four times in their homes during the school year: once before their children began Reading Recovery tutoring, twice during the time their children were in Reading Recovery tutoring, and once after their children completed Reading Recovery tutoring. All interviews were audiotaped and transcribed. Open-ended and prompt questions were used across all four interviews. Parents were assured confidentiality, were free to leave the parent research project at anytime without penalty to their Reading Recovery children, and were told that they would be given written summaries of all interviews to check before the final report. Four families left the project during the year because of moving, family emergencies, and illness. Thirteen of the seventeen families were able to complete all four interviews. The children in this study progressed at different rates through the Reading Recovery program: three finished the program in early January; six finished in the spring; and four did not complete the program by the end of the school year.

Of the thirteen remaining families, six were black and seven were white Appalachian. One black family was Appalachian. Family income levels ranged from five families below $10,000 to five families between $10,000 and $20,000 to three families between $25,000 and $40,000. For four families in the highest income groups, both parents worked outside the home. Single parents were heads of household in six families, while seven were two-parent families. Several generations lived together in one household for four families, while one household was composed of two families.

Interviews were always by appointment, which parents could cancel at any time without giving reasons. Interviews, usually at the kitchen table or the family sofa, most often included mothers, but grandmothers and some fathers participated. Younger preschool siblings were often present. At the second interview school report cards had just arrived and parents shared these with me as well as their impressions of the grading. By the third interview parents felt comfortable enough to show me where children's home literacy materials were kept. I met all family members in each family through the course of the four interviews.

All seven Reading Recovery teachers of the thirteen children agreed to participate in the project. This circumstance allowed closer investigation of home-school communication patterns concerning the Reading Recovery children and their literacy development at home and in Reading Recovery tutoring. Six Reading Recovery teachers also served as classroom teachers for some of their Reading Recovery children during half of the school day. However, emphasis in these teacher interviews was placed on their role as Reading Recovery teachers and communication about that program to parents. Teachers did not know which families were part of the parent research project. These seven Reading Recovery teachers were interviewed at the beginning and end of the school year. Interviews with teachers usually occurred in the Reading Recovery tutoring room during the lunch period.

Several kinds of information were collected during the study from parents and Reading Recovery teachers:

1. Formal audiotaped interviews.
2. Informal interviews.
3. Written and audiotaped field notes.
4. Questionnaires about household members, parent literacy histories, parent-teacher communication, and future Reading Recovery parent participation.
5. Collection of writing samples.
6. Home Literacy Context Checklist.
7. Observation of family story reading.

In this study, the following strategies were used to ensure trustworthiness: prolonged site engagement, audit trail, triangulation, member checks, and peer debriefing.

FAMILY LITERACY CONTEXTS

All parents considered reading and writing to be the most important abilities for success in education, employment, and future life. Reporting personal experiences with illiterate adults either in their own families or among friends, parents said that they realized the consequences of illiteracy and enumerated these to be no high school degree, inability to obtain job security, dependence on others for literacy assistance, vulnerability in work or business interactions, and inability to provide for one's family. Parents could not imagine their children having a successful future without acquiring the abilities to read and write.

Every child was supported by family members in reading and writing activities. From the data, family literacy support was organized into the following eight roles: (1) models, (2) providers, (3) readers, (4) spellers, (5) listeners, (6) scribes, (7) receivers, and (8) interpreters. Each of the roles will be described with examples.

1. *Models.* Materials such as the Sunday newspaper, magazines (for example, *True Romance, Detective, Ebony*), and the Bible were common to most families. Children often saw adult family members reading them. Although three parents read books regularly and two occasionally, most parents reported that they did not like to read books. In writing, adult family members paid bills, filled in business forms, and wrote greeting cards and letters. Two mothers were themselves involved in educational programs and children saw them studying and writing homework assignments. Siblings often modeled reading and writing more than adult family members, since they were completing school homework assignments. Older female siblings modeled book reading more than did adults in the families. Siblings read their own books at home and sometimes shared them with younger siblings. Most families had nightly homework sessions. While older siblings were completing their written homework, the younger children would pretend they had homework and copy, draw, or write.

2. *Providers.* Most families purchased reading materials (e.g., books and tapes, books and records) as gifts during the school year, especially for Christmas, adding several new books to their family book collections each year. In five families children were regularly taken to the public library. The school was not a regular source of library books. Writing materials, such as little tables, chalkboard erasers, paper and pencils, were available in five families. For most of the families, there was not a continuous supply of writing materials available for children to use.

3. *Readers.* Female family members (mothers, older sisters, and grandmothers) took most of the responsibility for reading books to children, but all family members acted as readers to help children interpret print in the environment. Children asked readers to read traffic signs, food products, coupons, TV commercials, junk mail, billboards, and advertisements.

5. *Spellers.* All family members who could spell were drawn into helping children spell words. When children wrote, they turned to older siblings and parents for spelling information, and those persons willingly spelled words out. At the same time children sought and used sources to interpret print in the environment. Children would spell the word out and older siblings or adults would tell them what they had spelled.

6. *Scribes.* Early in the year, when children were drawing pictures, adults and older siblings were called on to write words or sentences on them. Older siblings served as scribes more often than did parents. Some parents or grandparents composed special messages for children, such as letters to Santa Claus or to extended family members.

7. *Receivers.* The younger siblings in these families played a "receiving" role for children's reading activities. These youngsters provided the Reading Recovery children opportunity for assuming the roles of model and reader. Children read their Reading Recovery books to younger siblings, thus sharing their newly acquired reading abilities. Often, when Reading Recovery children finished a book, younger siblings took it and read it back by the illustrations, "reenacting" the reading. These younger siblings "received" Reading Recovery children's reading and modeling behaviors and then used them.

8. *Interpreters.* Children gave parents messages that parents could not read. These messages with invented spellings were given back to children to read for parents. On other occasions, children handed parents a piece of writing they had tried and asked parents, "What does it say?" When parents did not know, the message was lost.

These complex family literacy support systems involved many players and roles. Schools and teachers tend to expect mothers to engage children in literacy activities, but this research indicates that many different family members provided support. One element often overlooked by schools and teachers proved to be important in this research—the literacy support provided by both younger and older siblings!

LITERACY MATERIALS IN THE HOME

Common items for children to use for reading and writing were available either in the surrounding environment or in family-owned or school-supplied literacy materials. All families read the environmental print which appeared as part of their everyday lives. With the help of family members, Reading Recovery children noticed and read junk mail, catalogues, coupons, and Sunday newspaper comics.

Family-owned reading materials generally consisted of four kinds of books: (1) Golden Books, (2) Walt Disney books, (3) Sesame Street books, and (4) popular television cartoon character books (e.g., Rainbow Bright, He-Man and She-Ra, Cabbage Patch Kids). Children's book collections remained generally the same throughout the school year. Most families owned between six and eight children's books. At the beginning of the study, parents were aware that their Reading Recovery children could not read any of the children's books in the home independently. Parents relied on outside sources for reading materials that children could read independently.

The public school served as a major source of children's reading materials for every family in the study. The literacy materials sent home by Reading Recovery teachers were the books children read independently at home. Assuming that their children could read whatever school reading materials were sent home, parents tended to depend on both Reading Recovery and classroom teachers to select appropriate reading materials for their children. The Reading Recovery natural language books sent home were by far the most popular independent reading materials in family literacy contexts. Basal reading materials sent home by classroom teachers were not read as often by the children. Children were often unable to read basals independently and needed the aid of parents or older siblings. In fact, usually they were associated with negative parent-child literacy interactions, because parents pushed children to read the whole basal book rather than individual stories.

School papers sent home by classroom teachers as part of classroom basal reading programs were children's primary reading activity at the beginning of the school year. These work papers included exercises related to color words, sight words and pictures, phonics activities, and activities related to the basal reading program. Every evening, it seemed that a "school paper ceremony" took place in each home. Children showed the work papers to parents who responded by identifying and correcting mistakes. Typical parents' comments were "Look what you did wrong! Let's fix it up!" Children erased errors and parents helped them correct the papers. As soon as the papers were corrected, the parents stored them away, gave them to their children to play with, or threw them away when children were not looking. School work papers were looked at only once.

School library books were brought home on a weekly basis by five of the children all located at the same school. Eight other children were not allowed by their two schools to bring home library books. For the five children who did bring school library books home, these books were initially used as read-aloud books by parents and older siblings. By March, these five children could read the school library books themselves and they began to use them as independent reading materials in the home. All parents remembered bringing home books from school libraries and wanted the same privileges for their children.

Writing materials available for children's use did not change over the year and seemed related to family income. All families had writing tools such as pencils and pens, and one-third had at least one coloring book and crayons. Two-thirds did not have paper in the home for children's use. Half of the families had one or more additional writing materials, such as plastic magnetic letters, store-bought workbooks, chalkboards, water paint, typewriters, and computers without printers. The higher the family's income, the greater the variety of writing materials.

For most families, the major source of writing materials was the school. When classroom teachers sent home school work papers, they were, perhaps unknowingly, supplying children with a major writing tool. School work papers had a long life in the hands of children. After parents had completed their correction practice, children took the papers, turned them over, and drew or wrote on the blank back side. Some children and their siblings acquired extra leftover school work papers and brought them home to write on and play with. School work papers were used to play school. According to parents, children wrote spelling tests, math problems, sentences, and drew on the back when playing school.

Reading Recovery teachers sent home cut-up sentences, which promoted more writing, usually in the form of copying. Parents encouraged their children to copy whole written texts. Parents were pleased because they believed copying would help children become better writers.

Classroom teachers sent home handwriting work papers. Parents took seriously classroom teachers' comments on these papers, usually material copied off the classroom blackboard. A happy face, star, or "Good Work!" were received as positive proof that children were developing stronger writing abilities. Sad faces, "Messy!" or "You can do better!" were interpreted to mean that children needed more practice at home, and parents often made children rewrite the entire exercise.

IMPACT OF READING RECOVERY ON
FAMILY LITERACY CONTEXTS

By December, children were bringing home Reading Recovery books and cut-up sentences. Each day children brought a new natural-language book for independent reading and their own written sentence cut up into word pieces for reassembly. These two new reading tools affected children, parents, and other family members.

Children were responsible for the care of each Reading Recovery book brought home. They were well aware they had to return the book to obtain another new book to take home the next day. These thin, paperback books had to be kept in a safe place away from younger siblings, pets, and accidents. During the year, more than seven hundred Reading Recovery books were taken home by these thirteen first-grade children, but only one child lost a book.

Children initiated reading sessions at home with these books on a daily basis, usually with more than one family member. Family members complied by listening to children's reading; the Reading Recovery book became a literacy tool that drew the whole family together to support the young reader's need to share reading. Even when parents or other family members were busy or preoccupied, children demanded reading time. They learned not to tolerate distractions from reading. Other family activities had to stop and the listeners were expected to concentrate on the books and to draw physically closer to the children. Children insisted, at times to the point of tears, that listeners comply with their desire to read. Even when no one was available, children read the books to themselves or to dolls, stuffed animals, and family pets.

Reading Recovery books provided children with the opportunity to behave as successful readers by reading their own books. Younger siblings were ready audiences, and children eagerly shared their power with younger brothers and sisters by attempting to pass on the newly acquired literacy skills.

The availability of Reading Recovery books seemed to confirm that children had entered the world of readers. They acted as readers by reading independently without help from older family members and other family members confirmed their role by acting as audiences. Because children could find and correct their own errors, parents did not have to correct. Younger siblings also supported confirmation by providing a contrast between readers and nonreaders.

These little, natural-language books that children could read provided access to lifetime reading behaviors and habits such as independent reading, recreational reading, reading aloud, and teaching others. These were available to children because they had the right kind of books. The Reading Recovery books were viewed as a positive family literacy activity in all families. As soon as children began bringing these books home on a daily basis, they became the central family literacy daily event, superseding school reading papers and basal reading texts in popularity as well as repeated readings among many family members.

The presence of these natural-language books had a negative side, however, that was revealed after children were released from the Reading Recovery program. Almost immediately, home reading activities decreased. While children retained their reading abilities, the loss of the daily book, specially selected by the Reading Recovery teacher, appeared to result in a shift within the family reading support system. Suddenly, no books were coming home; established family reading habits had centered on the books as a consistent resource. Once the center was removed, nothing replaced it; and those customs changed. Most of the children in this study did not have an outside source of books, and they were not able to read the more difficult trade books available in the home. As a result, a novel situation was created: readers without books!

In the Reading Recovery program children wrote a message or story everyday as part of their half-hour tutoring session. No writing materials were sent home. The cut-up sentence went home as a reading activity in which children reassembled their sentences and read them aloud to their parents. Any writing associated with the cut-up sentences usually took the form of copying, which all parents held in high esteem as helping their children become better writers. Parents tended to demand that children practice handwriting daily. They seemed unaware of the importance of story writing.

Through Reading Recovery, children increased in writing ability and more writing appeared in the homes. At the time of the first interview, before Reading Recovery tutoring began, children were drawing pictures, writing their names, and practicing alphabet letters at home and school. They were not writing messages in either place. By January, after Reading Recovery tutoring was underway, children's writing at home had dramatically increased. They wrote words and sentences on their drawings as well as messages to family members and friends at school. They no longer wanted to copy writing.

The Reading Recovery Program helped parents to support their children's reading by providing adequate reading tools to use at home. Since the family owned books and library books were too hard for children to read independently, the specially chosen Reading Recovery books were easy for children to handle. The program also helped children meet parents' expectations for error-free reading. The books children took home were very easy for them, so children could read them alone, virtually without errors. To the delight of parents, children could correct their own errors and they read with fluency, expression, and attention to punctuation. The Reading Recovery teachers carefully analyzed children's reading and provided harder and more complex reading levels as appropriate. Parents no longer had to worry about finding books that their children could read. A new one was always available and family members could become involved with books.

A problem related to Reading Recovery books, however, was the decreasing emphasis placed on parents reading *to* their children. When children fervently demanded "to be the reader," parents capitulated and gave up their role of reader. On the other hand, hearing children read made parents conscious of children's abilities. By the third interview, almost all parents believed their children were acting like good readers.

HOME-SCHOOL COMMUNICATION

Parent-teacher communication patterns were influenced by previously developed attitudes on the part of each group. Parents tended to follow the Reading Recovery teacher's lead in home-school communication and they reacted to these teachers' styles of communication.

TEACHERS' VIEWS OF HOMES • Reading Recovery teachers expressed frustration about the literacy backgrounds of children they taught. They blamed not parents but poverty for children's reading and writing problems. Reading Recovery teachers guessed that children from poor homes probably had not been read aloud to during preschool years, did not own books, had few experiences with books, and had little writing experience. Teachers described many of the families as barely able to keep up with the basic necessities of life, such as food, clothing, and shelter. Reading Recovery teachers viewed children from poor homes as having noisy, chaotic, and unstable family lives, tending to move frequently, having single parents, and often living with extended family members.

All seven Reading Recovery teachers had in years past been required to make home visits; they believed these had helped them better understand children, parents, and family literacy contexts, but they did not want to make them as part of the Reading Recovery program. They said they were afraid of making home visits, especially alone, and they much preferred that parents come to the school. Some reasons cited were the increase in violence in society at large and lack of time without being released from teaching. If home visits were to become a Reading Recovery program requirement, they would be willing to go during working hours but would hope to go in partnership with another teacher.

PARENTS' VIEWS OF THE SCHOOL • Parents expressed fear of school, teachers, and teachers' judgments. Unless either Reading Recovery or classroom teachers contacted them first, parents tended not to initiate contact with the school. More than half the parents studied did not finish high school. Many held bitter memories of teachers and schools, feeling that they had been unfairly treated. Parents reported that when they went to school, these emotional scars surfaced and confronted them. Report cards were taken very seriously by all families and in some instances negative school evaluations shook parents' own confidence in their children's capabilities. Parents were afraid to express to both Reading Recovery and classroom teachers their feelings of anger and frustration and said they believed teachers would punish their children as a consequence. Parents wanted to avoid that at all cost.

Parents also expressed a sense of powerlessness concerning their children's education. Children were at the school all day with classroom and Reading Recovery teachers and parents had little knowledge of what was happening there or what represented normal school literacy progress. Parents expected all teachers to give them guidance in helping their children develop literacy but did not understand how either classroom or Reading Recovery teachers taught reading and writing. In feeling unsure about how to support their children's literacy development, parents used their own memories of learning to read and write and continued those actions unless teachers told them otherwise. Some Reading Recovery teachers took the time to tell parents exactly what to do at home; these teachers increased in parent regard and parents diligently followed their instructions.

Parents had practical reasons for not getting to school for conferences. They needed transportation and baby-sitting services. Parents who worked at hourly wages during the day needed flexible appointment scheduling, which was not available from the school. Reading Recovery teachers expected parents to come to the school to talk, but teachers in this study did not offer to come to homes to talk about children's progress in reading and writing. When parents did go to the school, they entered unknown territory where they felt powerless to do anything about problems that arose.

TEACHERS' STYLES OF COMMUNICATION

Reading Recovery teachers at each of the three schools varied in the ways they communicated with parents, as illustrated in Table 7–1. Three Reading Recovery teachers could be characterized as "passive." They were content to send home formal notes and did not persist when parents failed to respond immediately. They tended to use only one type of communication and did not usually accommodate conference times to parents' schedules. They gave few, nonspecific suggestions for parents to work with children. These teachers generally had little rapport with parents and did not generate a high degree of trust.

In contrast, four Reading Recovery teachers used a parent communication style that could be characterized as "active." These teachers were able to generate a high level of parent participation and positive regard. Examining these "active" styles can provide helpful suggestions for reading teachers who want to enhance home-school relations.

ACTIVE SCHOOL-TO-HOME COMMUNICATION • Active Reading Recovery teachers used a personal, persistent, and flexible style of communication. They made communication with parents during the first month of children's participation in the program. Communication took the form of telephone calls, handwritten notes and/or invitations, and face-to-face encounters. These Reading Recovery teachers persisted in obtaining contact with their parents. If one form of personal communication did not work, another was tried over and over again until parents responded.

When contact was made with parents, these Reading Recovery teachers had a specific message they relayed to parents: "I need your help to teach your child to read and write. We have to work together for your child's success." Teachers then sought specific appointment dates and times to meet with parents to inform them about Reading Recovery and their children's progress in reading and writing. These teachers were flexible and demonstrated respect for parent's work schedules.

Active Reading Recovery teachers viewed parent observation as an integral part of the child's reading program. They wanted

TABLE 7–1   STYLES OF TEACHER-PARENT COMMUNICATION

ACTIVE APPROACH	*PASSIVE APPROACH*
1. Persistent follow-up communication.	1. Communication sent one time only.
2. Personal (phone calls, notes, and face-to-face encounters).	2. Formal (Reading Recovery letters or parent-teacher conferences).
3. Early communication during first month of children's tenure in Reading Recovery.	3. Early formal notification letter with no follow-up.
4. Message: "I need your help to teach your child to read and write. We have to work together for your child's success."	4. Message: "Come in if you want to do so."
5. Specific appointment dates and times sought at teachers' initiations.	5. General open-ended invitation, "Come in anytime," leaving initiative to parents.
6. Flexibility and respect for parents' schedules, especially working parents. Parents are allowed to set appointment time and dates within the confines of the regular school day.	6. Lack of flexibility or respect for parent schedules.
7. Expect parent to observe a lesson with their children as an integral part of their Reading Recovery Program.	7. No expectation of parent lesson observation as an integral part of Reading Recovery Program.
8. Reading Recovery books and cut-up sentences not sent home at one school until parents understand proper literacy support procedures. Parents at this school do not confuse usages of Reading Recovery materials at home.	8. Reading Recovery books and cut-up sentences sent home without directions. Parents overemphasize traditional literacy support behaviors with books and used flash card methods with cut-up sentences.
9. Parents understand the Reading Recovery program and their roles as literacy supporters of children at home.	9. Parents are confused about Reading Recovery program and their roles as literacy supporters of children at home.
10. Strong rapport and trust between parents and teachers.	10. Less rapport and trust between parents and teachers.

parents to understand the school program and the importance of their roles as literacy supporters at home.

PARENT OBSERVATIONS • The active Reading Recovery teachers in this study tried to arrange for parents to observe their children in reading lessons; a total of six children were so observed. As reported in interviews, the experience had a powerful impact on all involved in this three-way collaborative event: parent, teacher, and child. Parents said this was the first time they had actually seen a professional educator teach their children. The observation provided parents with a shared school literacy context on which to base their talk with Reading Recovery teachers. Parents were amazed at what they saw teachers and children doing in the Reading Recovery lesson and at the competence demonstrated by children. Observations convinced parents that Reading Recovery teachers really cared for children's success in school. Parents observed and listened carefully to teachers and used Reading Recovery teacher behavior as "measuring sticks" for their own support behaviors. They questioned teachers about actions they did not understand, followed through on teachers' suggestions, and, when necessary, changed their own way of working with children.

This observation seemed to empower parents as literacy supporters of children. They better understood their roles because Reading Recovery teachers modeled behaviors and gave specific suggestions. Parents left observation sessions with the confidence that they could help their children at home in reading and writing. They felt their help was important to their children's progress in Reading Recovery. Parents also told family, friends, and coworkers about the positive new reading program at the public school system.

Reading Recovery teachers had opportunity to demonstrate professional teaching to parents. They could explain the Reading Recovery Program to parents, communicate concern for children's progress in reading and writing, teach parents how to use books and other materials, and clarify parents' confusions about literacy support. Just as parents were closely observing them, Reading Recovery teachers were closely observing parents. When parents demonstrated unproductive literacy support behaviors during the lesson, teachers could suggest alternative ways of helping children. Reading Recovery teachers had their own reasons for wanting to form an alliance with parents: they hoped strong family literacy support would help children make faster progress. They wanted parents to understand their important role in children's reading and writing development.

With the Reading Recovery teacher's support, children had opportunity to show their literacy skills and to share school literacy experiences with their parents. When their parents and Reading Recovery teachers met together in their presence, children saw concern about their well-being and value for their literacy work concretely demonstrated.

This collaborative venture among parents, Reading Recovery teachers, and children contrasted sharply with parents' previous experiences in formal parent-teacher conferences (see Table 7–2). The simple idea of sharing a school literacy context with parents and children powerfully and concretely created a shared meaning of the Reading Recovery program and its importance in children's literacy development.

TABLE 7–2 COMPARISON OF TRADITIONAL PARENT/TEACHER CONFERENCES AND READING RECOVERY LESSON OBSERVATION

TRADITIONAL PARENT/TEACHER CONFERENCES	*READING RECOVERY LESSON OBSERVATIONS*
1. *Participants:* parent and teacher.	1. *Participants:* parent, teacher, and child.
2. *Time:* 20–30 minutes.	2. *Time:* 30–60 minutes.
3. *Focus:* Child's literacy behaviors in the school context.	3. *Focus:* Reading Recovery lesson under observation and parent literacy support role.
4. *Emphasis:* Teacher directed.	4. *Emphasis:* Collaboration among parent, teacher, and child.
5. *Parent Role:* Listens to teacher's report of child's school progress and may have chance to ask questions.	5. *Parent Role:* Observation of lesson, discussion of home literacy activities, receiver of teacher's specific suggestions, and participant in conference with teacher about child's progress and further needs.
6. *Field:* Separate contexts of school and home not shared by parents and teachers.	6. *Field:* Shared context of Reading Recovery lesson in progress.
7. *Tenor:* Teacher as powerful entity and source of knowledge concerning child's literacy progress.	7. *Tenor:* Power is shared among parents, teacher, and child concerning child's literacy progress.
8. *Mode:* Speaking and listening.	8. *Mode:* Speaking, listening, reading, and writing.

TABLE 7–3   SCHOOL MATERIALS SENT HOME

STUDENT	MATERIALS SENT HOME
Scott	School papers, Good Behavior lunchroom awards, report cards, Reading Recovery books, and cut-up sentences
Chuckie	School papers, Reading Recovery books and cut-up sentences, *Birds Fly Bears Don't* (first primer), *Across the Fence* (second primer), report cards
Clifton	School papers, Reading Recovery books and cut-up sentences, report cards
Shontell*	School papers, report cards, Reading Recovery books and cut-up sentences, *Little Dog Laughed* (first preprimer), *Fish and Not Fish* (second preprimer)
Sally	School papers, report cards, *Fish and Not Fish* (second preprimer), Reading Recovery books and cut-up sentences, school awards for passing basal texts
David**	School papers, end-of-year school awards (field day ribbon and Reading Recovery completion certificate), report cards, *Fish and Not Fish* (second preprimer), Reading Recovery cut-up sentences
Fred	School papers, Reading Recovery books and cut-up sentences, *Fish and Not Fish* (second preprimer), *Inside My Hat* (third and last preprimer), school music song book, three dittoed nutrition books, report cards
Ciniqua	School papers, *One Potato Two* (old kindergarten basal reading book), Reading Recovery books and cut-up sentences, report cards
Brad	School papers, school library books, Reading Recovery books and sentences, report cards, Scott-Foresman Level One preprimer (old kindergarten textbook)
Willy	School papers, school library books, Reading Recovery books and cut-up sentences, *Birds Fly Bears Don't* (first primer), report cards
George	School papers, school library books, Reading Recovery books and cut-up sentences, report cards, school awards, completed writing journal
Bradley	School papers, school library books, Reading Recovery books and cut-up sentences, report cards, school awards, completed writing journal
Danny	School papers, school library books, Reading Recovery books and cut-up sentences, report cards, school good behavior awards, Reading Recovery certificate

* Shontell lost a Reading Recovery book and lost her privileges to take them home for nearly two months

** David was the only child in this study who did not take Reading Recovery books home

IMPLICATIONS

Just as teachers look at young children's preschool literacy experiences for evidence of positive family literacy support behaviors, they might also examine their current school practice and consider the impact, if any, on the families of their students. Evidence from this study indicates that teachers' communication styles and school materials sent home can have a profound impact on home literacy environments and on the nature of home-school relations. Teachers' persistence in making positive, face-to-face communication can have a big payoff in help for children. Good materials, such as natural-language books children can read independently, can take on a life on their own once they are established in home environments. A simple inventory of literacy materials sent home by teachers (see the example in Table 7–3) might increase educators' awareness of ways to influence the family literacy context. What are we sending home with our students? How are families interpreting and engaging with these literacy materials? This study suggests certain conditions to help strengthen home and school literacy contexts.

Recommendations for parents and teachers are summarized below:

1. Parents need the tools to provide literacy support for their children at home. Teachers and school districts can help by sending high-quality, well-selected natural-language books home with children every day.

2. Parents need the opportunity to observe their children in actual school literacy instruction and they need guidance in this observation. Teachers can arrange these experiences.

3. Parents should be advised to continue reading aloud even after children can read independently. Teachers should prepare parents and children for the child's release from special supplementary literacy programs like Reading Recovery and offer assistance in maintaining support.

4. Parents should be encouraged to help children write messages and stories rather than simply copying and practicing handwriting.

5. Parents need more opportunities to participate in collaborative literacy conferences involving themselves, teachers, and their children. Teachers can help by taking the trouble to arrange these sessions when parents can come.

6. Siblings should be encouraged to provide family literacy support.
7. Male family members should receive more invitations to participate in school literacy programs.
8. Parents should be given specific tasks with reasonable time limits for their work with children. Teachers can demonstrate and talk about these tasks in collaborative sessions.
9. Parents need help in selecting and acquiring books for children even after they are released from special programs such as Reading Recovery.
10. Teachers need to be active, personal, persistent, flexible, and positive in initiating communication with parents.
11. Teachers need to learn about family literacy support systems and home literacy contexts.
12. Teachers should be actively encouraged by the school district, perhaps through some released time, to make home visits.

Children need not play the lonely role of ambassador between home and school literacy contexts. Parents and teachers, too, need to move in and out of both home and school literacy contexts. When people work together to share knowledge, information, and ways of communicating, then teachers, parents, and, most importantly, children are empowered. When home and school literacy contexts are brought together, children can gain the literacy abilities they need.

REFERENCES

Clark, M. 1976. *Young Fluent Readers*. Portsmouth, N.H.: Heinemann.
Durkin, D. 1966. *Children Who Read Early*. New York: Teachers College Press, Columbia University.
Heath, S. B. 1983. *Ways with Words: Language, Life, and Work in Communities and Classrooms*. New York: Cambridge University Press.
Holland, K. 1987. *The Impact of the Reading Recovery Program on Parents and Home Literacy Contexts*. Ph.D. diss., Ohio State University, Columbus, Ohio.
Wells, G. 1986. *The Meaning Makers: Children Learning Language and Using Language to Learn*. Portsmouth, N.H.: Heinemann.

3

On Teaching and Teachers

• • • • • • • • • • • • •

This section examines teachers as learners in their own right, working in the classroom to build a dynamic literacy community.

Gay Su Pinnell discusses the importance of Reading Recovery as a model of ongoing learning for teachers as well as for children. Woolsey examines how participation in Reading Recovery can profoundly change teachers' attitudes toward reading instruction and affect their conduct in the regular classroom. Lyons illustrates the dangers of applying the label of "learning disabled" too readily to a child. She describes how one Reading Recovery teacher came to realize that her failure to reach a child came from her own preconceptions about the child's limited abilities. Finally, Huck and Pinnell suggest ways of applying the insights we have gained from Reading Recovery in traditional classrooms.

EIGHT

·················

Teachers and Children Learning

GAY SU PINNELL

························· *E* ························

E xperience is often said to be the "best teacher." Current educational situations, however, may lead teachers to learn the following from experience:

- Stacks of activity sheets are the easiest way to keep children busy and quiet and simultaneously please administrators.
- Following the scripted directions in the reading system effectively absolves them of personal responsibility for children's learning.
- The curriculum should consist solely of teaching to the test.

These understandings are commonly developed during student teaching and the first few years. But, worse, teachers may learn other things from experience:

- "Some" children, because they do not respond to the prescribed curriculum, cannot learn.
- "Some" parents, because they do not come to school or know how to teach reading at home, do not care.

The primary goal of literacy education is to make a difference for children and society. There is only one way to accomplish that goal: find ways to increase the expertise of teachers. We need to know more about what teachers need to know, how they make decisions, and how they learn. The staff development course that is an integral part of Reading Recovery offers a productive arena for studying these processes. In this course, teachers often change their views of teaching, of literacy, of learning, and of the competence of the children they teach. They learn they can make a difference.

Conscious attention to teacher development is required; a single preparation program plus "experience" is inadequate. In children's language and literacy development, the knowledge base has been considerably expanded through research in the past two decades. The next two decades offer unprecedented challenges for literacy education related to a rapidly changing elementary-school population (Hodgkinson 1986). Ongoing preparation is necessary in addition to experience. In other words, professional development must be an integral and ongoing part of the teacher's job.

Few argue about the need; many argue about how professional development can most effectively be accomplished. Researchers and educational commentators from a range of theoretical perspectives are recommending approaches that emphasize the teacher's own learning (Shulman 1986; Berliner 1986) and awareness of such learning (Duckworth 1986). Berliner (1986) recommends a "pedagogical laboratory," which includes a range of inquiry-oriented activities. Others (Mayher and Brause 1986; Heath 1983; Clay and Watson 1982) have recommended involving teachers in research in the educational contexts in which they operate. Duckworth (1986) has articulately described the value of teachers' "discovery" learning.

This chapter describes an interactive staff development model based on principles of learning that apply both to children and to teachers. In this interactive system, the learner (teacher or child) is acting, observing, talking, responding, and negotiating. Out of these activities we hypothesize that the same learner is engaging in "in-the-head processes" needed to construct a generative system, one that will allow the learner to keep on learning independently. The model is derived from an analysis of the unique staff development program designed for the Reading Recovery program. Research (Clay 1985; Pinnell, DeFord, & Lyons 1988) indicates that when the program is implemented as described, including the teacher training and implementation procedures required, the result is more learning for students. The purpose of this article is to present some basic principles for designing staff development. These principles are based on the Reading Recovery program but have potential for wider application.

THE CHILD AS LEARNER

Through early experiences with written language, such as hearing stories read aloud and writing to accompany family activities, children construct their own ideas about reading and writing. As they read and write for their own purposes, they learn to use their knowledge to solve problems and to construct meaning. Gradually, they learn about how texts are organized and how print works. In this constructive process, they are usually supported by adults: parents and preschool, kindergarten, and primary teachers. The child, however, is the active learner who does the necessary work.

In each Reading Recovery lesson, children engage in reading and writing their own messages and stories, assisted by specially prepared teachers. The instructional situation is one-to-one; teachers and children know each other well. While reading and writing, they engage in an ongoing dialogue that surrounds and supports the literacy activities. The child does the work; the teacher "follows the child," searching for opportunities to help the child extend his or her knowledge and further understand how the child is learning. Knowledge of the particular child and of the processes involved in learning to read and write serve as guidelines for this process.

THE STAFF-DEVELOPMENT PROGRAM

To learn how to work with children, teachers are engaged in a yearlong staff-development program, with continuing contact sessions on a regular basis after that. No time is lost in service to children because participants begin to tutor children immediately. During the training year teachers meet weekly in seminar sessions, usually held after school, at a special facility equipped with a special viewing mirror. This facility enables the group to watch through a one-way glass, analyzing and discussing as they observe.

After teachers learn diagnostic techniques (Clay 1985) and get started using a few procedures with children, behind-the-glass sessions begin. The weekly seminar has two basic parts: (1) *talking while observing*, in which participants observe the lesson or lessons, talking among themselves as they do so; then (2) *reflective discussion*, in which participants meet with the demonstrating teacher and discuss the lesson. Both processes are led by a trained teacher leader who guides discussion, raises challenging questions, and uses the observed behavior of the child and teacher to help the group develop skills in describing, analyzing, and making infer-

FIGURE 8–1   SET-UP FOR CLINICAL CLASS

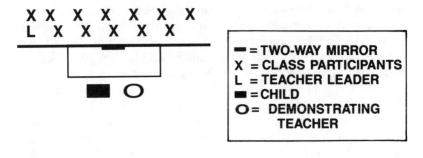

```
X X  X  X  X  X  X
L  X  X  X  X  X
```

■ = TWO-WAY MIRROR
X = CLASS PARTICIPANTS
L = TEACHER LEADER
■ = CHILD
O = DEMONSTRATING
      TEACHER

FIGURE 8–2   SET-UP FOR DISCUSSIONS

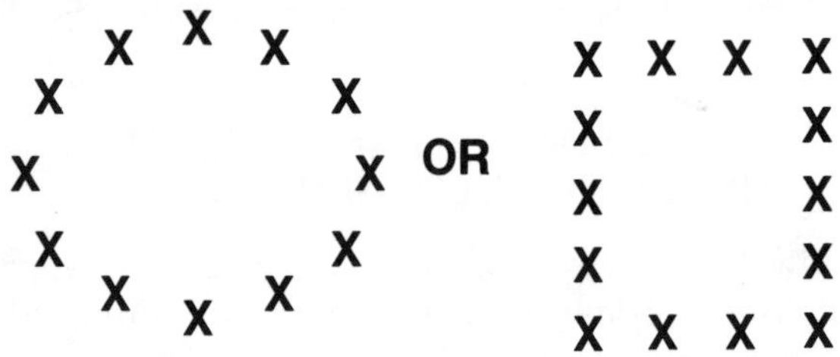

```
      X  X  X              X  X  X  X
   X           X           X        X
   X           X  OR       X        X
   X           X           X        X
      X  X  X              X  X  X  X
```

ences. In this way, the teachers begin to develop their own theories, grounded in the specifics of teaching.

In behind-the-glass sessions, teachers sit close to the glass (see Figure 8–1). A sound system enables observers to hear the teacher and child, but the group can talk without disturbing the ongoing lesson. They can see the text being read, eye and hand movements, and every detail of the teacher-child interaction. In the reflective discussion, teachers sit in a circle or around a table so that interaction among participants is facilitated (see Figure 8–2).

The inservice process is sometimes disconcerting to first-time visitors. Most of us are accustomed to silent observation, perhaps with note taking and with discussion afterwards. Reading Recovery, however, is based on the theory that learning takes place through action and that language facilitates the development of important concepts. As teachers struggle to express their ideas and theories in language, they refine and make them more explicit. Group support is important. The Reading Recovery teachers work together to construct a language that can in turn be used as a tool for learning.

In the following transcript of an inservice session, a teacher is working with Sara, who has just begun her Reading Recovery program. The child is reading a simple book, *All Fall Down* (Wildsmith 1983), which she has read several times previously. On the other side of the glass, observers—the leader, Diane, Linda, and Viviane—are responding to some questions from the leader.

OBSERVERS	LESSON
LEADER: What is Sara bringing to this reading?	SARA (*reading*): "A ball and a butterfly . . . and a bee . . ." (*Sara substitutes "rate" for "mouse."*)
VIVIANE: She's searching for meaning by using the pictures?	
LEADER: Is she?	
VIVIANE: No, she's just substituted "rate" for "mouse".	
LINDA: She's rerunning.	TEACHER: Try that again from here, Sara.
LEADER: And what does that suggest?	
DIANE: She's confirming her sense of language. She's trying to get the way the sentence sounds.	SARA (*reading*): "I see a ball and a butterfly and a bee . . ." (*long pause*)
LEADER: Is she using language structure?	(*Sara loses her place, stops, starts over.*)
VIVIANE: I think so. Sometimes we forget how powerful that is to help children predict.	(*Sara tries again, but loses her place in the sentence.*)
LEADER: What do you think is getting in the way?	SARA (*reading*): ". . . a butterfly, (*omits an "a"*) ball" (*looks at picture*)
DIANE: The sentences are too long and it's hard to get the sense of language.	TEACHER (*pointing to the ball*): What's this?

VIVIANE: Maybe she needs a bit more support.

DIANE: She's having difficulty matching up one-to-one and also knowing all the labels for the things in the pictures. The pictures aren't helping.

VIVIANE: The teacher might come in and read with her, and I would check on her one-to-one correspondence.

LEADER: What opportunities is this giving Sara to practice what she knows?

VIVIANE: She's mastered using language structure to help her read.

DIANE: I'll challenge that. Is she really using her language knowledge or is she just trying to name words?

LEADER: Does this text really give her a chance to use language structure?

SARA (*hesitates*): Bee.

TEACHER (*pointing*): What is this?

After the observation, the teacher group meets with the one who demonstrated the lesson. The demonstrating teacher gets feedback on the lesson and has a chance to ask questions about what the group observed and discussed. The observers provide valuable information because, from their vantage point (and without the pressure of instruction), they are able to observe aspects of child behavior that the teacher does not ordinarily see. Often, aspects of teacher-child interaction are uncovered that have important implications for further decision making.

In the example above, the teacher learned that she had given Sara a text with a syntactic structure that was difficult for the child to predict. This difficult text structure confused the child, who was not able to use her own knowledge of language. The teacher's responses were guiding Sara to labels or words but were not helping her deal with the difficult structure. Based on group feedback, the teacher was able to select reading material and work more effectively with Sara.

In another case, the teacher was concerned about the dependent behavior of a child with whom she was working. Jeffrey, unwilling to guess at words, constantly appealed to the teacher. The group noticed that the teacher's responses were rewarding dependent behavior. She did not wait for Jeffrey to respond, gave quick answers to his appeals, and paid little attention when he did risk a guess. Through feedback, she learned to value Jeffrey's own attempts, even when he did not achieve the accurate answers, thus encouraging him to take on the task of reading independently.

In the discussion session, teacher and participants can check the accuracy of their observations and provide useful information for the demonstrating teacher. The following comments, taken from a discussion transcript, illustrate the group's reflection on a demonstration session. The text was: "I will go to town on my jumping stick, my super silver jumping stick." The child had read, "I will go to town . . . " and then hesitated; he went back to the beginning of the line, reading, "I will go to town on my jumping stick, my powerful silver jumping stick," substituting "powerful" for "super."

JAN: I noticed that he read "I will go to town," then went back and reread that line.

KAREN: Then he read "my powerful . . . " and went back again. He obviously knew that something was wrong.

JEANNE: You noticed that after he read the book I went back and asked him what he was thinking about on that word (*super*). He said, "The *p.* " Isn't that something?

KAREN: I couldn't imagine how he got powerful out of that, but now I can see it. He was noticing the *p* in *super.*

JAN: But the substitution also fit with the meaning and the language structure. It sounded good, but he said he was thinking about the *p*. When he went back, he had his finger right on the word (*super*). He was really paying attention to everything there.

KAREN: Maybe you should have pointed that out to him—how it was a really good guess because it made sense. That pogo stick is going over a semitruck in the picture and *powerful* was a very good guess. Make him realize he was using other cues, too.

JAN: The point is, you have the opportunity because you are there one-on-one with the child and you can get into that kid's brain and see what may be happening to him back in the classroom. It gives you information about his thinking that a [classroom] teacher just doesn't see. For example, a teacher might be tempted to correct him on that error and tell him to pay more attention to sounds, meaning the *first letter*. Well, he already is paying attention to sounds, but the teacher might not realize it.

In addition to teaching the clinical course for an entire year, the leader is responsible for providing individual help to teachers in training and for those previously trained. The leader assists teachers through regular visits to their schools and individual observation of lessons. In these sessions, the leader is able to give specific, critical feedback to teachers and to engage with them in solving problems about the progress of individual children.

Monitoring is integral to the program and takes place at many levels. Leaders monitor the behavior and understandings of teachers; teachers assist each other by monitoring through observation, analysis, and discussion; teachers monitor children's progress through ongoing analysis of reading and writing behavior. And all participants, including children, learn to monitor their own progress.

Research on teachers who have been involved in Reading Recovery provides evidence that the training program has a powerful impact on participants. Individuals generally experience a shift in theoretical orientation, moving from a "skills-oriented" view of reading, which focuses on materials and sequential learning of specific aspects of reading, toward a holistic orientation, which suggests that children "orchestrate" a range of skills and knowledge when they learn to read and write.

A year-long qualitative study of one group of teachers revealed continuous shifts in teachers' focus of attention throughout the training period (Pinnell and Woolsey 1985). The data for the study consisted of transcribed group discussions, which were held every two weeks following training sessions. This study of teacher language in an informal setting revealed teachers' concerns, their growth of concepts, and the complexity of ideas with which they dealt at various points in the inservice process. In general, the study supported the idea of long-term training to help teachers develop their own theoretical ideas. The trends noted in teacher talk are illustrated in Figure 8–3.

At the beginning of the training, teacher language centered on the logistics of implementing a new program. They wanted to know "how to do it" and to be told the "right way." They were concerned about management and materials and about the inevitable conflicts, questions, and stresses surrounding most

FIGURE 8–3   CHANGE IN TEACHER FOCUS OVER A PERIOD OF READING
RECOVERY TRAINING (PERCENTAGE OF TEACHER COMMENTS FALLING
INTO EACH CATEGORY DURING GROUP DISCUSSIONS)

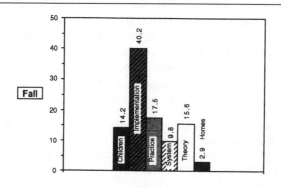

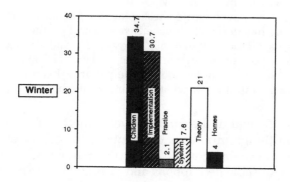

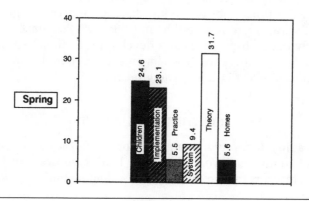

innovations. Whatever the topic, what we called "logistics" crept in and consumed attention. It is no wonder that college professors find it so difficult to require teachers to deal with theoretical concepts or to apply theory to practice within a two-week course.

This surface-level focus continued for several months. Then, as teachers became comfortable with their teaching, they began to focus on their own discoveries and insights. They reported detailed observations of children; they created and shared metaphors; they learned about each others' students and told "stories" about their work. This example comes from Anne in February:

> Tim had the "Helen Keller" experience: he just put his hand under the faucet and felt the water. Tim never even used visual cues. He was great on meaning and great on using language structure, but he didn't check the visual information. So, one day Tim is reading *Sam's Mask* [Cachemaille 1983]: " 'Help,' said Mom." And he goes on to the next page and then he says, "Wait a minute!" I said, "What do you mean?" He said, "That doesn't say 'Mom.' Mom is *M-O-M*."
>
> Anyway, now he cross-checks, looking for visual cues; so, I think he has definitely touched water and he's the one, he says to me, "It's so neat to be able to read." He said, "You know with these books you can pile them in my box." He said, "I like to flip through them and look at the pictures. I can read the name at the top. I know what the name of the book is."

Toward the end of their training year, another shift could be observed in the group's focus of attention. In their discussions, they began to generalize and to make theoretical statements and hypotheses. Specific descriptions and "stories" were still evident but were fewer, and teachers began to link their ideas into more cohesive statements. The increased theoretical understanding was not evident in teacher talk until they had been immersed for a long time in the process of observing, talking, and challenging. This study indicates that if, as Shulman (1986; 1987) suggests, teachers must change in their views and develop professional knowledge, then staff developers and teachers must be prepared to invest time and unusual effort in the learning process.

CONTINUED SUPPORT

The Reading Recovery training lasts for one full academic year, but support continues beyond that time. During subsequent years of service, teachers meet regularly to view demonstration lessons and discuss new insights about children. Teachers report that during this second year, their understandings deepen. Leaders provide continuous contact and support. Reading Recovery is a continuous learning process; teachers from the first year of training report that they are still learning about the reading process and about children.

In summary, the Reading Recovery staff-development program combines some important elements. Here are a few:

1. Careful observation of children and teachers.
2. Talking while observing.
3. Documentation and monitoring of progress.
4. Group support under skilled leadership.
5. Clear communication of learning processes related to expected outcomes.
6. An intensive year of training and follow-up sessions in subsequent years; ongoing learning.

AN INTERACTIVE MODEL FOR STAFF DEVELOPMENT

The outcome of effective staff development must be the growth of a set of theoretical understandings, based on which the teacher will make decisions and take action. Lists of "good" teaching behaviors, performed in mechanical ways in response to supervisors' observations, are useless without this underlying knowledge. At the same time, staff development must assist teachers in putting their understandings to work in specific actions and decisions with the supportive feedback of their peers.

If teachers are reflecting with understanding on their own decisions, they are always tentative in their definition of good teacher responses. This hesitancy reflects two things: (1) the stance of continued inquiry, and (2) the complexity of the reading process and its relationship to the social situation. For example, an action might be productive, appropriate, or powerful, depending on the child. A behavior considered effective in one context might not be effective in another. In the training process, teachers become aware of and skillful at assessing the child's strengths and needs, as well as the complex elements present in the social context of instruction. They develop a repertoire of possible actions and responses, but the real task of teaching is selecting and applying those actions relative to the needs of the child at that particular time. Through observing others and through reflection, teachers develop a heightened awareness of their own moment-to-moment actions and decisions. Being an effective teacher, then, means having a well-developed set of understandings which one can apply in practical ways based upon the special needs of the situation. This knowledge is constructed by only one person: the teacher who must use it.

The definition of effectiveness proposed here is consistent with a general view of learning that suggests that the learner constructs knowledge from experience, building a kind of "theory in the head," which makes sense to him or her. From a Piagetian perspective, Duckworth (1986) applies this view to teachers' learning as well. Beliefs about teaching and learning, she claims, are complex and deeply held. Duckworth goes on to suggest that teacher educators "structure experiences in which prospective teachers learn, try to explain, and hear other people's ideas" (1986, p. 482), but they must make sense of it for themselves. While not fully exploring the role of language in learning, Duckworth strongly suggests that "much of the learning is in the explaining" as learners propose tentative ideas and, in negotiation with others, think them through (p. 483).

The last twenty years of research on language learning has illuminated the theory of learning as a constructive process by providing specific descriptions of the way children learn the rules and structures of language while they *use* language to communicate meaning. Halliday (1975) has described the process as "learning how to mean"; others (King 1980; Bissex 1980; DeFord 1980; Harste, Woodward, & Burke 1984) have noted the same "meaning construction" processes in children's development of literacy.

The staff-development model described here is based on the assumption that language is a key factor in building theories, because language is used to represent our experiences to others and to refine and extend it for ourselves. Through language interactions with other people, we expand our experiences, try out our ideas, and formulate or reformulate understandings of a particular phenomenon.

As they teach reading and writing (as well as other areas), teachers continually develop and refine their own theories. This process goes on whether or not the teacher is involved in any formal inservice or graduate education program, because the theories are largely constructed from information encountered on a case-by-case basis during practice. Teachers' theories, often held implicitly, are constructed from their own experiences; these theories encompass views of the nature of learning, the processes of reading and writing, the definition of teaching, and theories about societal factors such as ethnic or economic group characteristics. Indeed, the theoretical base out of which teachers act is complex and continuously developing.

As illustrated in Figure 8–4, learning is a social event and the social context is carefully designed. The child, learning about reading and writing in a one-to-one situation with chances for rich oral interaction, focuses on stories and messages. Teacher learning takes place in two contexts, in work with children and in the inservice session. Staff development is specific to the context of the particular learner: the teacher focuses on the child responding to specified literacy activities; and teachers, assisted by a leader who encourages and facilitates group interaction, focus on the dynamics of the teacher-child interactions they observe.

There are parallel processes in child and teacher learning, although these processes must be inferred from observation of very different contexts and sets of activities. Among the many complex processes at work here, I will discuss three: (1) developing strategies, (2) analyzing to solve problems, and (3) scaffolding the learning process.

DEVELOPING STRATEGIES • "Strategies are the in-the-head processes which are involved in making sense of any situation" (Clay 1985). A reader uses strategies to construct meaning from

••

FIGURE 8–4 AN INTERACTIVE MODEL FOR STAFF DEVELOPMENT

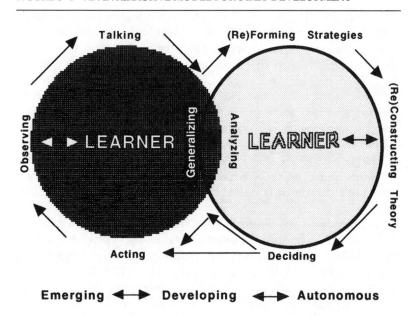

printed language, a process called "reading work" by Reading Recovery teachers who try to foster this kind of work. Strategies cannot be directly observed and we can only guess at their nature; however, the child's behavior does provide clues to the kind of problem solving going on. The detailed observation which is part of the inservice program helps teachers to make hypotheses about children's use of strategies and guides their responses to the child. Specific questions ask that children begin to articulate their own thinking. Some examples of the kind of strategies teachers try to foster are self-monitoring while reading, searching for information to help in reading, and checking one kind of information against another. An effective reader must learn to "orchestrate" or integrate many strategies simultaneously while focusing on the meaning of the message.

Teachers also develop processes for making sense of the instructional situation. Assisted by their peers, teachers learn to (1) monitor their own behavior in instructional settings, and (2) search for probable explanations for children's behavior on a daily basis and by demonstrating for their peers. Gradually, they develop a repertoire of responses and a theoretical base from which they act. They are not learning a series of behaviors in a linear way; instead, they are building a set of understandings from their interactions with a learner and responses from their peers. These understandings frame and guide their responses to children.

SOLVING PROBLEMS • Throughout the instructional process, both teachers and children solve problems. In children, this "reading work" happens when they are working on a text that allows them to keep the focus on meaning but yet is difficult enough to provide challenge. Children solve problems through developing and using strategies that are "generative"—that is, they enable the reader to become a better reader.

Teachers engage in problem solving during every lesson and in behind-the-glass sessions. We might call this "teaching work." Teachers develop the ability to analyze and make decisions as they build up a personal knowledge of individual "cases" through their work with children (daily *and* behind-the-mirror at inservice sessions) and discussion with peers. Early in the process, teachers learn procedures for working with children more effectively, but this is only the beginning of the staff development program. Learning to become a better teacher of reading takes time. Procedures can be taught in a few weeks, but the program is designed to help teachers learn deeply and to develop a "generative" decision-making system based on their own observations and knowledge.

SCAFFOLDING • In Reading Recovery the teacher becomes aware of helping the child develop a theory in the head about the basic processes of reading and writing. The teacher is also aware that the most powerful teaching takes place in conversation with the child during reading and writing activities. In many ways, this mirrors the learning that takes place in the home during the child's early years.

Vygotsky's (1978) notion of the "zone of proximal development" is important for both teachers and children in Reading Recovery. This concept suggests that the most productive learning takes place when learners use support of a more skilled "other" to extend their performance beyond the boundaries of what they can do alone. This kind of support occurs naturally in early language learning and has been called "scaffolding" by Bruner (1983), Cazden (1988), and others. The learner does the major acting, but another person provides strong support. In Reading Recovery lessons, the teacher consciously supports the child's reading and writing. From the first day, these "nonreaders" are expected to behave like good readers and the teacher skillfully supports this process. As the child reads and writes the teacher closely follows and consciously structures responses to provide the kind of moment-to-moment assistance children need to build and act upon their developing theories of reading. This process, of course, requires responding differently to each child, based on the teacher's hypothesis about what the child knows about reading and the contexts of varying texts.

Teachers receive support or "scaffolding" as they struggle to describe and analyze children's behavior and to make their own theories explicit. By working with children and talking about it, teachers move beyond their previous boundaries, extending the "edge" of their understanding. Support for the process is critical, both for the child and the teacher. Language (in the form of conversation rather than lecture or direct instruction) is the vehicle through which support is given. The goal for both child and teacher is independent, informed decision making as they pursue their tasks.

ONGOING LEARNING

The Reading Recovery teacher tries to help *children* change their views of themselves as readers and to give them power over the process. This kind of interactive staff development also changes *teachers'* view of themselves and what they do. They are empowered in a very positive and real sense, through their personal knowledge and ability to solve problems and make decisions.

The interactive staff-development model has potential for use in many content areas and for various age groups. Detailed observation, peer demonstration, talking while observing, practice and feedback, and scaffolding of learning can help teachers develop their own knowledge base. Such a knowledge base is the foundation of personal and professional empowerment. The model described here has been developed through research and it involves all participants in research. It suggests one way to involve teachers in the inquiry process and to help them develop an inquiring attitude toward all of their work with children; it provides a model of ongoing learning.

REFERENCES

Berliner, D. 1986. "In Pursuit of the Expert Pedagogue." *Educational Research* 15(7): 5–13.

Bissex, G. 1980. *GNYS AT WORK: A Child Learns to Write and Read.* Cambridge, Mass.: Harvard University Press.

Bruner, J. 1983. *Child's Talk: Learning to Use Language.* New York: W. W. Norton.

Cazden, C. 1988. *Classroom Discourse.* Portsmouth, N.H.: Heinemann.

Cachemaille, C. 1983. *Sam's Mask.* Illus. Terence Taylor. Reading to Read Series. Wellington: School Publications Branch, New Zealand Department of Education.

Clay, M. M. 1979. *Reading: The Patterning of Complex Behavior.* 2d ed. Portsmouth, N.H.: Heinemann.

———. 1985. *The Early Detection of Reading Difficulties* 3d ed. Portsmouth, N.H.: Heinemann.

Clay, M. M. & B. Watson. 1982. "An Inservice Program for Reading Recovery Teachers." In M. M. Clay, *Observing Young Readers: Selected Papers,* 192–200. Portsmouth, N.H.: Heinemann.

DeFord, D. E., ed. 1980. *Learning to Write: An Expression of Language (Theory into Practice).* Columbus: College of Education, Ohio State University.

Duckworth, E. 1986. "Teaching as Research." *Harvard Educational Review* 56: 481–95.

Halliday, M. A. K. 1975. *Learning How to Mean.* London: Edward Arnold.

Harste, J., V. Woodward, & C. Burke. 1984. *Language Stories and Literacy Lessons.* Portsmouth, N.H.: Heinemann.

Heath, S. B. 1983. *Ways with Words: Language, Life and Work in Communities and Classrooms.* New York: Cambridge University Press.

Hodgkinson, H. L. 1985. *All One System: Demographics of Education, Kindergarten Through Graduate School.* Washington, DC: Institute for Educational Leadership.

Huck, C. S. & G. Pinnell. 1985. *The Reading Recovery Project in Columbus, Ohio: Pilot Year, 1984–1985.* Technical Report. Columbus: Ohio State University.

King, M. L. 1980. "Learning How to Mean in Written Language." In D. DeFord ed., *Theory Into Practice*, 163–70.

King, M. L. & V. M. Rentel. 1981. "Conveying Meaning in Written Texts." *Language Arts* 58: 721–28.

Mayher, J. & R. Brause. 1986. "Learning Through Teaching: Is Your Classroom Like Your Grandmother's?" *Language Arts* 63 (6): 617–20.

Pinnell, G., D. E. DeFord, & C. A. Lyons. 1988. *Reading Recovery: Early Intervention for At-Risk First Graders*. Arlington, VA: Educational Research Service.

Pinnell, G. & D. Woolsey. 1985. *Report of a Study of Teacher Researchers in a Program to Prevent Reading Failure*. Report to the Research Foundation of the National Council of Teachers of English.

Shulman, L. S. 1987. "Knowledge and Teaching: Foundations of the New Reform." *Harvard Educational Review* 57 (1): 1–22.

———. 1986. "Paradigms and Research Programs for the Study of Teaching." In M. C. Wittrock, ed., *Handbook of Research on Teaching*. 3d ed., 3–36. New York: Macmillan.

Wildsmith, B. 1983. *All Fall Down*. New York: Oxford University Press.

Vygotsky, L. S. 1978. *Mind in Society*. 1938. M. Cole, V. John-Steiner, & E. Sonberman, eds. Cambridge, Mass.: Harvard University Press.

NINE

Changing Contexts for Literacy Learning: The Impact of Reading Recovery on One First-Grade Teacher

DANIEL P. WOOLSEY

*E*very day teachers of young children make a multitude of decisions as they organize and implement the classroom literacy program. They determine goals, select materials and learning activities, evaluate student progress in reading and writing, and make plans for ongoing instruction.

How do they make these decisions? A strong line of recent research suggests that these decisions are influenced by teachers' implicit theories and beliefs about literacy and learning in general (cf. Bussis, Chittenden, and Amarel 1976; Clark and Peterson 1986; DeFord 1985; Harste and Burke 1977; Shavelson 1983).

We are just beginning to understand how teachers create their theories, translate them into classroom practice, and develop them over time. Qualitative studies of practicing teachers as they interact in and outside of their classrooms hold great promise for further insights and understandings about these issues.

The implementation of the Ohio Reading Recovery project offered an excellent opportunity to explore the impact of involvement in a major research project and an intensive inservice effort on teachers' theories and classroom practice. Throughout the school year and in addition to their daily work with children, the Reading Recovery teachers attended weekly inservice sessions, in which they learned and practiced the diagnostic techniques and teaching procedures used in Reading Recovery.

How do these teachers change during their participation in Reading Recovery? How do the ideas and techniques utilized during work in individual Reading Recovery lessons "spin off" into their teaching in the regular classroom setting? What forces facilitate these changes and what forces work against them? These were some of the questions underlying a study of fourteen teachers involved in the first year of the Ohio Reading Recovery program (Pinnell and Woolsey 1985) and a yearlong follow-up study with Sue Anderson, then in her second year of work with Reading Recovery (Woolsey 1986).

In order to gain insights into the complex and shifting theories held by the teachers as well as the ways in which these theories were realized in their classrooms, both studies made use of naturalistic research techniques: classroom observation and teacher interviews in the first study (Pinnell and Woolsey 1985); and participant observation, interviews with the teacher and her students, and videotaping and subsequent analysis of key literacy events in the second (Woolsey 1986). In both studies DeFord's Theoretical Orientation to the Reading Process (TORP) was used to provide specific data on the teachers' belief systems on reading process and practice. (For a more complete description of the methodology and conclusions of each study, see Pinnell and Woolsey 1985 and Woolsey 1986.)

FORCES FOR TEACHER CHANGE

Data from the first-year study indicated that all of the teachers involved in the first year of Reading Recovery in Ohio made important changes in the ways in which they thought and talked about literacy instruction. The most dramatic changes in theory and in practice were evidenced by Sue Anderson, the subject of the second study and this chapter. Sue worked with her colleague, Joan Krakoff, in team teaching a first-grade class; both teachers were also involved on a daily basis with the implementation of Reading Recovery lessons with children from that class. Following the model generally used in the Ohio Reading Recovery project, Sue taught reading and language arts in the morning to her first graders while Joan worked individually with four "at-risk" children, using the ideas and techniques of Reading Recovery. After lunch they switched roles and Joan worked with the first graders on math, science, and social studies while Sue worked with Reading Recovery students.

This dual role and the intensive on-the-job training, which was an important part of the Ohio Reading Recovery program, exposed

Sue to many new insights about literacy learning and forced her to reconsider her routines and practices as a teacher. According to Sue, "As I trained in Reading Recovery, I experienced many frustrations because I was teaching one approach to reading in the morning and another in the afternoon" (Anderson 1986). The ideas and techniques of Reading Recovery were at odds with Sue's rather traditional and skills-oriented approach. The resulting discomfort was an important force for change.

Interestingly, this desire and willingness to change may have been strengthened by her work with Reading Recovery. A firm belief undergirding the inservice training and the daily work with children is that teachers must be willing to examine acts of teaching in a reflective and critical way and to change ineffective practices (see Pinnell's chapter, this volume). Sue maintained this stance in her regular classroom teaching as well as in her Reading Recovery lessons. As a result, this classroom offered an especially rich opportunity to observe teacher change.

CHANGE IN THE TEACHER AND HER CLASSROOM:
THE FIRST YEAR

Evidence of Sue's evolving thinking and classroom practice during the first year of her work with Reading Recovery is found in several places: results of the TORP (administered in September and June), structured interviews, and classroom observation. All three sources suggest a teacher and a classroom in transition. Table 9–1 presents the results of the TORP from thirteen teachers in the first-year study. The September data reveals that more than any of her peers, Sue held traditional beliefs about reading instruction, her score hovering between the phonics and skills orientations. However, in June, her responses indicate a significant move toward a whole-language orientation. In fact, Sue's score shifted thirty-one points in the whole-language direction, while the average change in her peers' scores was eleven points.

Interviews provide further evidence of this move away from a traditional phonics/skills approach and toward a more meaning-based and whole-language approach. Near the end of the second year, Sue described her literacy learning program prior to her work with Reading Recovery:

> In September of 1984, when I first started working in Reading Recovery, I always wanted a quiet, controlled classroom. . . . My attitude was that's the only atmosphere you can read in. I

TABLE 9–1   TORP SCORES FOR YEAR ONE READING RECOVERY TEACHERS*

R.R. TEACHERS	SEPT. SCORES	JUNE SCORES
WM	115	116
OD	110	104
GR	108	102
ER	107	117
TT	106	120
HK	98	101
SL	94	99
JA	93	113
MS	85	101
GJ	77	94
KJ	74	100
WD	71	89
Sue	65	96

*Pinnell and Woolsey 1985.

was a firm believer in the basal approach. I frequently did not have time to read stories to the class, but we did all the dittos. The children copied words and sentences from the board, but they weren't encouraged to do any of their own writing or to use any invented spelling. (Interview 3/4/86, Woolsey 1986)

Excerpts from October and May interviews provided in Table 9–2 underscore Sue's shift away from a basal and skills emphasis and reveal the influence of her Reading Recovery training. These excerpts indicate that in October, Sue's theories and practice were letter and word based; she relied on the basal to provide a "step-by-step sequence." In May she continued to make use of the basal series to structure reading instruction. However, there were clear differences in the ways that she thought about and made use of the basal materials. In the later interview, she was thinking of reading as a language process. She mentions the orchestration of the different cueing systems, emphasizes the value of placing new words and texts in meaningful contexts, and prizes the importance of interest and sheer pleasure in reading. Readers who are familiar with the writings of Marie Clay (1979; 1985) and Reading Recovery lesson procedures will detect the clear influence of Reading Recovery training in these responses.

Two activities mentioned by Sue mirror Reading Recovery procedures: her introduction of new stories prior to reading them and

TABLE 9–2   CHANGES IN ONE READING RECOVERY TEACHER'S VIEWS ON READING

INTERVIEWER'S QUESTION	OCTOBER, 1984	MAY, 1985
Could you describe the way you teach reading in your classroom?	I first begin with letter recognition and from there we go to the words. Of course, we follow the Ginn series, so that there is some formal format. And then I do work on rhyming word families aside from that, but basically I follow the text that the school has selected.	I have five reading groups and we basically read from the basals and then some days we do the worksheets which we discuss and then the children go and do individually. Before we read a new story we talk through it, looking at the pictures and introducing words in our conversation. I never isolate the words. The children each read a page and no one can interrupt or correct. That way, I have a chance to watch them work through it.
What kinds of writing did the children in your classroom do last week?	Writing? Now, a lot of them are no further than their ABCs. We did a lot with color words and number words from the board. I had one girl write the beginnings of a good Halloween story.	We build sentences using word families. They also wrote entire books this week, with a beginning, middle, and ending. They wrote one sentence on each page and then worked with a mother volunteer to fix the mistakes. They are also writing individual stories daily.
How can you tell when a child is going to be a successful reader?	They seem to be able to put their letter sounds to work in digging out a word. They have good word retention. Usually I only have to help them with a word once and they have it.	When you first discover that they are enjoying reading, that they can get pleasure out of it. They're attentive, interested, and self-motivated. They can put the cues together when they read.
What are the most important things for the child to learn in order read well?	I believe that they've got to start with their alphabet and their sounds, so they have the tools to dig words apart. . . . I really think that most children need a step-by-step sequence of learning.	They need to know how to use all the cue systems: meaning, visual, and structure. They need experiences with language because things like the alphabet will come through experiences with reading. They also need to be motivated and to love reading.

her daily practice of having children write individual stories. Daily writing by all students is a major change from her earlier practice of having all students copy from the board and encouraging personal writing from only the more capable students.

Pinnell and Woolsey (1985) concluded that change in ideas and the ability to verbalize those ideas usually precedes tangible changes in actual classrooms. However, classroom observations carried out at regular intervals during the first year of Reading Recovery indicate that Sue's new understandings were, indeed, translated into practice.

Observations in Sue's classroom in the fall noted an emphasis on skills work in small ability groups and independent seat work, in which Sue made extensive use of basal worksheets and other duplicated materials dealing primarily with phonic and word analysis. There was a classroom library of approximately one hundred trade books, but these were available to students only when their assigned seat work was completed.

In January and February the reading program remained much the same, but there were indications that Sue was including other literacy activities, such as story writing, rather than just having students copy from the board or fill in blanks. In March it was noted that Sue set aside part of reading time to allow the children to read self-selected trade books with a partner or on their own. After the final observation in late May, the observer made the following notation: "I was thinking about the first time I came into Sue's room—it was so regimented and basal/phonics oriented. Between that time and this last visit I have seen much more reading and writing" (Woolsey and Pinnell 1985).

CHANGE IN THE TEACHER AND HER CLASSROOM: THE SECOND YEAR

The more extensive and focused observation of literacy instruction in Sue's classroom during the second year of her work with Reading Recovery indicated that ideas and practices from the program continued to be carried over into the regular classroom. Not surprisingly, this influence was seen in her work with reading groups, though at the beginning of the year Sue handled reading instruction much as she always had.

In September Sue had grouped her students into three groups of six to eight children. She also worked individually with two girls who were very proficient readers. Reading instruction took place every morning following morning exercises and story time, generally for about two hours. Work in reading groups was highly structured and routinized. Typically, oral reading from the basal readers alternated with skills work. Depending on the ability level of the group, skills work consisted of playing games involving letter recognition and letter/sound correspondences, orally working through basal worksheets, or using large sheets of chart paper draped over an easel on which Sue wrote words and sentences. In September Sue tried to meet with each group on a daily basis. When not meeting with Sue, the first graders worked at their desks on three or four "morning jobs." Generally, the jobs included copying a short group-composed story from the board or making a personal journal entry in which they were asked to respond to the story read during story time, and then working on two or three dittos. The worksheets involved traditional skillsheet activities, including filling in blanks, matching, coloring, etc., with a focus on letters, words, and numbers.

Whether they were reading orally or previewing a worksheet in reading group, the children took turns, always working "round robin" starting with the child on Sue's left. In oral reading, each child read one page of text while all of the other members of the group read along silently, pointing to each word as it was read. However, if the reader stumbled on a word or was stuck, other children were discouraged from piping up with the correct word.

Sue applied the same rules to herself in working with children who were struggling. When children were stuck she allowed a few minutes to let them "do their own reading work," but if they continued to need help, she used one of several approaches:

> If a child gets stuck I try to think through what I know, how that child has processed what he already has read, and I see if I can help him dig the word out for himself. I'll try everything that I can think of without getting too laborious for the rest of the children, to try to find something, some way to help the child dig that apart rather than just tell. (Interview 10/9/85, Woolsey 1986)

A review of field notes indicates that Sue usually waited until a child had read the entire page before she interrupted with prompts or questions. According to her, "this gives them every opportunity that the page will give them to correct their own error." At this point, Sue often asked children to reread a sentence or the entire page. If the child made the same miscue, she asked questions designed to get children to attend to certain aspects of the text (e.g., "Does that look like went?"; "Does that sound right to say 'Came Ana said Grandma'?"; "You read 'Do not make it in said Grandma.' Does that make sense?"—all taken from video transcript 9/25/85). As a last resort she would simply provide the correct word and allow the oral reading to continue. This practice of allowing the child time for doing work on unknown words is clearly the result of Sue's work with Reading Recovery, as are the prompts that focus children on various language cueing systems.

For the first month of school Sue's methods of reading instruction continued relatively unchanged. However, in early October some changes were evident, particularly in her work with the two lowest groups—the groups that included the Reading Recovery children. Earlier in the year, this group seldom read whole texts, focusing instead on letters and sounds and high-frequency words using flash cards, games, and worksheets. By mid-October all of the children were reading whole texts during small-group instruction. However, rather than reading from the basal, this group often read from supplementary paperback reading materials, such as the highly patterned Price-Merrill Instant Readers and the Breakthrough to Literacy books. Sometimes they engaged in enthusiastic choral readings of well-known and loved story-time books, such as *Brown Bear, Brown Bear, What do You See?* (Martin 1967). Since these were the simple and predictable books with which the children enjoyed much success in Reading Recovery lessons, it was not surprising to find them also cropping up in classroom instruction.

In late November and December another change was seen: all of the groups read from the basal series. Further, though the students still read orally for at least part of the group time, more time was devoted to skills work utilizing the skill sheets provided by the basal series. Conversations with Sue during this part of the year showed that she was consciously giving more attention to skills work, acutely aware of the forces that drove her to it and torn by it all:

> You know, I was trying to decide what worksheets the various groups would do, and I realized that [the basal] has you. I kept saying, "I won't do that one or that one," but then I realized that I had to do some of them or these kids would never be able to take the tests. So there are things I don't like in the way I teach reading. There is a real pull here. You know, you're a hypocrite because you're doing one thing because you're expected to and then you're torn to do another. I've had to zip back to more of those dittos because it was just said in a staff meeting the other day that we've got to send scores in on each child. I've not turned a test in . . . so the heat's starting to come.

I would much rather spend all of my time reading with these kids but I can't get them through what they have to know for that stupid reading series. (Interview 12/12/85, Woolsey 1986)

Sue was caught in a dilemma. Her beliefs about reading and literacy instruction and her usual ways of structuring that instruction were being challenged by her work with Reading Recovery and other university classes. However, she also was keenly aware of the expectations and priorities being pressed upon her by the school system and by her administrator. Although Sue had some freedom to create and implement literacy instruction in her classroom, the presence of the curriculum selected by her school district and the expectation of regular testing weighed heavily upon her. Obviously, there were numerous and sometimes conflicting forces influencing the work of Sue and her first graders.

Outside of formal reading instruction where there were no test scores to report to the principal, Sue had more freedom to experiment with the ideas and methods learned in her inservice classes. As the year progressed, Sue's wider literacy program showed more reliance on a rich variety of genuine experiences with reading and writing and less upon the structured instructional materials provided by her school system. As we shall see, this experimentation even took over the formal instruction in the spring.

One example of increasing freedom and the use of authentic reading materials lies in the use of trade books rather than the basal. Over the summer Sue and Joan had worked hard to build the classroom library up to about four hundred titles and, in contrast to previous years, story time became a daily event. In September, trade books were read only in the free time after the "morning jobs," but soon they began to appear in reading group as well. Further, Sue gave the children steadily increasing opportunities to select books and to read independently or with their peers.

Independent reading took place at two points in the morning: just after arrival and simultaneously with classroom business, and during reading work time. Starting in October, children found a book on their desks when they entered the classroom in the morning. Mostly these were the little paperback books from the classroom library, including caption books from Price-Merrill Instant Readers and supplementary readers from various basal series. Sue selected them especially for each child with the intent of providing recreational reading. Again, we see the influence of Reading Recovery in the regular classroom, for Sue's motives and decision-making process in selecting books for each child were very similar to those involved in the daily selection of a new book for a Reading Recovery student, with attention given to what the child knows and can do with print.

The children were invited to read their books on their own and then again for their neighbors, and they were allowed to continue while Sue took lunch count. A steady hum filled the room as children read and talked about their books, often exchanging books or selecting other books from the chalk tray.

Sue referred to these as "practice books" and the children were encouraged to make use of them at several points in the morning. One of the "jobs" often assigned during reading work time was to read these books again by themselves or with a friend. On several occasions, though exclusively with the two lower-ability groups, She had children bring their practice books to reading group where they took turns reading for each other.

Independent reading provided a special time when all children were encouraged to engage in reading. As such, it was an advance from the previous when-your-work-is-done method. As would be expected, children were given the opportunity to make their own selections as the year progressed. In December and thereafter Sue encouraged students to make their own selections and to keep these books in their desks.

Another move toward authentic reading came in December and thereafter when time was devoted exclusively to reading and sharing, so that children did not have to carry on in hushed tones and a divided ear while business was conducted. Although it was called sustained silent reading, it seldom was silent. Children moved about the room as necessary to look for books or other literacy materials. While there was a special emphasis on reading with a friend, individual reading was also valued and a steady buzz of voices filled the room. During this time Sue moved among the children, helping them to locate books, serving as an audience for their readings and encouraging them.

In February and March, independent reading was enhanced by the addition of a richer variety of reading materials, including special book collections from the public library, big books, and poems, captions, and story charts mounted on the walls. An excerpt from the field notes provides a snapshot of this busy time:

> April uses a pointer to read *Velveteen Rabbit* captions, moving left to right across the length of the bulletin board and reading out loud. She is soon joined by Conchata. They read in unison, April wielding the pointer.

Steven, Kelly, Randy, Antiwonne, and Cindy crowd around the new book collection in the reading center, pulling books out, glancing through them, and exclaiming about what they're finding.

Scott, Angela, and Todd are looking at books at their adjacent desks. They have stumbled on three copies of *Little Bear*. They exult in this discovery, flipping through the books, finding illustrations that interest them and making an effort to stay on the same page. They point out that they have the same book to everyone who comes by, and eventually settle down side by side on the front rug. Scott, who is clearly the leader, begins reading out loud while the others follow in their copies.

Carlos and Steven are in the reading center. Steven sits on a chair with the big book of *Mrs. Wishy Washy* on his lap. Carlos stands beside him and both children read aloud.

Sue is excited by all of the reading that's going on. She has been talking and reading with various children. As she walks by she mutters, "Oh, how I hate to cut this off." Five minutes later she turns the lights off to call the children to order, telling them, "I hate to stop all this beautiful reading and sharing, but we have to take lunch count. We'll do some more after that." She takes a very quick lunch count while children continue to look at books and chatter at their desks. After three or four minutes, she turns them loose on reading again, and the children respond with continued enthusiasm. (Field notes 4/5/86, Woolsey 1986)

As the school year progressed scenes like this one generally took place at least two times during the morning: just after arrival and before story time, and once again toward the end of reading work time. Gradually, independent reading, story time, and shared writing experiences consumed the lion's share of the morning. By the end of February, Sue met less and less with the reading groups, preferring instead to circulate around the room and work with individual children. One day as they stood in the room looking at children busily at work all around them, she commented to me, "Why should we have reading groups? The children have already done all kinds of reading today!" (field notes 2/25/86, Woolsey 1986). Rather than meeting with reading groups she worked with individual children all morning, having them read their stories to her and helping them work on writing their own stories. Several days later, Sue decided to do away with reading groups for the three weeks that remained before Easter vacation:

> I'm sending them the wrong messages . . . Last Friday I was
> very involved with the children, but yesterday didn't go so well
> and part of it was that . . . I was doing something else with the
> reading groups. (Field notes 3/5/86, Woolsey 1986)

In April Sue resumed basal work with the reading groups
because, as she explained, "I'm getting the word from the principal
that I have to really dig in and see what these kids can do in terms
of what [the basal] wants them to do" (field notes 4/9/86, Woolsey
1986). However, she also managed to come to a compromise that
allowed the children to work independently and in small groups on
genuine literacy tasks. Typically, she met with reading groups with
basal materials two or three days a week and then she concentrated
on "whole-language" activities on the other days.

Although she was taking time with the basal because she felt
she had to, it was apparent that Sue placed the highest value on the
learning that was taking place as children read and reread favorite
and familiar stories, as they talked and worked together on writing
and reading. Sue herself was quite aware of the ways in which this
scenario contrasted with her reading program early in the year:

> At the beginning of the year I was torn between following the
> [basal] or going with whole language. Now, I basically tolerate
> the basal, but I've gone much more with whole language. You
> know: reading aloud and shared writing, letting the children do
> a lot of discussing and developing their own language, whether
> they discuss with me or whether they share and talk with one
> another . . . I find myself not preplanning lessons as much, but
> listening more to what the children are talking about and key-
> ing in on teaching them right there and then what they bring
> up. (Interviews 3/20/86 and 4/17/86, Woolsey 1986)

This move away from activities prescribed by a basal series and the
teacher to activities that centered upon and emerged from children's intentions, is another instance of the influence of Reading
Recovery training. Rather than relying on a sequence of activities
created by the experts (i.e., basal authors), Sue was making on-the-
spot decisions about student strengths and needs and planning
instructional strategies accordingly.

In this chapter I have presented a picture of the ways in which
one first-grade teacher was influenced in her beliefs about and
actual practice of literacy instruction as a result of her work with
Reading Recovery. Obviously, the impact of Reading Recovery was

great, but it was offset by other forces at work on this teacher and her classroom. Figure 9–1 represents a summary of the forces, external as well as internal, that impinged upon the literacy learning program in this classroom.

Helpful insights into the nature of these forces for change are provided by George Kelly in his work *A Theory of Personality: The Psychology of Personal Constructs* (1955). Like other theorists (e.g., Piaget, Britton, F. Smith, J. Bruner) Kelly posited that to be human is constantly to seek to make sense of our experience in the world. He argued that personal constructs are the templates with which we shape and organize our representations of that experience.

• •

FIGURE 9–1   EXTERNAL AND INTERNAL FORCES FOR TEACHER CHANGE

INTERNAL FORCES:

Personal history of
literacy learning

Personal experience
as a learner

Personal experiences
as a teacher

Ongoing observations
of students

Reading, thinking
and talking

EXTERNAL FORCES:

Systemic expectations
and mandates

Colleagues' expectations

Pre-service and
in-service training

Community expectations
and pressures

TEACHER:

Understandings, beliefs and theories

Techniques for organizing instruction

Strategies for implementing instruction

Expectations of children and their potential progress

Self-perceptions as a teacher and learner

Kelly wrote about the conditions that are favorable to the formation of new constructs and those that are unfavorable. These are pertinent to our discussion of the changes seen in Sue's classroom. Kelly's conditions are as follows:

Favorable Conditions	*Unfavorable Conditions*
1. Use of fresh elements.	1. Threat to core constructs.
2. Experimentation with limited consequences.	2. Preoccupation with old constructs.
3. Availability of validating.	3. No laboratory.

Reading Recovery and other coursework at Ohio State University offered Sue a set of fresh elements and a laboratory setting (i.e., the Reading Recovery inservice sessions and teaching) in which to experiment with new ideas and ways of approaching literacy instruction. When she was asked how she could explain changes in her literacy program, Sue responded:

> Well, certainly Reading Recovery, working with you and Joan [her team teacher], Dr. Huck, and other classes at Ohio State . . . the readings that I've done, like *Becoming a Nation of Readers* [Anderson et al. 1985] and studies of children who are successful in learning to read, what Marie Clay was saying about what they do in New Zealand schools. I had to rely on those readings and those people to have the nerve to change from what the school system is saying is Gospel, and then once I had the nerve to change, I guess the thing that sparked me from there on was the children's enthusiasm and their success. (Interview 4/17/86, Woolsey 1986)

This quotation also indicates the presence of the third element conducive to changing constructs; in observing her students' success and enthusiasm for reading and writing, Sue received support and confirmation of her decision to try new approaches to instruction.

Obviously, unfavorable conditions were also present and competing with the positive conditions noted above. There was subtle as well as very direct pressure from administrators and peers to follow the basal's sequence of skill-learning activities and tests. These pressures, particularly the demand for test scores, created a situation in which Sue's new constructs were threatened and she could no longer "experiment with limited consequences" except in her informal literacy program.

In the spring, with a rich foundation of readings, two years of inservice training, and collaboration with her team teacher and the researcher, Sue had the support that she needed to make changes even in her formal literacy program. She developed ways to meet the demands of the system while still implementing her own "underground" literacy-learning program. Change is seldom painless or quick. In order to implement new approaches to literacy instruction teachers need the fresh ideas and long-term support provided by inservice programs such as Reading Recovery. Further, those supervising that inservice training need to be sensitive to other forces and pressures that affect literacy instruction.

REFERENCES

Anderson, S. 1986. "Creating a Supportive Classroom." Paper presented at Ohio Reading Recovery Conference, Columbus.

Anderson, R., E. Hiebert, J. Scott, and I. Wilkinson. 1985. *Becoming a Nation of Readers: The Report of the Commission on Reading.* Washington, D.C.: National Institute of Education.

Busis, A., E. Chittenden, and M. Amarel. 1976. *Beyond Surface Curriculum: An Interview Study of Teachers' Understandings.* Boulder, Colo.: Westview Press.

Clark, C., and P. Peterson. 1986. "Teachers' Thought Processes." In M. C. Wittrock, ed., *Handbook of Research on Teaching,* 3d ed., 255–96. New York: Macmillan.

Clay, M. 1979. *Reading: The Patterning of Complex Behavior.* 2d ed. Portsmouth, N.H.: Heinemann.

———. 1985. *The Early Detection of Reading Difficulties.* 3d ed. Portsmouth, N.H.: Heinemann.

DeFord, D. 1978. "A Validation Study of an Instrument to Determine a Teacher's Theoretical Orientation to Reading Instruction." Ph.D. diss., Indiana University.

———. 1985. "Validating the Construct of Theoretical Orientation in Reading Instruction." *Reading Research Quarterly* 20: 351–66.

Harste, J., and C. Burke. 1977. "A New Hypothesis for Reading Teacher Research: Both the Teaching and Learning of Reading are Theoretically Based." In D. P. Pearson, ed., *Reading: Theory, Research and Practice* (26th Yearbook of the National Reading Conference), 32–40. New York: Mason.

Kelly, G. 1955. *A Theory of Personality: The Psychology of Personal Constructs.* New York: Norton.

Martin, Bill, Jr. 1967. *Brown Bear, Brown Bear, What Do You See.* Illus. by Eric Carle. New York: Harper and Row.

Pinnell, G. S., and D. P. Woolsey. 1985. "Report of a Study of Teacher Researchers in a Program to Prevent Reading Failure." Report to the Research Foundation of the National Council of Teachers of English.

Shavelson, R. 1983. "Review of Research on Teachers' Pedagogical Judgments, Plans and Decisions." *Elementary School Journal* 83: 392–413.

Woolsey, D. P. 1986. "First Grade Children's Responses to Teacher Change in Literacy Contexts." Ph.D. diss., Ohio State University.

TEN

·············

Helping a Learning-Disabled Child Enter the Literate World

CAROL A. LYONS

··························· T ··························
he learning disability field has
been plagued by contradictions and controversy for the past
twenty-five years. A major reason for the obvious confusion is that
leading researchers in the field have never agreed on how to define
learning disability or how to identify children as learning disabled
(Ysseldyke, Algozzine, & Epps 1983). Berry and Kirk (1980) evaluated the best scientific studies in the field and concluded that the
results were uninterpretable because the subjects in the studies
could not be clearly defined. Yet in some school districts in the
United States, children are tested by local professionals and classified as learning disabled at the beginning of first grade (Lyons 1989).

In addition to the problems associated with a term that defies
definition, the learning-disability field has been marked by a lack of
effective instructional programs with well researched successful
results (Gittelman 1985). In a review of the research on various
treatments for learning disabilities, Clay (1987) concludes that children who are below their classmates in reading achievement are
learning to be learning disabled, because the teaching they receive
in class is not appropriate for their idiosyncratic needs. Furthermore, when special small-group or individual instruction is available, it is focused on small segments of reading and writing, rather
than directed toward reconstructing and restoring the whole, integrated response network involved when one reads (Clay 1987).

There is, however, an early intervention program, Reading Recovery, that has been rigorously researched (Lyons 1989a; 1989b) and found to be very successful with first-grade children who fall into the bottom 20 percent of their respective classes and who are further classified as learning disabled by professionals prior to placement in the program. A research study (Lyons 1989b) compares two groups of Ohio first-grade students having reading difficulties. The students in one group were diagnosed as learning disabled; the other group was composed of students who were *not* diagnosed as learning disabled but who were having reading difficulties. Both of these groups received daily, thirty-minute Reading Recovery instruction in the first grade. Examination of their reading strategies at the beginning of the Reading Recovery program showed that the group identified as learning disabled tended to overrely on visual/auditory cues and to ignore supporting language, while the group not identified as learning disabled tended to overrely on meaning and structure and to underemphasize visual/auditory cues. In an average of 63.13 lessons of Reading Recovery instruction, 73.3 percent of the students identified as learning disabled reached average reading levels in their respective classrooms and were discontinued (released) from the program. These results suggested that students identified as learning disabled often received exactly the wrong kind of special early instruction, which typically stresses limited reading strategies. Reading Recovery offered a promising way to help such students develop the full range of reading strategies they needed to become successful readers and thus prevented many of them from being mislabeled as learning disabled.

Reading Recovery is *not*, however, a learning-disability program. The program is designed to provide instruction to the least able 20 percent of first-grade readers in the education system—not excluding anyone—and to help them reach a level of achievement equal to the average of their class, thus placing them out of the remedial track. Research (Lyons 1989a) also suggests that the program can help educators define the term *learning disabled* more accurately and thus provide a way to eliminate some of the burgeoning population of students diagnosed as learning disabled (Singer & Butler 1987).

Reading Recovery *is* a second-chance first-grade program with daily, thirty-minute individual lessons supplementing regular classroom instruction for twelve to twenty weeks. It was developed and initiated in New Zealand by Marie Clay, a developmental child psychologist. The goal of the program is accelerated progress.

Acceleration is achieved as the child takes over the learning process and works independently, continuously discovering new things and relating them to prior knowledge.

According to Clay, "acceleration depends upon the teacher's selection of the clearest, easiest, most memorable examples with which to establish a new response, skill, principle, or procedure" (1979, p. 53). It is essential that the teacher follow the child, designing a superbly sequenced program determined by the child's needs and then making highly skilled decisions throughout the lesson, moment by moment, to help the child make accelerated progress.

Reading Recovery teachers learn how to observe and assess the reading and writing strengths of children and design intervention strategies to meet individual learning needs in a yearlong inservice program. Some Reading Recovery teachers, however, become more skillfull in implementing *effective* individual programs than others. For example, during the 1986–1987 school year, 25 of the 310 Reading Recovery teachers in Ohio successfully discontinued three or more children in forty lessons (eight weeks) or less (Lyons 1987). Further examination of their instructional programs revealed that these teachers recognized the teachable moments throughout the lesson: moments when the students could be taught how to use what they knew to develop new understanding. These effective teachers used a repertoire of actions and responses to facilitate accelerative progress. One of these very successful teachers, however, failed in her attempts to help Ryan, a child identified in kindergarten as learning disabled. Mary initially thought Ryan's inability to accelerate was the result of his learning disability. In this chapter you will learn how and why Mary changed her mind.

INSTRUCTIONALLY DISABLED, NOT LEARNING DISABLED

Mary was very concerned about the lack of progress of a first-grade boy she had been tutoring in the Reading Recovery program for six weeks. Ryan had been stuck on level 5, equivalent to a preprimer 1, for more than three weeks. This was the first time Mary had ever experienced difficulty in accelerating a child in the three years she had been teaching Reading Recovery.

Mary had asked several colleagues to observe her teaching Ryan. All concluded that the major reason Ryan was not accelerating was that he belonged to that group of children Marie Clay refers to as third-wave children, who need to be referred to professionals for further testing and placement (Clay 1987). Decisions for removing a student from the program are always carefully weighed and require a second opinion from an experienced teacher leader. (Teacher leaders prepare Reading Recovery teachers). Therefore I was asked to confirm the teacher's suspicions and recommend that Ryan be removed from Reading Recovery and placed in a special program. Before making that decision, however, I asked to observe not only Ryan's lesson but the lessons of the other Reading Recovery students Mary taught. The following portions of each of the four childrens' lessons reveal how Mary enabled all but one of her students to develop strategies that facilitated accelerative learning. That one student was Ryan.

MARY AND MELISSA • Melissa is in her third week of lessons. She is attempting to integrate the meaning, structure, and visual cuing systems. To become an independent reader, the child must learn to search for and use all three types of cues in flexible ways. Mary's questions and Melissa's responses demonstrate early stages of developing the strategy to search for cues in sentence structure (syntax), cues from the message (semantics), and cues from the letters (graphics). The text reads: "I wave to my friend, the car driver."

MELISSA: *(Reading)* "I will to my friend, the car driver."
MARY: You said, "I will to my friend, the car driver." Does that sound right?
MELISSA: No.

The teacher is developing the child's ability to search for cues in sentence structure. Melissa is a competent language user and Mary is teaching her to use her oral language and personal grammar to read the words.

MARY: "I will to my friend, the car driver." Does that make sense?
MELISSA: No, that sounds silly!

The teacher is developing the child's ability to search for meaning cues. Mary is asking the question "Does that make sense?" to help Melissa understand that reading involves messages expressed in language that must make sense. The teacher, through appropriate questioning, is demonstrating that when Melissa reads, she should use her knowledge of oral and written language to gain meaning. Melissa is being taught a set of operations or strategies for problem solving in order to read more difficult bits of text. Mary is deliberately teaching Melissa how to solve new problems (figuring out the word *wave*) with familiar information.

MARY: You said, "I will to my friend, the car driver." Does this word (*points to the word* wave) look like the word *will*?

MELISSA: No.

MARY: What letters would you expect to see if the word was *will*?

MELISSA: W, L.

MARY: What letters do you see?

MELISSA: W, A, V, E.

MARY: Look at the picture. What is the boy doing? What is the car driver doing?

MELISSA: They are waving to each other.

MARY: What do you think that word could be?

MELISSA: *Wave*.

MARY: Does *wave* make sense?

MELISSA: Yes. "I wave to my friend, the car driver."

MARY: Does "wave to my friend, the car driver" sound right?

MELISSA: Yes.

MARY: Does the word look right?

MELISSA: The letters make *wave*.

MARY: I like the way you figured that all out.

The teacher's questioning shows the child how to cross-check the meaning and structure cue with graphic information. Melissa is able to predict the letter she expects to see if the word is *will*. She knows that the word can't be *will* because she doesn't see any *l*'s. The teacher redirects her attention to a meaning cue (the picture on the page) and then asks her to cross-check the meaning cue with a structure cue ("Does that sound right?"). The teacher is teaching for the cross-checking strategy. She is teaching Melissa how she can search for and use structure, meaning, and visual cues to predict an unknown word and then how to check one kind of cue against another. The preceding questioning techniques focus on meaning while Melissa is reading connected text. There are no isolated word or letter drills.

MARY AND MARK • Mark is in his tenth week of lessons. He has read level 9 fluently, searching for and integrating the meaning, structure, and visual cues as Melissa is attempting to do. However, when reading his new text (level 10), Mark hesitates and shows signs of uncertainty when he comes to a difficult word. The text reads: "Lamb went to the bull."

MARK: "Lamb went to the . . ."

MARY: Why did you stop?

MARK: I don't know that word.

MARY: (*Attempts to direct Mark's attention to meaning*) Look at the picture.

MARK: Lamb went to the cow.

MARY: (*Fosters cross-checking one cue [meaning] with another cue [visual] by covering the word* bull *with her finger*) If that word was *cow*, what would you expect to see?

MARK: C.

MARY: (*Uncovers the word*) Could that be *cow*?

MARK: No, it doesn't begin with a C.

MARY: Can you think of another word that would make sense in the sentence and begins with a *B*?

MARK: *Bull.*

MARY: Check to see if what you read looks right [visual], sounds right [syntax/structure], and makes sense [meaning].

MARK: "Lamb went to the bull." Yes, that is the word.

MARY: How do you know?

MARK: Because there is a picture of a bull [meaning cue] and the word begins with a letter *b* [visual cue].

MARY: Great, I like the way you worked at that all by yourself.

Mary's first question, "Why did you stop?" tells Mark that she wants him to monitor his own reading. The fact that he is checking on his own behavior and recognizes that something is wrong is positive. Mary's next set of questions develops Mark's ability to search for and use meaning and visual cues to cross-check one kind of cue against another. She reinforces his self-monitoring and cross-checking attempts.

MARY AND JANIS • Today is Janis's fifty-sixth lesson. She has been in the program for eleven weeks and is reading at level 15. Mary notes that Janis is monitoring her reading, searching for and cross-checking at least two types of information, and self-correcting most of her own errors. This evidence suggests that Janis is ready to be discontinued from the program, but Mary is concerned that Janis relies on her too much. Today Mary is attempting to make Janis more independent by not asking questions when she stops at the word *splits*. The text reads: "The pupa splits. A butterfly comes out."

JANIS: "The pupa (*long hesitation*) spits. A butterfly comes out."

MARY: You made a mistake on that page. Can you find it? (*Janis points to the word* splits.)

MARY: Yes, how did you know?

JANIS: It doesn't make sense.

MARY: What are you going to do?

JANIS: Start over and think of a word that sounds right and makes sense and has the right letters. "The pupa (*long hesitation*) splits. A butterfly comes out."

MARY: I like the way you solved that all by yourself. How did you do it?

JANIS: I know another word that started with *spl* and that word is *splash*. I knew a little word in *splits*—*its*. Then I just put everything together.

Mary had previously taught Janis how to analyze words in text visually by helping her read in chunks. Janis independently applies this knowledge (attaching the *spl* sound to a group of letters rather than each letter) in order to figure out an unknown word (*splits*) from two known words (*splash* and *its*). Janis has demonstrated strategies for independent problem solving.

MARY AND RYAN • Ryan is beginning his sixth week of lessons and has been reading level 5 books for the past three weeks. Ryan relies on visual information exclusively and does not attempt to make sense of what he is reading by using meaning or structural information as Melissa is learning to do in her third week of lessons. In this story, Fantail, a bird, is offered several things to eat. Ryan's substitutions are noted in brackets.

RYAN: "Fantail, Fantail, have some [said] cheese [church]."
"No. No. No. I don't like [little] cheese [church]."

MARY: Look at this word (*points to* some). Look at the third letter. What is that letter?

RYAN: *M.*

MARY: What sound does *m* make?

RYAN: Mmmmm.

MARY: Does the word *said* have the *m* sound?

RYAN: No.

MARY: That word is *some*. Look at this word (*points to* cheese). Look at the fifth letter, what is that letter?

RYAN: *S.*

MARY: What sound does *s* make?

RYAN: Sssss.

MARY: Does this word have the letter *s* in it?

RYAN: No.

MARY: Could that word be *church*?

RYAN: No.

MARY: The word is *cheese*. Look at this word (*points to* like). What is the third letter?

RYAN: *T.*

MARY: Say your alphabet. What comes after *J*?

RYAN: *K.*

MARY: "What sound does *k* make?"

RYAN: Tuh, I mean kuh.

MARY: The word is *like*.

RYAN: "Fantail, Fantail have some [said] peas."
"No. No. No. I don't like [little] peas."
"Fantail, Fantail, have some [said] pie."
"No. No. No. I don't like [little] pie."
"Fantail, Fantail, have this [said] fly."

MARY: (*Spells the word* said *with magnetic letters*) Ryan, here is the word *said*. Does this word (*points to the word* some *in the text*) look like this (*points to word* said)?

RYAN: No.

MARY: What do you hear at the end of the word *said*?

RYAN: *D.*

MARY: Does this word (*points to* some) have a *D* sound in it?

RYAN: No.

MARY: The word is *some*. Find the word *some* in the book. (*Ryan points to the word* some.)

MARY: Find the letter *m*. (*Ryan points to the* m.)

MARY: What is that word?

RYAN: *Some.*

MARY: How do you know?

RYAN: Because it has the letter *m* in it.

MARY: Good.

When the lesson is over I ask Ryan what reading is. He replies, "Saying the right letters."

After the observation, Mary and I discussed Ryan's progress. Mary recalled only one real strength Ryan had—little difficulty in generating a sentence for the writing portion of the lesson. She was quick to add, however, that Ryan experienced more difficulty generating the sentence as the weeks progressed. This concerned her because Ryan had adequate language and was one of the more articulate children she had worked with in the Reading Recovery program over the past three years. She attributed this to the fact that he was in a literature-based reading program and had many classroom opportunities to discuss and share ideas orally.

Mary was able to discuss and describe in detail Ryan's problems. Ryan's major weakness, demonstrated in all parts of the lesson, was his the inability to use visual information. He did not integrate the meaning, structure, and visual cuing systems as the other three children did, because "he did not know his sounds." Lately, he was even experiencing difficulty remembering the letter names and sounds, which I observed in the lesson. This too was a surprise because he had scored 50 out of a possible 54 in letter identification on the Diagnostic Survey (Clay 1985).

Ryan seemed to have control of some of the early strategies (e.g., one-to-one matching, directional movement), but he couldn't locate an unknown word or letter even when prompted with a visual cue. Since Ryan did not have control of these very early strategies, Mary was not having any success teaching for strategies. He did not monitor his reading, search for other cues, cross-check one cue with another, or self-correct. Mary concluded that Ryan was "stuck because he could not use visual information."

As I listened to Mary discuss Ryan's lack of progress, several questions came to mind. First, why, when working with Ryan, did Mary abandon what she knew about teaching for strategies? Second, why did she have a less flexible view of Ryan's strengths? Third, why did Mary's attitude about Ryan's ability change? Finally, why did Mary change her instructional program so drastically when she taught Ryan?

I repeated some of the specific questions Mary asked Ryan, commenting on how they differed from ones she asked the other three children. Mary said that she had to shift her questioning techniques because Ryan was learning disabled and therefore needed a firm foundation in sound/symbol relationships before she could begin to teach for specific strategies. When Ryan began to regress in spite of an instructional program specifically designed to meet his needs, Mary concluded that Ryan should be placed in a learning-disabled class.

I supported Mary's concerns about Ryan's lack of progress and opened our conversation by repeating something she had said at the beginning of the conference: Ryan had adequate language and was one of the more articulate children she had ever taught in the Reading Recovery program. If he was a competent language user in the classroom and brought his knowledge of the world and experience to gain meaning in the beginning of the program, why had his behavior changed to exclude the supportive language he had good control of? We discussed the parts of the lesson that demonstrated Ryan's overattention to visual information. I asked Mary what Ryan had said at the close of the lesson when I asked him what reading is. Mary recalled that Ryan said "saying the right letters." She concluded that he was behaving in a way that really supported what he thought reading was—that is, he was saying the right letters.

Next I asked Mary what reading is. She quickly responded, "Gaining meaning from the printed page." We then looked at the type of questions Mary asked Ryan throughout the lesson. It didn't take her long to realize that she was confirming Ryan's assumption that reading is "saying the right letters"!

In examining parts of the other three children's lessons, it was obvious that Mary's questions supported the integration of all three cuing systems and were meaning-driven. For three of the four children, Mary's actions supported her definition of reading. For the fourth student, Ryan, Mary thought she needed to devise a different instructional plan. After examining her teaching decisions, Mary understood that once she taught Ryan how to use and integrate strategies for independent problem solving, he too would accelerate.

The following week I observed Ryan's lesson. The text reads: "Up, up, up came little spider, to see what he could see."

RYAN: "Up, up, up can, I mean came, little spider, to see what he can, could, see."

MARY: I like how you changed *can* to *came*. Why couldn't that word be *can*?

RYAN: Because "up, up, up can little spider" doesn't sound right.

MARY: That's right! I like how you started over and tried to make the sentence sound right. Does it make sense too?

RYAN: Yes.

MARY: You also made another good self-correction when you said to see what he could see. How did you know to change that?

RYAN: Because if it were *can*, I would see an *n* and there is no *n*, so it has to be a word with a *d* and *could* is the word with a *d* that sounds right.

MARY: I am so proud of how you are making sense of what you read and checking to see if the words look right. That is just what good readers always do.

It was obvious that Mary had started to teach for strategies and that Ryan was now on his way to accelerative learning. Seven weeks later he was discontinued from the program.

CONCLUSION

Ryan's initial oral pattern of response, overattention to visual information, is consistent with studies examining oral reading behaviors of "learning disabled" students receiving Reading Recovery instruction (Lyons 1989b). Students diagnosed as learning disabled tend to rely on visual information and ignore or exclude the supportive language they control. Once the teacher brings in the language side, as Mary did, accelerative learning does occur.

The findings in this study also suggest that differences in reading patterns of behavior among "learning disabled" and other failing children are learned, and therefore can be unlearned. The earlier the instructional emphasis is changed, the sooner the child shifts to more appropriate responses. Clay (1987) argues that only a small percentage of low-achieving readers (1–2 percent) will not make accelerative progress in the Reading Recovery program. Although not the case in the data analyzed here, this small percentage of children may have neurological problems and require more extensive testing.

Finally, Ryan's definition of reading may have contributed to his reading problems. Unwittingly, Mary reinforced and confirmed his notion of reading by asking questions that focused on visual information to the exclusion of meaning and language structure. The instructional program thus helped Ryan learn to be learning disabled. If he were placed in a program for learning-disabled youngsters, would his concept of reading be confirmed and reinforced?

In every classroom in the elementary school, teachers are confronted with children who are having difficulty learning to read. In light of the findings reported in this chapter, classroom teachers should ask themselves several questions. First, what is their definition of reading? Second, does the instructional program they implement adequately reflect and support what their definition of reading implies? Third, do they believe the concept of reading is different and must change to meet the needs of specific populations of children such as learning-disabled readers? Fourth, does their instructional program change to fit a different concept of reading for special populations? Finally, are they excellent teachers who may have fallen into the same trap Mary did?

We need to reexamine our beliefs and instructional programs for all at-risk readers, especially those classified as learning disabled. Perhaps some of these children are not learning disabled but instructionally disabled, and, as Marie Clay (1987) argues, learning to be disabled.

REFERENCES

Berry, P., & D. A. Kirk. 1980. "Issues in Special Learning Disabilities: Towards a Data Base for Decision-Making." *Exceptional Child* 27: 115–25.

Clay, M. M. 1979. *The Early Detection of Reading Difficulties.* 2d ed. Portsmouth, N.H.: Heinemann.

———. 1987. "Learning to Be Learning Disabled." *New Zealand Journal of Educational Studies* 22: 155–73.

Gittelman, R. 1985. "Controlled Trials of Remedial Approaches to Reading Disability." *Journal of Child Psychiatry* 26: 843–46.

Lyons, C. A. 1987. "Helping Slow Readers Make Accelerated Progress: Teacher Responses and Knowledge." Paper presented at the annual meeting of the National Reading Conference, St. Petersburg, Florida.

———. 1989a. "Reading Recovery: An Effective Early Intervention Program That Can Prevent Mislabeling Children as Learning Disabled." *Spectrum* 7: 3–9.

———. 1989b. "Reading Recovery: A Preventative for Mislabeling Young 'At-Risk' Learners." *Urban Education* 24: 125–39.

Singer, J. D. & J. A. Butler. 1987. "The Education for All Handicapped Children Act: Schools as Agents of Social Reform." *Harvard Educational Review* 57: 125–82.

Ysseldyke, J., B. Algozzine, & S. Epps. 1983. "A Logical and Empirical Analysis of Current Practice in Classifying Students as Handicapped." *Exceptional Children* 50: 160–66.

ELEVEN

••••••••••••••••••••••

Literacy in the Classroom

CHARLOTTE S. HUCK   GAY SU PINNELL

*H*ow can school make a differ-
ence in the lives of young children? One obvious answer is by
teaching literacy and doing it so effectively that they become
lifelong learners who can continue to learn while they read and
write and, in the process, become better readers and writers. The
question is particularly important for those children who, for lack
of experience or other reasons, find their first school introduction
to reading and writing very difficult. Most children move quickly
into reading and writing, but some appear to lag behind, to be
confused, and to profit little from class instruction. We see them
sitting in classrooms, dawdling for hours over impossibly complex
exercises. Patient teachers try with the best of intentions to teach
those children the requisite items of knowledge (for example,
"blends") and understanding of their use in reading and writing,
but many children continue to struggle.

Wells (1986) illustrated children's search for meaning in all they
see, hear, and read. In his first sample, Wells studied 128 children,
observing them from the time they spoke their first words through
to the age of seven. He then followed 32 of them as a group through
their elementary schooling. Two children were highlighted to illustrate his findings: Rosie, the child with the lowest scores on all the
tests administered (including Marie Clay's *Concepts of Print* [1985])
and Jonathan, who had the highest scores. After five years of
schooling their respective positions had not changed. The children

who entered school in the lowest class rankings remained in the lowest rankings throughout their elementary education.

The purpose of this chapter, the last in the collection, is to report ways we have tried to apply the insights gained from Reading Recovery to our work in classrooms. Our goal was to construct knowledge by bringing together what we had learned about teaching young children to read, particularly children who were having difficulty in the beginning stages. Those children need a great deal of support, but they also need to become independent, that is, to "learn how to learn" in reading and writing. In this chapter, we will describe several frameworks and some general approaches for classroom practice that have grown out of our deliberations.

INSIGHTS FROM READING RECOVERY

Reading Recovery provides intensive, individual instruction to help low-achieving children make accelerated progress and catch up with their peers, so that they can profit from ongoing classroom instruction. The general instructional approach of Reading Recovery is to immerse children in reading and rereading little books and in writing and reading their own messages. The teacher works alongside the child to "teach for strategies" while the child is actually engaged in reading and writing. A general lesson framework is used for Reading Recovery; however, within that framework, the program is individually tailored to suit each child's base of knowledge and strengths (see Pinnell, DeFord, & Lyons 1988).

Reading Recovery teachers try to "follow the child" and to make powerful instructional decisions. Through intensive staff-development experiences, teachers sharpen their skills at making and using inferences while teaching. They build a repertoire of teaching techniques and a theoretical framework that serves as a foundation for decisions about using those techniques. The heart of Reading Recovery lies in the moment-to-moment interactions between the teacher and child. The teacher's decisions must be the most powerful for the particular child at the particular point in time in reference to the particular text being read or written.

The instructional techniques used by teachers are designed to help children orchestrate a range of strategies in reading so that they can develop what Clay calls "a self-improving system," the kind that good readers appear to develop without the need for individual, intensive teaching.

Reading Recovery is intended for a particular group—those children who are not making progress even though they are receiv-

ing sound classroom programs. The procedures are specially designed for *individual* teaching and would be impossible to duplicate
in group teaching. While Reading Recovery has many characteristics consistent with New Zealand classroom instruction, for example, using graded natural-language texts or having children write
their own messages, Clay has made it clear that "most children (80
to 90 percent) do *not* need these detailed, meticulous and special
Reading Recovery procedures *or any modification of them:* They will
learn to read more pleasurably without them" (1985, p. 47).

It was not our intent in this project to transplant specific Reading Recovery techniques to the classroom. But we were trying to
use some *classroom* techniques from New Zealand education. We
wanted to promote more engagement in reading and writing meaningful text and at the same time use insights that we and the
teachers had developed through participation in Reading Recovery
teacher training. Concepts such as the orchestration of strategies or
connecting reading and writing apply to successful classroom experiences for all children. Our problem was to define and refine those
ideas that could inform classroom teaching, recognizing that we
did not want to duplicate the combination of procedures necessary
for individual work.

Some simple questions served as a starting point:

1. How could we get more children *actively* involved in reading
   text?
2. How could we help children develop knowledge of the structure of written language, that is, the syntax as well as the story
   structure?
3. How could we help children connect writing and reading?
4. How could we help children examine the visual details of written language without losing purpose and meaning?
5. How could we provide challenge so that children would learn
   to become independent?

Beginning in the fourth year of the project, some experienced
Reading Recovery teachers attempted, with researchers' support,
to use their knowledge and experience to improve their instruction
in settings other than one-to-one tutoring. They had already developed skills for observing and analyzing children's reading and writing behavior and had also learned to interpret those behaviors
through discussions with peers. All had a strong commitment to
teaching children who were having difficulty in school, and all had
experienced success teaching such children in one-to-one settings.

A positive support was that Reading Recovery, and its impact on students and teachers, had captured the attention of administrators in the district. Thus, in this district, the climate was open to change in literacy education.

The researchers were experienced teachers who were teaching children as part of their involvement in the Reading Recovery project. During their two years of trial and reflection, the teacher/ researcher group attempted to bring together four basic frameworks:

1. The group drew insights from their collective experience in implementing the Reading Recovery program in Ohio. They attempted to identify and articulate principles of learning on which their Reading Recovery instruction was based; that is, they utilized Clay's (1979; 1985) work as a starting point for their deliberations.

2. They examined research related to how young children learn to read and write (see Bruner 1983; Vygotsky 1978), including the body of research on emergent literacy (see Teale & Sulzby 1986).

3. Sample instructional plans were drawn from some models for teaching literacy, including (a) *informal education* in the British tradition (King 1974); (b) *integrated, literature-based curriculum* (Cochran-Smith 1984; Holdaway 1979; Huck, Hepler, & Hickman 1987; McKenzie 1988); and (c) *whole language* (Goodman, Smith, Meredith, & Goodman 1987). Those models, or adaptations of them, were generally consistent with the accepted theoretical base. They provided a beginning framework for planning and organizing instructional as well as a rich source of recommendations concerning instructional materials and activities. Using the identified instructional frameworks, teachers then borrowed some skills from the Reading Recovery program, for example, close, systematic observation of reading and writing behavior and the repertoire of teacher-child interactions suggested as "teaching for strategies." In other words, teachers tried to attend to the instruction at two levels: (a) how they planned and organized the general activities used, and (b) how they interacted with individuals and groups during these activities.

4. Group members based their own study procedures on the Reading Recovery staff-development model, which suggests that rather than hearing about and then doing a set of activities or step-by-step procedures, teachers need to develop and use

their analytical skills to adjust and frame instruction for individual children. Reading Recovery teachers' interactions with students come out of a knowledge base that is established through experience and constantly checked with evidence from children's responses. Teachers learning processes were supported by observation, analysis, and group discussion, processes that were used by all three groups of teachers (see Pinnell, DeFord, & Lyons 1988; Pinnell, Fried, & Estice, this volume; Rentel & Pinnell 1987).

Teachers in the group were experienced Reading Recovery teachers and thus were grounded in the theoretical framework developed during their training. All reported that, with varying degrees of success, Reading Recovery had influenced their teaching in classrooms and/or Chapter I settings (see Pinnell, Fried, & Estice, this volume). Members of the study group knew that Reading Recovery was designed for a one-on-one teaching situation and their own experience had told them that (1) the procedures were not directly transferable to group or classroom contexts, and (2) they were not appropriate or necessary for all children. Yet, all teachers taught in urban schools with high proportions of inexperienced readers and they needed to improve their teaching of all of those children. Reading Recovery alone was not sufficient in such settings, because it was not designed to take the place of the classroom experience, even where Reading Recovery was available.

As a result of involvement in Reading Recovery, teachers in the group were dissatisfied with a strict basal reader approach. They believed the system did not meet the needs of the children they taught. A literature-based approach was suggested by Ohio State University faculty for several reasons:

1. Children's literature texts were structured in a way that would provide springboards for shared writing as well as providing a rich source of written language.
2. Children's literature texts would be most likely to interest children so that they would want to hear them and read them a number of times.
3. In the district and among participating teachers there was strong interest in developing curricula for literature-based reading programs.
4. Children's literature offered material most like that used in the Reading Recovery program, from which basic principles were to be drawn.

5. Children's literature offered an alternative to the basal approach with which Reading Recovery teachers were now dissatisfied.

CONSTRUCTING LITERACY LESSONS

During the first year, teachers identified and tried a lesson framework for small-group instruction. In the second year, the framework was refined and extended, and teachers began to puzzle out the kinds of interactions that would be powerful within each of the components. In this section, we will use this framework as a set of recommendations for classroom practice. Although this framework is still being tested empirically, research exists to support the components. We will define, describe, and provide a rationale for each component.

The framework included six recommended approaches or components; however, the order of these components was not specified. Teachers found that they established routines that suited them and their students, but they could vary components according to the way activities developed. It was not necessary, or even desirable, to use every component each day. Longer periods of concentrated time were required for activities such as shared writing, so other activities were skipped to make room. Teachers recommended that reading aloud to children and rereading of familiar stories be included every day, but other activities were varied. Teachers made sure that all components were included over the course of a one-week period. The content of the activities varied according to the teachers' decisions and interests of the children.

Instruction within the lesson framework was based on the premise that at any time, teachers and children had a complex range of options to attend to. Learning opportunities of various kinds were inherent in each component. For example, in a shared-reading activity, children enjoyed repeating a story in unison or noticed words that began with the same letters as their names. Teachers asked children to examine the picture, searching for what would make sense in the text, or to look at a word to confirm their predictions. In shared writing, the teacher might attend to the text structure of a known story or worked to help children write words by saying them slowly and using sound-to-letter correspondence. Decisions were based on the teachers' knowledge of individual children's needs.

READING ALOUD • A key element of any literacy program is the necessity of reading to children every single day, several times a day. Reading to children is probably one of the most researched and proven practices for developing literacy. Thorndike's study of *Reading in Fifteen Different Countries* (1973) showed that children who came from homes that respected reading and who had been read aloud to since an early age were the best readers. This finding was supported in Margaret Clark's study of *Young Fluent Readers* (1976) in Scotland. She showed that children who learned to read before they came to school came from homes that valued reading, for all of them had been read aloud to by their parents or siblings. Many of them used public libraries and one father told wonderful fairy tales every single night. Dolores Durkin's (1966) two studies of *Children Who Read Early*, in both California and New York, showed the same two factors to be operating; she also found that the early readers had the opportunity to do lots of writing. Finally, Gordon Wells (1986) attributes much significance to the power of young children hearing stories read aloud. His longitudinal study focused on four activities that he thought might account for children's differences in reading ability. These included looking at picture books, drawing pictures, writing, and listening to stories. Only the last activity was significantly related to the acquisition of literacy and later to reading comprehension at age seven. Wells estimated that Jonathan, who was at the top of his group throughout school, had heard approximately 6,000 stories read aloud before he started school. Rosie had not heard one.

What is so powerful about this experience? First of all, reading aloud provides a time for children to learn to associate reading with pleasure, with love. Then, hearing the language of a story helps children to explore new structures and uses of language.

Ninio and Bruner (1973), in examining the reading of picture books by a mother and her 8½-month-old child, discovered one of the first consistent language frames in their dialogue. In this interactive pattern, the mother would say, "Look!" and the child would attend to the picture. Then the mother would ask, "What's that?" If the child could not answer, the mother might answer the question herself by saying, "Yes, that's a cow." If the child said, "Cow!" the mother would give immediate feedback and would say, "Good for you! Yes, that's a cow. Remember the cow we saw last week at the farm?" The mother adjusted her language pattern to include and also to extend what the child knew. Bruner used the word *scaffold-*

ing to describe this interaction process. The mother gave support where needed, withdrawing it when the child could do it alone.

Besides building a rich vocabulary by listening and interacting with stories read aloud, children develop a sense of story. They learn that stories have a beginning and an end. They learn to use past tense and develop knowledge of how particular characters will act in a story, such as what a princess, a fox, a wolf, a grandmother, or a stepmother will do. One teacher was reading a story about a sick old lion to a six-year-old. He no longer could hunt, so he had to entice various animals into his cave. He had already eaten an unsuspecting hen and a dog, when a fox came down the road. The child reading the story said, "Bet he won't catch the fox." The teacher said, "How do you know?" "Oh!" he said, "Foxes are the clever ones in stories, they never catch them." Knowing about particular characters helped this child predict the ending of the story.

Finally, in the process of hearing stories, children incidentally learn a great deal about the concepts related to print: for example, where to begin, the directionality of print, what a word is, and the one-to-one relationship of printed words to spoken language. Through experience with literature, children develop what Don Holdaway (1979) refers to as a "literacy set" for learning to read.

If children's preschool experiences have not prepared them for learning to read with ease, then the school must provide the necessary experiences so that children can make the links. Cohen (1968) explored the effects of a yearlong read-aloud program on second-grade children's learning to read in school. This study was later replicated by Cullinan, Jaggar, and Strickland (1974) with the same results. Cohen's study in New York City included ten experimental classes and ten control classes. Teachers of the experimental classes were sent a list of books and asked to read aloud every day for twenty minutes. They also agreed to do something with the story to make it memorable: to dramatize it, to make paper-bag puppets, to retell it, to discuss it—something to revisit that story. At the end of the year, the experimental group was significantly ahead of the control group in reading vocabulary and reading comprehension, at least as measured by standardized tests. Evidently, reading to children had helped them to learn to read.

In this literacy project, teachers read to the children daily, often several books each day. Some books were new; others were favorites they wanted to read again. Through hearing written language read aloud, children increased their knowledge of text structure and of the syntax of written English. The teacher provided a model of oral reading; often the children joined in on predictable phrases.

The books were carefully selected to support children's linking of one text with another and to build knowledge of text structure.

SHARED READING • Holdaway (1979) developed and wrote about a way to help inexperienced children participate in the act of reading by joining in as the teacher reads. He called this process shared reading. All the children can see the text. They see the teacher pointing to the words just the way a parent would, showing where to begin, predicting what will happen, joining in on the refrain, and, ultimately, helping children act like readers.

In New Zealand classrooms five- to six-year-olds have many big books. These books are first introduced carefully and then read and reread. Using pointers, children in groups of twos and threes read big books together. Many of these books have patterned texts, such as Bill Martin's well-loved *Brown Bear, Brown Bear, What Do You See?* (1983). Favorite nursery rhymes such as Jack and Jill and songs such as "The Old Lady Who Swallowed a Fly" or "Over in the Meadow" are also used. One of the very easiest patterned books is Brian Wildsmith's *Cat on the Mat* (1983). It begins simply: "The cat sat on the mat." The story builds with different animals sitting on the mat until the cat hisses, scaring them all away. Children get to the page just before the cat spits and frightens all the other animals away, and become so excited they can't wait to make the cat sound. A simple story, yet it has a recognizable climax and a satisfying ending.

Another story that the children love is *The Greedy Cat* by Joy Cowley (1983). In this tale, a young mother goes off shopping followed by a thin greedy cat. By the end of the story, the thin greedy cat is a fat cat who has stolen mother's sausages, sticky buns, potato chips, bananas, and chocolate. On the next trip, the mother buys a large pot of pepper—and this is the end of Greedy Cat's thievery!

REREADING STORIES • In each classroom, there was a collection of books for children to use for independent reading. This collection included literature that had been read aloud to the children; some of these selections were too difficult for the children to read independently (such as Jacobs' *The Story of The Three Pigs* [1980]) but they could read familiar refrains or approximate the texts. For most of their own reading, however, they chose to go to the texts over which they had more control. They selected books from a collection that included big books made by teachers and children, published little books with natural language texts, and books written by children.

In familiar rereading, children had a chance to use searching and checking strategies "on the run" while reading extended texts. They could work out problems for themselves because the reading was at a very easy level. This experience allowed them to use their knowledge of letter-sound relationships, language structure, words, and the like, along with their knowledge of the story to check whether it made sense. Every child had a chance to read fluently with phrasing—in other words, to behave like a "good reader."

The value of the experience was evident. Once a week, one of the first-grade teachers copied down the names of the books the children were reading during reading time. The teacher used to be concerned when week after week children would give the title of *The Very Hungry Caterpillar* (Carle 1981) or *Where's Spot?* (Hill 1980) until she realized that this was a book that they were really reading, and they were enjoying the power of reading it over and over again. As children share the excitement of books with a teacher who is equally enthusiastic, they become members of what Smith (1978) refers to as the "literacy club."

Up to this point we've talked about reading aloud both at home and at school, and ways to replicate the home read-aloud situation in school through the use of big books and shared reading. We also want to emphasize the importance of having time every day for children to read books of their own choosing. Frank Smith's (1978) statement "We learn to read by reading" is true. Children must have time to read, to reread, and to share ideas about their reading. Today, there is pitifully little time in reading class devoted to actual reading. R. C. Anderson, E. Hiebert, J. Scott and I. Wilkinson report in *Becoming a Nation of Readers* (1985) that the average amount of time spent in reading at home is four minutes a day. Compare that to the latest figures on television viewing in which the television is supposedly on seven hours and ten minutes per day. We used to say that children learn to read at school and become readers at home. That is no longer true. If they are going to become readers they have to become readers at school.

WRITING • We have learned from Reading Recovery that writing is a key activity in literacy learning. Anderson (1985) decried our overreliance on workbooks and skill sheets, maintaining that 70 percent of children's entire reading instructional time is devoted to this kind of activity and that it is totally unrelated to year-by-year gains in reading proficiency. He urged teachers to encourage children to do more independent reading and real writing rather this kind of senseless activity, which frequently fragments the reading task.

Moira McKenzie (1985) and teachers in London have been highly successful in providing shared writing experiences for children. This "shared writing" parallels the shared reading experiences previously discussed. A group of children help to dictate a story as the teacher writes. In that way, the process is like the language experience approach, but there are some important differences. The collaboratively composed text is usually based on literature that has been read to children. The text is first discussed and planned by teacher and children. The final result is a text that is structured in a way that children in the group can easily reread it. During the process of writing the story, the teacher may chat about where she begins, whether she capitalizes this word, or where she ends a sentence. The story may guide children's use of rich language and imagination or it may be more teacher directed, providing a patterned text for children's future reading.

One classroom took Bill Martin's *Brown Bear* (1983) and related it to the story of *The Three Bears* (Cauley 1981), since they were studying folktales; they also included *The Little Red Hen* (Galdone 1973). The story read: "Papa Bear, Papa Bear, what do you see? I see Mama Bear looking at me. Mama Bear, Mama Bear, what do you see? I see Baby Bear looking at me. Baby Bear, Baby Bear, what do you see? I see the dog looking at me." And then the question was asked to the cat, then to the red hen. Obviously, they could read *Brown Bear*, and they could turn around and read their group-made altered text as well.

In one first-grade class, the children had difficulty in dictating a story. Perhaps they had had limited experience hearing stories. The teacher began sharing favorite traditional fairy tales such as *Little Red Riding Hood* (Grimm Brothers 1983), *The Sleeping Beauty* (Grimm Brothers 1979), and *Cinderella* (Perreault 1954). The children in that room had also read *Where's Spot?* (Hill 1980) and they titled their story "Spot the King" (see Strong 1988). Listen to the way they have incorporated their knowledge of literature into this dictated story:

> Once upon a time there was nobody in the world except Spot, the king, his queen and his guards. He was the strongest king in the world. He could get anything he wanted. He had the beautifulest castle and the beautifulest queen. He was the kindest king. One night he woke up and a dragon came into his castle. He blew flames at Spot and Spot died. The dragon ate him up. His queen ran for help and got the guards. Spot used

his magic to get out of the dragon's stomach, but he was still dead when he came out of the dragon's stomach. They tried to wake him up from the dead. The queen kissed Spot and he came alive. He thought he had had a dream. The guards killed the dragon with their swords. They took off the dragon's skin and they made a gown for the queen for saving Spot's life. Then they had a dragon party and they ate dragon bones and they lived happily ever after.

This story incorporates a beginning and ending as well as the traditional use of the number three and the hyperbole of fairy tales—"the strongest king," "the kindest king," "the beautifulest castle." There were motifs from *Little Red Riding Hood* (Grimm & Grimm 1983), *The Sleeping Beauty* (Grimm & Grimm 1979), *Cinderella* (Perreault 1954), and *Saint George and the Dragon* (Hodges 1984), all of which they had heard. In both shared reading and shared writing, teachers make explicit the process or strategies that they or the children are using. Teachers may ask such questions as "Where do I begin to write our story?" or "What else do we know about this king?" Or they may ask the children about their knowledge of reading with such questions as "How did you know that word was *kindest?*"

Children also had the opportunity to write independently. There were several types of independent writing, including "balloon writing" to indicate direct speech on wall displays or in student-made big books, letters to characters, recipes, lists, and individual stories. Once an innovative text was created by the group, children often wrote their own versions. Journals were a regular part of the classroom work. Some teachers organized journal writing so that they could observe children writing and occasionally help with a word or an idea. Children used invented spelling in their individual writing but had opportunities to see and participate in producing standard spelling in the group writing situation. Teachers' opportunities for teaching are illustrated in the comment below:

> The children's own writing became a powerful source for learning how to work simultaneously on elements of story structure, letter-sound relationships, punctuation, and other components of writing. As in Reading Recovery, the child's behaviors provide a guide for teacher decisions. We observe and analyze what the child does and then make teaching points based on that information. With one student, we may be working on hearing the sounds in words in sequence; another may be ready for hearing one sound and representing it with a letter. A third

child may be able to use a known word to generate a word needed in the story. Providing time for independent writing helps the teacher focus on each child as an individual learner. (Glasbrenner 1989, p. 5)

ASSESSMENT

Literacy lessons included talking, writing, and reading activities. These suggested activities were used flexibly, but teachers structured their work and the children's work to be sure that every child engaged with the reading and writing processes at an appropriate level. Within the lesson framework, teachers attempted to gather knowledge about children's strengths and, through their interactions and directions, allowed children to use that knowledge in group settings. They used diagnostic techniques learned in Reading Recovery to provide baseline information, and they set up systematic, manageable monitoring systems to track progress. Running records and writing samples were collected at least every two weeks and added to children's assessment portfolios. In addition, teachers kept notes on children. There was an emphasis on collecting information on every child. A regular schedule was followed so that every child would be noticed, and his or her reading behavior analyzed to provide information for teaching.

HONORING CHILDREN'S READING AND WRITING

There is an old Chinese saying, "What is honored in a country will be taught there." We can go into any classroom and tell you what is honored there. If real reading and writing is honored, there will be an attractive reading corner with books displayed in a way that will make children want to read them. Children's interpretations of those books will be displayed along with the books. Their paintings, their puppets, their own books, and pictures will be carefully mounted with children's captions written under them for their own reading. There will be a message board that children will use to write real notes to other children. Art and writing will relate to what is going on in that classroom, and there will be writing to describe all of the children's creative products. Teachers recognize the interrelationship between children's reading and writing in their learning about literacy.

We have enough research to prove that all children can learn to read. But we must take time to read to them so that they will learn that reading is enjoyable. We must give them quantities of easy, predictable books with refrains that help them learn to read. We must build on what children know about oral language, reading, and writing by using shared reading and shared writing. And we must emphasize the meaning of a story and encourage the use of all strategies in context rather than drilling on isolated words and skills. Our major goal would be to help children to learn to read and learn to love reading in the process, to help them become lifetime readers, who can say, as did one seven-year-old boy, "Reading is easy once you do it; you can do it forever."

REFERENCES

Anderson, R, C., E. H. Hiebert, J. A. Scott, & I. A. G. Wilkinson. 1985. *"Becoming a Nation of Readers."* Washington, D.C.: National Institute of Education, U.S. Department of Education.

Bruner, J. 1983. *Child's Talk: Learning to Use language.* New York: Norton.

Carle, E. 1981. *The Very Hungry Caterpillar.* New York: Putnam.

Cauley, L. B. 1981. *Goldilocks and the Three Bears.* New York: Putnam.

Clark, M. 1976. *Young Fluent Readers.* Portsmouth, N.H.: Heinemann.

———. 1979. *Reading: The Patterning of Complex Behavior.* 2d ed. Portsmouth, N.H.: Heinemann.

———. 1985. *The Early Detection of Reading Difficulties.* 3d ed. Portsmouth, N.H.: Heinemann.

Cochran-Smith, M. 1984. *The Making of a Reader.* Norwood, N.J.: Ablex.

Cohen, D. 1968. "The Effect of Literature on Vocabulary and Reading Achievement." *Elementary English* 45 (February): 209–13, 217.

Cowley, J. 1983. *The Greedy Cat.* Illustrated by Robyn Belton. Ready-to-Read Series. Wellington: New Zealand Department of Education.

Cullinan, B., A. Jaggar, & D. Strickland. 1974. "Language Expansion for Black Children in the Primary Grades: Research Report." *Young Children* 29: 98–112.

Durkin, D. 1966. *Children Who Read Early.* New York: Teachers College Press, Columbia University.

Galdone, P. 1973. *The Little Red Hen.* New York: Seabury Press.

Glasbrenner, C. 1989. "Elements of a literacy lesson." *Literacy Matters* 1: 3–6.

Goodman, K. S., E. B. Smith, R. Meredith, & Y. M. Goodman. 1987. *Language and Thinking in School.* 3d ed. New York: Richard C. Owen.

Grimm, Jakob, & Wilhelm Grimm. 1979. *The Sleeping Beauty.* Retold and illus. by W. Hutton. New York: Atheneum.

———. 1983. *Little Red Riding Hood.* Illus. by T. S. Hyman. New York: Holiday House.

Hill, E. 1980. *Where's Spot?* New York: Putnam.

Hodges, M. 1984. *Saint George and the Dragon.* Illus. by T. S. Hyman. New York: Holiday House.

Holdaway, D. 1979. *The Foundations of Literacy.* Sydney, Australia: Ashton Scholastic.

Huck, C., S. Hepler & J. Hickman. 1987. *Children's Literature in the Elementary School.* New York: Holt, Rinehart and Winston.

Jacobs, J. 1980. *The Story of the Three Little Pigs.* Illus. by L. B. Cauley. New York: Putnam.

King, M. 1974. *Informal Learning.* Bloomington, Ind.: Phi Delta Kappa Educational Foundation.

Martin, Bill, Jr. 1983. *Brown Bear, Brown Bear, What Do You See?* Illus. by E. Carle. New York: Holt, Rinehart and Winston.

McKenzie, M. G. 1985. "Shared Writing." *Language Matters* (Inner London Education Authority, Center for Language in Primary Education) Nos. 1 & 2: 1–33.

———. 1988. *Journeys into Literacy.* Huddersfield, England: Schofield & Sims Limited.

Ninio, A., and J. Bruner. 1973. "The Achievement and Antecedents of Labeling." *Journal of Language* 5: 1–15.

Perrault, C. 1954. *Cinderella.* Illus. by M. Brown. New York: Scribners.

Pinnell, G. S., D. E. DeFord, & C. A. Lyons. 1988. *Reading Recovery: Early Intervention for At-Risk First Graders.* Arlington, Va.: Educational Research Service.

Rentel, V., & G. S. Pinnell. 1987. "A Study of Practical Reasoning in Reading Recovery Instruction." Paper presented at the National Reading Conference, St. Petersburg, Florida.

Smith, F. 1978. *Reading Without Nonsense.* New York: Holt, Rinehart and Winston.

Strong, E. L. 1988. "Nuturing Early Literacy: A Literature-Based Program for At-Risk First Graders. Unpublished Ph.D. diss., Ohio State University.

Teale, W. H., & E. Sulzby. eds. 1986. *Emergent Literacy: Writing and Reading.* Norwood, N.J.: Ablex.

Thorndike, R. L. 1978. *Reading Comprehension: Education in 15 Countries: An Empirical Study.* International Studies in Education. vol. 3. New York: Holstead Wiley.

Vygotsky, L. S. 1978. *Mind in Society.* 1938. Ed. by M. Cole, V. John-Steiner, & E. Sonberman. Cambridge, Mass.: Harvard University Press.

Wells, G. 1986. *The Meaning Makers: Children Learning Language and Using Language to Learn.* Portsmouth, N.H.: Heinemann.

Wildsmith, B. 1982. *Cat on the Mat.* New York: Oxford University Press.

CONTRIBUTORS

....

....

MARIE M. CLAY *professor, Auckland University, and president of the International Reading Association. Marie developed the Reading Recovery program, which became a national program of intervention for New Zealand.*

DIANE E. DEFORD *associate professor, Educational Theory and Practice, Ohio State University, Columbus, Ohio. Diane teaches courses on reading and writing methods and evaluation in addition to codirecting the Reading Recovery program for the state of Ohio.*

COLIN DUNKELD *professor, Portland State University, Portland, Oregon. Colin teaches courses in reading and language arts instruction for the university, and directs the Reading Recovery program for the state of Oregon.*

ROSE MARY ESTICE *resource teacher and Reading Recovery teacher leader, Columbus Public Schools, Columbus, Ohio. Rose Mary teaches Reading Recovery classes for her school district, overseeing Reading Recovery teachers in their training year and continuing contact sessions for experienced teachers.*

MARY D. FRIED *resource teacher and Reading Recovery teacher leader, Columbus Public Schools, Columbus, Ohio. Mary helps the Reading Recovery staff at Ohio State University, and coordinates teacher leader activities for the state of Ohio.*

KATHLEEN E. HOLLAND *Kathleen is a special reading teacher for the Amherst school district in Massachusetts. She was involved in the Reading Recovery program during her doctoral studies at Ohio State University.*

CHARLOTTE S. HUCK *Charlotte is retired and living in Redlands, California. Before retiring, she was professor of children's literature at Ohio State University and was instrumental in bringing the Reading Recovery program to Ohio State University.*

CAROL A. LYONS *assistant professor, Educational Theory and Practice, Ohio State University, Columbus, Ohio. Carol teaches courses in developmental reading, reading evaluation, and supervision of teachers; and* directs the Martha L. King Language and Literacy Center. She also codirects the Ohio Reading Recovery program and is the director of the National Diffusion Network dissemination effort at Ohio State University.

BARBARA PETERSON lecturer, Ohio State University, Columbus, Ohio. Barbara teaches courses in children's literature, language arts, and linguistics and works on the Reading Recovery staff.

GAY SU PINNELL associate professor, Educational Theory and Practice, Ohio State University, Columbus, Ohio. She teaches courses in language learning, children's literature, and language arts in addition to codirecting the Ohio Reading Recovery program.

KATHY GNAGEY SHORT assistant professor, University of Arizona, Tucson, Arizona. Kathy teaches courses in reading, language arts, and children's literature. Kathy became involved in Reading Recovery when she was a postdoctoral fellow at Ohio State University.

DANIEL P. WOOLSEY assistant professor, Seattle Pacific University, Seattle, Washington. Dan teaches courses in reading and children's literature. He became interested in Reading Recovery during his doctoral work at Ohio State University.